Understanding Children
as Consumers

Understanding Children as Consumers

Edited by

David Marshall

Los Angeles | London | New Delhi
Singapore | Washington DC

SAGE Publications Ltd
1 Oliver's Yard
55 City Road
London EC1Y 1SP

SAGE Publications Inc.
2455 Teller Road
Thousand Oaks, California 91320

SAGE Publications India Pvt Ltd
B 1/I 1 Mohan Cooperative Industrial Area
Mathura Road
New Delhi 110 044

SAGE Publications Asia-Pacific Pte Ltd
33 Pekin Street #02-01
Far East Square
Singapore 048763

Library of Congress Control Number: 2009936891

British Library Cataloguing in Publication data

A catalogue record for this book is available from the British Library

ISBN 978-1-84787-926-4
ISBN 978-1-84787-927-1 (pbk)

Typeset by C&M Digitals (P) Ltd, Chennai, India
Printed in Great Britain by TJ International Ltd, Padstow, Cornwall
Printed on paper from sustainable resources

Mixed Sources
Product group from well-managed
forests and other controlled sources
www.fsc.org Cert no. SGS-COC-2482
© 1996 Forest Stewardship Council
FSC

Contents

Notes on Contributors

Gary Cross is Distinguished Professor of Modern History at The Pennsylvania State University (USA) and author or editor of 13 books, including *Time and Money: The Making of Consumer Society* (Routledge), *Kids' Stuff: Toys and the Changing World of Modern Childhood* (Harvard), *An All-Consuming Century: Why Commercial Won in Modern America* (Columbia), *The Cute and the Cool: Wondrous Innocence and Modern American Children's Culture* (Oxford), *The Playful Crowd: Pleasure Places in the Twentieth Century* (with John Walton, Columbia), and *Men to Boys: The Making of Modern Immaturity*.

Teresa Davis is a Senior Lecturer at the University of Sydney, Australia. Her main research interests lie in two areas. The first focuses on the discourses around children, childhood and consumption. The second examines the intersections of culture and consumption. Related areas of research are the socio-historical analyses of culture and consumption. Teresa has published articles in *Consumption Markets and Culture*, *Advances in Consumer Research*, *Journal of Consumer Marketing* and *Journal of Brand Management*. She was also the co-editor of the *Advances in Consumer Research Asia-Pacific Volume 7* and co-editor of a special issue of *Consumption Markets and Culture* on the historical perspectives on production and consumption in the Asia-Pacific (forthcoming 2010). She is on the programme committee of the Consumer Culture Theory conference for 2010. She has co-authored the 2007 textbook *Consumer Behaviour: Implications for Marketing*, which won the 2008 Australian Publishers' award in the 'tertiary education' category. She serves on the editorial boards of *Journal of Consumer Behaviour* and *Young Consumers*.

Valérie-Inés de La Ville is a professor in organization studies, business policy and marketing innovation at the University of Poitiers (France). She is the founder of The European Centre for Children's Products – a training and research unit focused on children-orientated markets – that delivers a Masters Degree in Plurimedia Management of Children's Products. She has edited in 2005 *L'enfant consommateur*, Vuibert, Paris, and coordinated as a guest editor a special issue on Child and Teen Consumption in the *Society and Business Review* in 2007. Her research areas are in the collective foundation of entrepreneurial and strategic undertakings, the dialogical processes of strategy formation, and the strategic innovations in children-orientated markets as well as in the ethical issues raised by addressing children as consumers within contemporary society. She currently supervises a national interdisciplinary research programme on *Children and Fun foods*.

Karin M. Ekström is Professor in Marketing at the School of Business and Informatics, University of Borås, Sweden. She is initiator and former director of the Centre for Consumer Science (CFK), an interdisciplinary consumer research centre. Her research concerns family consumption, consumer socialization, collecting, design and the meaning(s) of consumption. She has edited several books, *Children, Media and Consumption, on the Front Edge* (2007), *Little Monster, (De) coupling Assemblages of Consumption* (2007), and *Elusive Consumption* (2004) and published in journals such as *Academy of Marketing Science Review, Journal of Consumer Behaviour, Journal of Consumer Research, Journal of Marketing Management* and *Research in Consumer Behavior*.

Stephen Kline is currently a Professor in the School of Communication at Simon Fraser University, and the Director of the Media Analysis Laboratory. His writing and teaching ranges widely through the fields of media analysis and audience research including media education, advertising and consumerism, toy and video game play, and most recently domestic consumption dynamics. His most recent book *Globesity, Food Marketing and Family: A Communication Analysis of a Lifestyle Risk Pandemic* (Palgrave-MacMillan) examines the processes of risk communication galvanized by the media's relationship to sedentary lifestyles, fast food culture and children's consumerism.

David Marshall is Professor of Marketing and Consumer Behaviour at The University of Edinburgh Business School and Head of the Marketing Group. His research interests and activities centre on understanding consumer behaviour, as a key component of marketing. This includes research on children's consumption, particularly food choice behaviour; and food availability and access in relation to health. He edited *Food Choice and the Consumer* (1995) and has published in a number of academic journals including *Consumption, Markets and Culture, Journal of Consumer Behaviour, Advertising and Marketing to Children (Young Consumers), Journal of Marketing Management, The Sociological Review, Public Health Nutrition, Appetite,* and *Journal of Food Quality and Preference*.

Agnes Nairn is Professor of Marketing at two of Europe's leading business schools: EM-Lyon in France and RSM Erasmus University in the Netherlands. Her area of expertise is the ethics of marketing to young people. She works as a consultant to a range of governments, NGOs, charities and corporations including Family and Parenting Institute, Consumer Focus, Care for the

Family, Coca-Cola GB, Unilever and Mothercare. She currently serves on two UK government expert panels for the Department of Children, Schools and Families and Department of Health. She is a frequent press, radio and TV commentator on the impact of the commercial world of children. Agnes' academic work has appeared in a wide range of international journals and she is author of a number of policy reports. Her co-authored book, *Consumer Kids*, appeared in 2009.

Clive Nancarrow, Professor Emeritus at Bristol Business School, University of the West of England, specializes in applied psychology and research methodology. He has been a practitioner for many years on both the research agency and client side. He has published widely in both academic and practitioner journals and carried out consultancy for Associa, Barclays Bank, Channel 4 TV, Chartered Institute of Marketing, Christian Dior, COI, The Royal Mail, Saitek, TNS and the Wellcome Trust.

Stephanie O'Donohoe is Reader in Marketing at the University of Edinburgh Business School. An interpretive consumer researcher, her PhD, completed at Edinburgh, explored young adults' everyday experiences of advertising, and her current research interests include advertising production and consumption, the role of consumption in the transition to motherhood, and bereaved consumers' interactions with the marketplace. Her work has been published in various edited volumes and international conference proceedings, and in journals including *Human Relations, European Journal of Marketing,* and *Consumption, Markets and Culture.* She is book review editor for the *International Journal of Advertising* and a member of the editorial boards for *Young Consumers* and *Marketing Theory.*

Maria Piacentini is Senior Lecturer in Marketing at Lancaster University Management School, UK. Her research focuses on the consumption behaviour of vulnerable consumers, a stream of research that emanates from her PhD research which focused on low income and disadvantaged consumers and their attitudes and motivations towards healthy eating. She has published her work in a number of journals, including the *Journal of Business Research,* the *Journal of Marketing Management, Advances in Consumer Research,* the *Journal of Consumer Behaviour, International Journal of Non-Profit and Voluntary Sector Marketing, International Review of Retailing, Distribution and Consumer Research, Appetite,* and *Food Quality and Preference.*

Jeanette Rasmussen is a PhD student at the Copenhagen Business School. Her thesis is about Tweens' perception of commercial messages on the internet. Her research centres on children's use of the internet and children, media and consumer research. She has published in *Journal of Consumer Marketing* and *Young Consumers.*

Christine Roland-Lévy is Professor of Social Psychology at the University of Reims Champagne-Ardenne, and Head of the Applied Psychology Research Laboratory. Her research interests and activities centre on understanding consumer behaviour, and especially via economic socialization, as well as on social representations. This includes research on children's understanding about money, consumption, and other related fields, as well as of economic behaviour. She edited a series of books in English, French and Japanese, on related themes, such as *Everyday Representations of the Economy* (2001), *Political Learning and Citizenship in Europe* (2003, and 2006 for the Japanese adaptation), *Psychologie Économique: Théories et Applications* (1998) and *Économie, Médias et Nouvelles Technologies* (2003), as well as three special issues of international scientific journals on the theme of Applied Psychology and Economic Socialization (*Journal of Economic Psychology, New Review of Social Psychology* and, *Applied Psychology: An International Journal*). She has published in a number of academic journals including the above mentioned, and *International Journal of Advertising and Marketing to Children, Consumer Behaviour,* as well as *Citizenship, Social and Economics Education: An International Journal, European Psychologist, European Review of Applied Psychology*. She is the President of the Consortium of Associations of French Psychologists, as well as the President of a European academic network on Citizenship and Identity.

Valérie Tartas is a lecturer and researcher in developmental psychology within the Octogone – Cognition, Communication and Development Laboratory at the University of Toulouse 2, France. Her principal interest topics are about the relationship between social context, mediation tools and learning. She is interested in socio-cognitive development through the appropriation of cultural tools by children with a special interest in the development of children's thinking and language. She has recently taken part in research about learning through argumentation supported by ICT tools in two European projects: Dunes (Dialogic and argUmentative Negotiation Educational Software, 2002–2004) and Escalate (Enhancing SCience Appeal in Learning through Argumentative interaction, 2006–2007). In 2009, she published a book on the construction of social time by children.

Julie Tinson is a Senior Lecturer in Marketing at the University of Stirling where she principally teaches Consumer Behaviour and Marketing Communications. Her research interests include family decision making and consumer socialization. She has recently published a book entitled *Conducting Research with Children and Adolescents: Design, Methods and Empirical Cases* and has published in a number of academic journals including the *International Journal of Market Research, Journal of Consumer Behaviour, Journal of Consumer Marketing, Advances in Consumer Research* and the *Journal of Marketing Management*.

Sarah Todd is Professor of Marketing and Pro-Vice-Chancellor (International) at the University of Otago. She is co-director of the Consumer Research Group and has been co-leader of the comprehensive study of New Zealanders' consumer lifestyles, undertaken on a five yearly basis. Within the broad area of marketing, Sarah's teaching and research has primarily been in consumer behaviour, with current research interests including children's consumption, particularly how children learn and understand the marketplace, and ethical consumption. Additionally, Sarah has acted as expert witness for NZ's Commerce Commission on a number of cases based on consumers' understanding of information.

Birgitte Tufte is professor at Copenhagen Business School. Her research is focused on Children, Media and Consumption. Her publications have been published in various academic journals such as the *Journal of Consumer Marketing, Society and Business* and the *International Journal of Advertising and Marketing to Children.* She has also authored a number of books including *Global Trends in Media Education* (Hampton Press, 2003), *Frontrunners or Copycats?* (Copenhagen Business School Press, 2005), *Children, Media and Consumption – on the Front Edge* (Nordicom, 2007). Her latest two books (in Danish) are: *Children, Media and Market* (Samfundslitteratur, 2007) and *Children growing up with Media and Consumption* (Samfundslitteratur, 2009).

Brian Young is a Research Fellow and consumer psychologist at the University of Exeter. A psychology graduate of the University of Edinburgh, he spent seven years in Hong Kong where he received a PhD in Chinese-English bilingualism. He has published extensively in the area of children and advertising with *Television Advertising and Children* (Oxford University Press, 1990) and with E.L. Palmer (eds) *The Faces of Televisual Media: Teaching, Violence, Selling to Children, 2nd Edition* (Erlbaum, 2003). Brian is Editor of *Young Consumers,* an Emerald Group journal. His interests are in consumer socialization and theories of promotional activity. He teaches at the University of Exeter in both the School of Psychology and the Business School in consumer and economic socialization, child development, and advertising and consumer psychology.

Preface and Acknowledgements

Someone asked me recently why I became interested in young consumers. The answer was simple and I did not have to think long and hard about it – because I had children of my own. As they grew up I became fascinated by their 'consumer' experiences, many of which I was responsible for, with a range of products from building blocks to breakfast cereals, trading cards to Tamogotchi pets, football (soccer) players to social networking sites. You may not have guessed but we have boys and I remember having to try to buy a present for my young nieces and realizing that there was another aisle in the toy store where we seldom ventured. Children, both boys and girls, seemed engaged, knowledgeable and 'experienced' in this commercial world and I felt that there was more to all this than the model of the passive vulnerable child depicted in many texts. Another reason for my initial interest can be attributed to one of my undergraduate students, Sarah (ffelhan) Case who was looking at the role of character merchandising in marketing to children and wrote an excellent dissertation on the topic. As part of her research into the role of media and character toys she lent me a copy of *Out of the Garden* by Stephen Kline, one of this book's contributors (I returned it only recently!), and this opened up a new field of research literature which was fascinating and intriguing. The more I read – a number of these books are briefly listed in the introduction – the more it became clear that the views of many experts did not always correspond with my own experiences and so I began to try to see what children made of this all by talking to them.

The idea for the book arose from a meeting with Sarah Todd, University of Otago, at the 2003 European Association for Consumer Research conference in Dublin, Ireland. At that time Sarah was looking at children's experiences with money and this started out as a joint project. Unfortunately due to other commitments Sarah had to withdraw from her editorial role but continued to offer invaluable comments on the structure of the book as it took shape. Her support and enthusiasm throughout the project have been invaluable and much appreciated. Thanks also go to Phil Harris, University of Chester, who supported the text as part of the Sage Advanced Marketing Series. I am especially thankful to Delia Alfonso the commissioning editor at Sage who embraced the idea with genuine enthusiasm and her unending patience was to prove a virtue as work commitments and pressure from the UK Research Assessment Exercise led to delay after delay as the project got pushed back. Without Delia and her colleagues at Sage this book would not have materialized.

Huge thanks go out to all the authors, who persevered amidst continual requests for chapters, revised submission schedules and delayed publication dates as the final pieces of the jigsaw were put together. Special thanks go out to those who stepped in at the last minute to contribute chapters to the book. Each author has made an individual contribution despite busy work – and in many cases, family – schedules, to bring their own perspectives on children as consumers that both review the field of study and offer new and interesting perspectives for the reader. I am grateful to John Dawson and Stephanie O'Donohoe at the University of Edinburgh Business School, Stephen Kline at Simon Fraser University and Agnes Nairn, University of EM-Lyon, who provided invaluable insights and constructive comments throughout the project and Rosemary Duff of Childwise who allowed me access to information on the UK children's market.

A number of anonymous individuals gave up their time to review the initial proposal and offer valuable and constructive suggestions on how to improve the book proposal. I endeavoured, where possible, to deliver on these requests and hope this is in line with your expectations. Special thanks go to the two anonymous reviewers who provided some excellent and extremely helpful comments on the manuscript draft and enabled me to revisit, with the help of the contributors, some of these issues and further develop the text.

Finally, I would like to thank my partner Linda and our children Shaun and Ben, who are always willing to offer their consumer perspective.

I hope this edited collection will provide insights and generate some of the enthusiasm that we have experienced in reading, researching, writing about and watching children as consumers. Knowledge should be empowering for us as students, academics, researchers and practitioners and the insights from each of the contributors allow us to understand children as consumers more fully by considering their perspectives on the commercial world. In the process children might benefit from having their voices heard. Ideally the contributions in this book will encourage readers to refresh their thinking and research methods by listening to children about how they engage with the commercial environment, but also reconsider when, where and how children need to be protected from its excesses.

David Marshall

1 Introduction

David Marshall

The aim of *Understanding Children as Consumers* is to look at how we view children as consumers and to consider the extent to which they are actively engaged in the marketplace as the buyers, users and recipients of consumer goods. This edited collection draws on recent research and academic expertise within the area of consumer behaviour and childhood consumption. It looks at a range of age groups but is primarily focused on children aged 8 to 12 years old. As a number of commentators have noted, childhood is firmly embedded in the commercial marketplace (Langer, 1994, 2005; Cook, 2004) and a major challenge is to understand the ways in which young consumers negotiate this terrain.

In (re)thinking children as consumers we need to recognize the ubiquity of the marketplace in children's everyday lives and consider the ways in which they experience this commercial world, be it through exposure to various forms of media, visiting retail stores, making requests for products, or purchasing goods with their own money. With direct and indirect marketing to children on the increase there is a question over how children engage with this commercial world. A number of discussions, for example, around food marketing and childhood obesity, online activity and sedentary lifestyles, or increased materialism among the young tend to place children as hapless victims subject to the onslaught of marketing activity. While we have often excluded children from debates about consumption, manufacturers and retailers have long recognized the role of children as consumers and acknowledged their contribution to family decision making (Kline, 1993; Cross, 1997; Cook, 2004).

With this growth in marketing to children some commentators have gone as far as claiming that children are suffering from 'marketing related diseases' and that we are witnessing the 'hostile takeover of childhood' in a 'toxic' commercial environment permeating all aspects of young lives (Schor, 2006, citing commercialalert.com; see also Linn, 2004; Palmer, 2007). Seen from this perspective, this once commercial-free arena of childhood is increasingly populated with attempts to 'lure' young consumers, and their parents, into ever more consumption, with a variety of devious tactics that include recruiting children to promote products in the playground and online through social networking sites, as well as by using a variety of promotional tactics that 'play on their dreams and exploit their vulnerabilities' (Mayo and Nairn, 2009: xvii). Underpinning this moralizing is an assumption about children as 'consumers' and a question over the extent to which they are either vulnerable and exploited in the commercial environment to which they are exposed or competent and savvied individuals. As Cook (2004: 7) notes, 'The dichotomous construction of the exploited child and the empowered child arises from a lingering tension between markets and moral sentiment: it is a tension which, at least since the beginning of industrialisation, continues to inform considerations of childhood'. Resolution of this tension, according to Cook, occurs where goods are considered beneficial and functional, as is the case with educational goods, or when children are seen as full *persons* who desire goods and can exhibit some degree of agency. Gunter and Furnham (1998: 7) argue that children resemble other (adult) consumers in many ways and exhibit a degree of sophistication and pragmatism in their approach to the marketplace to the extent that they are both 'active and discerning' in their consumption. Similar views are expressed by David Buckingham (2000, 2008; Buckingham and Willett, 2006) in his accounts of children and media. One only needs to consider their knowledge about latest toys, or the hottest characters on collectible cards, the 'best' sports players, or the coolest websites.

These issues form the basis of what this book is trying to do in looking critically at children[1] as active consumers, but it differs from previous accounts by trying to address the key issues and uncover what being a consumer means to children themselves – namely, from their perspective![2] This attempt to give children some voice in the debate is sympathetic to the idea that they should have some say, that their opinions matter, and that they have some 'agency' as consumers and 'social beings' in their own right (James et al., 1998).[3]

Marketing to children

To put this idea of vulnerable or competent consumers into context let us consider where much of the discussion about children as consumers has been centred thus far – on marketing to children. One of the most influential writers in the field remains James McNeal. His books include *Children as Consumers: Insights and Implications* (1987) and *The Kid's Market Myths and Realities* (1999) in which he offers interesting insights into young consumers. These, along with texts like Guber and Berry's *Marketing to and through Kids* (1993), raised the profile of the children's market and generated interest in the notion of children as consumers. Much of their focus was on how to market to children as opposed to what children are doing with marketing.

Later texts such as Acuff's (1997) *What Kids Buy and Why: The Psychology of Marketing to Kids*, or Del Vecchio's (1997) *Creating Ever Cool: A Marketeer's Guide to a Kid's Heart* attempted to unpack the key to successful marketing. Cross offers an historical account of childs' play in *Kid's Stuff: Toys and the Changing World of American Childhood* (1997) and *The Cute and the Cool: Wonderous Innocence and Modern American Children's Culture* (2004) where he looks at changes in the children's market in the USA. Cook's historical account of the commercialization of children's fashion with *The Commodification of Childhood: The Children's Clothing Industry and the Rise of the Child Consumer* (2004) shows that the idea of marketing to young consumers is not some new phenomenon but part of a gradual process of integrating children into the marketplace. Gunter and Furnham provide an excellent psychological analysis of the young consumer entitled *Children as Consumers* (1998) in which they detail the nature of the children's market and their role as consumers. McNeal's *Kids as Customers: A Handbook of Marketing to Children* (1992) and more recently *On Becoming a Consumer: The Development of Consumer Behavior Patterns in Childhood* (2007) look at how children develop as consumers. Ellen Seiter's (1993) treatise on the children's toy market, *Sold Separately: Children and Parents in Consumer Culture*, focuses on children's creative use of consumer goods and media. David Buckingham in *After the Death of Childhood: Growing Up in the Age of Electronic Media* (2000) looks at children and the media environment at the start of the century, a theme developed with Rebekah Willett in their (2006) edited text *Digital Generations*. In contrast to this academic approach, Martin Lindstrom and Patricia Seybold (2003) offer a practitioner's perspective on global kids in *Brand Child* looking at contemporary market research with young consumers.

But as an interest in marketing to children grew so too did concerns over the way in which this was developing. Stephen Kline's excellent history of marketing to children, *Out of the Garden* (1993), maps out a detailed historical trajectory of children's play culture and the role of the mass media in building up the 'children's' market. His account ten years later of the development of new media in *Digital Play* (Kline et al., 2003) reveals the emerging relationship between technology, culture and marketing in the games and video industry. Susan Linn's (2004) *Consuming Kids* and Juliet Schor's (2004) *Born to Buy* both raised important questions over this increasingly commercialized world of childhood and the pervasive nature of marketing. More recently the UK National Consumer Council's (Nairn et al., 2007) study on materialism and marketing towards children concluded that children who spend more time in front of the television or computer tend to be more materialistic and have lower self-esteem, raising further concerns over the impact of marketing to younger consumers. Mayo and Nairn's (2009) *Consumer Kids: How Big Business is Grooming our Children for Profit* leaves little doubt as to the sentiment of the text. They provide an insightful account of the latest marketing tactics and the impact on children's wellbeing[4] in an increasingly commercial world and also look at some of the positive ways in which children are responding to this consumer world.

A large part of the debate on marketing to children has focused on advertising, primarily in relation to mass media advertising and the ways in which children engage with television and, more recently, online advertising. Research from over thirty years ago showed that children's ability to distinguish between persuasive advertising and television programmes was related to age (Robertson and Rossiter, 1974). While some would argue that children lack the life skills and experience to resist the persuasive nature of commercial advertising others claim that promotional messages provide information to allow for informed choice (Moore, 2004). Inherent in this debate is the idea that advertising to children is 'unfair' and one approach has been to look for a 'magic age' at which children can understand the persuasive intent of these commercial messages. While it has commonly been assumed that teenagers are less vulnerable to advertising, recent research suggests that they may be just as persuadable as younger children when it comes to digital marketing. The persuasion model relies on explicit mental processes and does not account for the formation of implicit attitudes when children encounter certain stimuli (Livingstone and Helsper, 2006; Nairn and Fine, 2008). Today's children are faced with a variety of new media where the distinctions between commercial and non-commercial material are increasingly blurred, for example, when advergames promote brands online (Moore and Rideout, 2007; Lee et al., 2009). For this generation, television advertising represents only one aspect of their consumption experience and more recent accounts have considered their engagement with a broader range of media including the internet (Livingstone and Helsper, 2004; Tufte et al., 2005; Schor, 2006; Ekström and Tufte, 2007; Livingstone, 2009).

As we ponder on the impact of advertising campaigns on children, few ask if younger children are actually interested in these ever more devious advertising campaigns or how they relate to them, and most importantly how they impact on their behaviour (Andersen, 2007). While most of the discussion around marketing to children has centred on exposure and the comprehension of commercial intent, we know much less about how children utilize that information and the impact on their behaviour (Lawlor and Prothero, 2002; Bartholomew and O'Donohoe, 2003). In a rapidly changing media environment we might also ask how children have learnt to deal with marketing as a consequence of this increased exposure to products and brands and try to understand that experience from their perspective.

Children and consumption

Over a twenty year period from the 1960s to the end of the 1980s, young consumer spending in the USA increased from $2bn to $6bn and their influence extended to a staggering $132bn of household expenditure (McNeal, 1992). This trend was to continue through the 1980s in the United States with an increasingly affluent teenage market, despite numbers of teenagers declining by 15.5 per cent (Gunter and Furnham 1998: 2; see also Davis, 1990; McNeal, 1992). By the end of the 1990s it was estimated that children in the USA accounted for $23bn in direct spending, almost all of this discretionary, and influenced a further $188bn in family purchases (McNeal, 1999). Ten years on the children's market (i.e. the annualized amount spent on child related goods and activities) is around $921bn[5] in the United States. The corresponding value of the UK market is around £117 bn.[6]

The most recent account of children's direct purchasing power in the USA is around $51.8bn (Schor, 2006). It is difficult to get similar figures for the UK but the most recent British pocket money survey from the Halifax[7] showed the following:

- Average pocket money in 2008 was £6.13 per week, versus £8.01 in 2007.
- Younger children aged between 8 and 11 years old got almost half the amount of their older counterparts (12 to 15 years old) receiving £4.34.
- Pocket money was out of step with inflation — there was a shortfall of £3.30 for 2008 s weekly allowance compared with three years beforehand.
- Whilst parents provided a weekly allowance they continued to pay for mobiles, iPods and gifts.
- Three in ten children saved some of their pocket money each week; however, if they wanted something in addition to their allowance they tended to ask for it as a 'present' (Halifax, 2008).

With an estimated 13 million children aged under sixteen in the UK (Office for National Statistics, 2009), and around 70 per cent receiving pocket money, this represents considerable spending power that does not include money gifted to children or the cash they earn for part-time jobs or individual enterprise. The *ChildWise Monitor Report*[8] (2009) found 84 per cent of UK children aged 5 to 16 years old received a regular income, with 72 per cent receiving pocket money or an allowance and a quarter earning income from a paid job. Average weekly income was £10.10, with children aged 5 to 10 years old getting around £4.70 per week on average and 11 to 16 year olds receiving £12.10 each. This gives a total value of children's annual income of £3800m,[9] with a further estimated £5100m in ad hoc handouts including birthday money. Taken together this represents a combined annual figure of £8900m per year (covering pocket money, allowances, paid jobs and ad hoc handouts) at children's disposal.

James McNeal (1987, 1992, 1999) discusses this potentially lucrative market of young consumers spending their money on a range of items such as confectionary, drinks, toys, fast food, magazines, movies and music and influencing family spending[10] (directly and indirectly) on products as diverse as breakfast cereals, family cars and holidays. The (2008) *ChildWise*

Report gave an average annual self spend for the UK's 5 to 16 year olds of £310m on crisps and snacks, £290m on soft drinks, £260m on sweets and chocolate, £1090m on clothing, £440m on music and CDs, and £340m on computer software – a grand total across these categories of £2730m. In a number of these areas children are seen as having their own 'needs' and also a willingness to spend money on such products, but to constitute a market they also need to have the ability and the authority to purchase, as well as some knowledge and understanding of that market.

This idea of a 'children's market' is a relatively new development in 'western' markets and up to the 1960s children were not seen as customers in their own right but as savers and future customers. While most of the focus has been on children's direct and indirect influence on family purchases, from breakfast cereals through to cars, an increasing number of products and promotions are being targeted directly at children. This has led to debates around pester power and persuasive kids, raising concerns over the ways in which this commercialization of childhood is impacting on family life (Wooton, 2003; Carauna and Vasello, 2004; Preston, 2004; Spungin, 2004). However, more recent views suggest that parent–child relationships are less confrontational and more collaborative in contemporary western societies. Finally, children are important as a future market for most goods and services and one to be cultivated early. Consider children's savings accounts offered by most banks, or children's food ranges on the supermarket shelves, or a British advert that reverses the parent–child role and has the kids commenting on the versatility of the family orientated MPV. No wonder that the relevant companies are interested.

One measure of this interest in the children's market is in the amount spent on advertising products to children. A 2007 report for the Advertising Association in the UK reported a 9 per cent (£26m) fall in advertising expenditure on confectionery, potato crisps and snacks, full sugar carbonates (fizzy drinks), breakfast cereals and fast food restaurants between 2003 and 2006. In the same period there was a corresponding 61 per cent increase in expenditure on fruit juice, water, fresh fruit and vegetables (albeit from a low base). The same report shows a fall of 29 per cent in the number of core category ads (all food, fast food and confectionary) watched by 4 to 9 year olds in the immediate period following the introduction of restrictions on UK advertising. From 1 January 2009 there was to be no advertising of high fat, sugar, or salt food products on children's TV channels. Yet advertising in other media (such as online) appears to be taking hold (Lee et al., 2009; Mayo and Nairn, 2009). In the USA, advertising aimed at children is estimated at $15bn annually (Linn, 2004). The Kaiser Family Foundation (2006, 2007) found food to be the most widely advertised product on the networks in their study. Almost half of the ads on kids' time television were for food products and the vast majority of those brands also had an online presence with websites using a variety of marketing tactics.

Children as consumers

However, this book is not simply about the size of the market or indeed what marketing does to children, but about children as consumers. It looks at what children do with marketing (as consumers of the advertising, promotions and products they are exposed to) and their consumption experiences. While marketers propose a view of children as relatively autonomous individuals making independent decisions, policy groups are more likely to see children in need of protection. This book stands outside those opposing adult views and looks at consumption from the child's perspective. More specifically, it presents the views of a number of leading experts in the field about children as consumers, and one that is *sympathetic* to the idea of looking at consumption from the child's perspective, despite the limited amount of research that adopts this approach. There has been a considerable body of work within the field of marketing that seeks to explore and examine the consumption practices of children, in many cases looking at ideas that have been applied to adult consumers and adapting them accordingly, but in all of this debate there remains a question around the extent to which children should be treated differently from adults.

A number of themes – besides the vulnerable-competent issue – emerge over the course of the book. One such theme is consumer socialization and the extent to which children are integrated into consumption practices either as individuals or as members of a 'family'. Socialization assumes that children are in some form of liminal state and childhood is part of a transition into adulthood, encapsulated in the idea of children as 'becomings'. But as we will see, there is some interest in children as consumers in their own right – as 'beings' – and a need to understand what consumption means to them. This transition and development theme is reflected in the cognitive development literature which has played an important role in how we approach children's consumption. This is evident across a number of chapters and references to the work of Piaget and Roedder-John appear throughout the text.

How we choose to conduct research with children as consumers is beginning to change and throughout the book there is increasing evidence of interpretivist approaches, the use of projective techniques, and looking at children's consumption from a consumer culture theory (CCT) perspective. These new ways of looking at young consumers are evident in a number of the chapters. Another theme to emerge is the issue of ethics, particularly around the growth in materialism and consumption among young children and the role that marketing plays in this development.

Finally, one cannot help but notice the impact of new mobile and internet technologies. Social networking sites, blogs, online gaming, advergames and web 2.0 are connecting consumers and creating new forms of dialogue between young consumers and companies. Increasingly companies are marketing through these new media channels as well as via the traditional media of television and print. This is an area that has drawn the attention of a number of researchers interested in how children engage with this new media. Evidence from the UK showed that young people (7 to 16 year olds) are engaged with a range of interactive and non-interactive media. Many have internet access at home, a mobile phone, games consoles and a television in their rooms[11] (ChildWise, 2008). Children spend twice as much time in front of the screen as they do in class (Mayo and Nairn, 2009).

Organization of the book

There are four sections and 14 chapters in the book (see Figure 1.1). Each chapter has a set of objectives and includes short vignettes that illustrate the issues discussed within, along with some discussion questions at the end of the chapter. The book is organized around the idea of children being actively engaged in the commercial marketplace and begins by looking at some of the ways in which we have conceptualized children as consumers, drawing on psychological and sociological models of childhood. These serve as the background for some of the ways in which children's marketing has evolved in response to the shift from 'cute to cool' and the role of branding, advertising and retailing in shaping their consumption experiences and engaging them as consumers, both directly and indirectly. Developments in marketing towards children force us to rethink some of our ideas around how they function and engage as consumers in the marketplace and this feeds back into our debate around development and socialization. The third section looks at a number of the products that are associated with young consumers, notably snacks, clothes, and the internet, as areas of consumption where they exercise some discretion. These represent specific examples of marketing to children that resonate with developments in Part II, but they also raise issues about children's abilities as consumers and their agency in certain categories of consumption. This leads into the final section that reflects on the moral aspects of these changes and conclude by revisiting the question of whether children are competent or vulnerable beings in a marketplace that is increasingly orientated towards them as consumers. In the end, these questions force us to reflect on, or rethink, the ways in which we look at children as consumers.

Contributors

This book is an edited collection with contributions from a number of international researchers actively engaged in theoretical and empirical work on the consumption practices of children. Contributions from Europe,

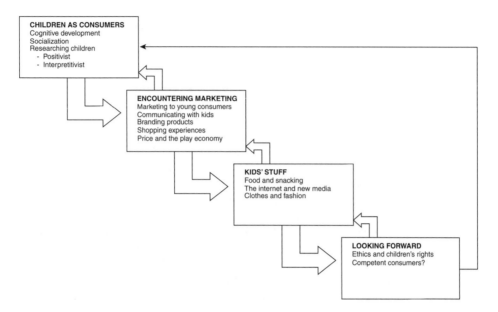

CHILDREN AS CONSUMERS
Cognitive development
Socialization
Researching children
  - Positivist
  - Interpretitivist

ENCOUNTERING MARKETING
Marketing to young consumers
Communicating with kids
Branding products
Shopping experiences
Price and the play economy

KIDS' STUFF
Food and snacking
The internet and new media
Clothes and fashion

LOOKING FORWARD
Ethics and children's rights
Competent consumers?

Figure 1.1   Understanding children as consumers

Scandinavia, North America, Canada, New Zealand and Australia offer a contemporary view of child consumers in developed western economies and provide valuable insights into different aspects of children's consumption. This is a rich and emergent field attracting a range of disciplines from business, commerce, and management through to other social science fields such as psychology, sociology, anthropology, education and history, and the text looks beyond children and advertising to consider how they engage and interact with consumption more broadly. There are clearly questions over children's competencies as consumers and the various contributors revisit the contemporary view of children as passive consumers. The book provides readers with a basis for looking at various aspects of children's consumption, supplemented with cutting-edge research insights that contribute to a better understanding of the ways in which children interact, respond and engage with marketing-related activities.

Part I looks at 'Children as Consumers' and has contributions from experts in the field of marketing to children. In Chapter 2 Valérie-Inés de la Ville and Valérie Tartas look at the contribution from three development psychology perspectives on understanding children as consumers. They offer a considered and insightful critique of the theoretical cognitive development frameworks that have informed much of our research into children as consumers and argue for the need to consider children's development as consumers as a function of environmental influences. They also look at some of the ways in which children acquire social skills through their interaction with others and offer a framework that brings together these ideas and recognizes the active nature of children's consumption and the role of the environment and socialization in shaping their cognitive development. For de la Ville and Tartas, children are very much active participants in the marketplace and they examine the ways in which children develop as economic actors in a complex cultural system that both enables and constrains their consumption activities. They challenge us to consider how children move from being peripheral to central participants in consumption. This chapter offers an excellent review and critique of the dominant approach to understanding children as consumers and argues convincingly for the need to consider critically what this tells us about children as consumers.

The third chapter by Karin Ekström picks up on this theme of consumer socialization within the specific context of the family, an important site of consumer socialization and one that appears throughout the book. Ekström looks at the mediating influence of the family unit and the extent to which this plays an important role in transferring and transforming children's consumption experiences. But she rejects this unidirectional, one-sided view and sees this process not simply as one where parents influence children but as a much more dyadic interaction whereby children can influence and change what their parents, and grandparents, consume through their provision of knowledge. In this respect children are much more agentive and can influence certain aspects of family consumption. In discussing this process of socialization, Ekström looks at the dualistic perspective of children as either competent or vulnerable and argues, like de la Ville and Tartas, for the need to look at this in a broader environmental context – not least in terms of developments in communication technologies, especially with the emergence of web space and social networking sites that have been enthusiastically adopted by young consumers. She offers ten different family types, derived from her own research, and considers a range of consumption scenarios that explore socialization in contemporary Swedish families. The chapter reveals the extent to which children's influence depends on the nature of family communication, supporting other research in this area. And what she shows, through this, is a relationship between influence and affluence, raising issues around socio-economic differences in the socialization of young consumers.

The challenge of researching young consumers is taken up by Teresa Davis. She discusses the methodological and ethical challenges in undertaking this type of research and offers an insightful and pragmatic approach to understanding children's consumption, drawing on both positivistic – which has dominated much of the consumer research with children – and more recent interpretative approaches. She considers the appropriateness as well as the strengths and weaknesses of each approach. Davis recognizes the extent to which the selection of a research method is dependent on a researcher's ontological perspective, with positivist approaches commonplace among the cognitive developmentalists and interpretivist approaches emerging in the field of sociology. In particular, she argues for the need to rethink our approach to the child as subject and how that impacts on our research method. The chapter provides an excellent guide to doing research with young children and offers a series of 'dos' and 'don'ts' that serve to guide researchers in either the positivist or interpretivist tradition. She draws on a range of contemporary studies of children and brands to illustrate the different approaches currently used in academic research to understand how children categorize and classify their own consumption. Positivist approaches include categorization and choice tasks, using shopping scripts, or simplifying and modifying research instruments. Interpretivists are utilizing projective techniques to look to unpack some of the complexity that lies beyond the surface response. Projective techniques covered in the chapter include drawing, online research methods, and using photography and comic book approaches. The chapter offers a balanced view on how to conduct research with young consumers and introduces some exciting new developments in how we conduct research that will be of interest to both academics and practitioners alike.

Part II, entitled 'Encountering Marketing', has contributions from academics looking specifically at how children engage with marketing. It looks at marketing toys, branding aimed at children, advertising and promoting to children, how children engage in shopping, and ideas about how they experience money. Chapter 5, by Gary Cross, offers a fascinating historical perspective in the marketing of toys to children in the USA. He is less receptive to the idea of asking children about what they consume and provides an alternative approach that considers the changing nature of the children's market over time, drawing on historical accounts and archive material of the children's toy market. He notes the relatively recent emergence of the children's market and the manner in which the marketing of toys has changed since the 1900s. With the emergence of the 'wondrous innocence' comes a celebration of the 'cute' and the first appearance of the child-centred holiday. Just as Ekström comments on children's influence across generations, so Cross notes the way in which nostalgia became part of the marketing around toys and the cross-generational 'retro' appeal linking parents and children. In contrast, the marketing of 'cool' as a rebellion against a parental imposition of the cute emerged in the early part of the twentieth century and saw the appearance of toy figures and paraphernalia based on media figures and fantasy characters. Marketing toys to children, especially boys, began to take on a new guise – aided and abetted by an emerging children's media in the form of movies, the radio, comic books and television. Girls are not immune to this influence and the arrival of the Barbie doll, and more latterly Bratz, saw a corresponding shift from cute to cool down to the tween market, something which Cross suggests we might look at more closely. His chapter illustrates the value of looking historically at what is happening in the children's market today.

Agnes Nairn takes this idea of branding and looks at how children relate to and use brands as part of their everyday existence in Chapter 6. She shows how brands and exposure to the commercial world are an integral part of contemporary childhood. Children are already familiar with brands of confectionary, clothing, and music and software at a young age. Like a number of other authors she is critical of the developmental perspective and argues that any understanding of how children use brands, as opposed to simply learning about them, requires us to consider other approaches. She turns to consumer culture theory (CCT) for an explanation into the ways in which brands are used, by young consumers, as part of their individual and group narrative. Like Cross she talks about the importance of 'cool' and looks at the central role of brands in this process. Drawing on her own research Nairn looks at the possessions and brands that matter to children by talking directly to them. In the process she finds that these brands are heavily marketed towards children across a range of media and marketing channels that extend far beyond the realm of television advertising. She unpacks some of the complexity in 'cool' and highlights the active and participative nature of children's engagement with brands that they deem relevant and meaningful. Once again Barbie appears but this time the complaints are coming from the children not the parents – she is no longer 'cool'. Brands appear to be a central part of gender and class identity but a key contribution of this chapter is the discussion around consumption and materialism. It appears that marketers are more astute and innovative in their online promotional activities and Nairn suggests that we pay close attention to developments in this area.

One area that has been under particular scrutiny is advertising to children, and in Chapter 7 Brian Young looks critically at this aspect of marketing. He outlines some of the anxieties around advertising to children and examines the ways in which children process this information by looking at materialism and obesity in young consumers. Young's chapter is firmly located in a developmental mode and he offers a Piagetian perspective on advertising that considers different cognitive developmental stages. He revisits the argument around informative and persuasive intent and in looking back at a classic study raises interesting questions about the nature of contemporary children's engagement in a much more cluttered world of marketing and media aimed directly at them. Young finds some evidence of media literacy in children around the ages of between 6 and 9 years old, but as he notes this understanding of advertising does not mean there is no effect on children's consumption. He goes on to suggest that there is a trajectory of development sequences through which children learn to understand advertising. However, Young is the first to recognize the danger of only looking at advertising and acknowledges that this is only one of a range of factors that have come to influence children's consumption. Like a number of authors he also argues that children are more actively engaged, and dismissive, of this medium than we may have given them credit for in the past. He picks up and develops this idea of materialism and childhood from a developmental perspective. He then finishes off with an examination of one of the most sensitive, and controversial, aspects of marketing – the promotion and advertising of fast food to children. Young offers an interesting perspective on the relationship between advertising and obesity in young people that suggests we may be looking in the wrong place for an explanation of childhood obesity, but the jury remain out on this.

In Chapter 8 Julie Tinson and Clive Nancarrow look at children and shopping. They are interested in how children behave in the context of the family unit but their focus is on the nature of the decision process and the role of children in this. Like Ekström they find evidence of the dyadic nature of the parent–child interaction in certain types of family units, in this case single parent, blended and intact units. They see children as more actively engaged in the decision process as opposed to being passive recipients. Their specific focus is on 8 and 12 year olds' involvement in family decision making. Tinson and Nancarrow are interested in the various stages of this decision process in relation to both the product and the age of the child. The authors discuss different types of family decision making, conveying the range of different approaches that may be adopted both within and across family units. What is clear from their account is that children are being included and are more directly engaged in a number of family decisions. Although the options and opportunities for their involvement are likely to be limited, children often believe the process to be more democratic that it is. Tinson and Nancarrow explore and unpack this idea of consumer savvy in relation to children, drawing us back towards the broader issue of whether children are vulnerable or competent in their shopping encounters.

This issue of becoming consumers and competence is further developed in the discussion around children and money by Christine Roland-Lévy in Chapter 9. She focuses on children's experiences with economic aspects of consumption and looks at how children acquire and manage their financial resources. Centring on economic socialization, she describes the process by which children acquire the skills and competencies that are relevant to the economic world. Like de la Ville and Tartas, she draws on both cognitive development and social learning theories to explore this aspect of consumption and outlines some of the differentiating factors that contribute to this learning process. In the process she argues for a need to look at what she calls the 'real economic behaviour' of children and the 'play-economy'. She reports on cross cultural research into young children's understanding of relatively complex financial issues, such as taxation and savings versus credit, highlighting some of the social and cultural differences in relation to their economic socialization. Roland-Lévy is sensitive to the specific research challenges of understanding this aspect of children's behaviour and the chapter illustrates some of the issues in this specific area of research.

Part III, entitled 'Kids' Stuff', looks at three key areas of children's consumption of food, fashion and the internet (toys are examined in the previous section). In Chapter 10, David Marshall and Stephanie O'Donohoe discuss the emergence of a distinctive children's food culture and growing concerns over what children are eating in an increasingly obesogenic environment populated with the marketing of foods that are high in fat, sugar and salt. Yet amidst this debate they examine the issue of fun food and consider children's ideas about snacking as part of their everyday food experiences and the extent to which this needs to be seen in relation to the overall family food system. They talk about the nature of the family meal occasion and report on research with children from Scotland, New Zealand and Canada in relation to eating at home. They explore children's own accounts of snacking and question the importance of food advertising in children's food preferences, echoing some of the ideas presented by Young in Chapter 7. They find some evidence of discretionary consumption, but argue that despite some of the concerns around snacking much of young children's food consumption continues to be mediated by parents rather than manipulated by marketing messages and advertising. Finally, they argue that food consumption offers an excellent opportunity to observe and understand various aspects of children's consumption behaviours.

In Chapter 11 Birgitte Tufte and Jeanette Rasmussen consider what has become one of the most contested aspects of children's consumption, the internet. They outline the emergence of the global high speed network and the more recent development of social networking sites before drawing on their research with Danish children into the relationship between media use and consumption. The authors highlight the increasing gulf between children and parents along with the differential use between boys and girls. The chapter provides valuable insights into how children are engaging with this virtual environment and contrasts the differences between internet use at home and in schools. Tufte and Rasmussen show how the emergence of new forms of media serve as a vehicle for marketing to children and outline some of the concerns around the commercialization of these new communication channels, echoing broader concerns over young people's media use. In an area of consumption where children are generally seen as more 'being' than 'becoming', they illustrate some of the complexity surrounding the ways in which children interact with and utilize this new form of media and how they engage with marketing activities online.

Maria Piacentini looks at children's ideas about clothing brands and fashion in Chapter 12, locating her discussion in the literature of symbolic consumption and self-identity and self-expression. She looks at the role that fashion and clothing play in young consumers' lives and how these are closely bound to ideas about the self and peer group influence. She critically examines the role of marketing and the fashion system in shaping choice and considers how clothing styles and brands allow young consumers to simultaneously pursue individual identities and create social distinctions that mark their place within a youth subculture. She considers the inherent social and cultural capital in this very visible and public consumption good. Piacentini looks at rituals surrounding fashion and unpacks some of the contextual aspects and the increasingly 'adultification' of children's fashion that touches on broader issues around marketing to children. The chapter lends some support to the socialization thesis but reveals some important differences in perspective between young consumers and adults in relation to fashion and clothing consumption.

The final part of the book, 'Looking Forward', considers some of the moral issues surrounding marketing to children and brings us back to the broader debate around marketing to children and how they, as consumers, respond to this commercial activity. Sarah Todd, in looking at the ethics of marketing to children, returns to the question of age and cognitive development in relation to young consumers' understanding of persuasive intent in marketing activities. She notes that a scepticism about marketing is an insufficient basis on which to argue that children are any less susceptible to marketing influences. Building on this idea, Todd examines children's rights and the relevant codes of ethics applying to those who research children. She picks up on the ill effects of marketing and most notably the growth of consumption and materialism in the young – a recurrent theme throughout this book – discussing the symbolic role of brands in building an emotional attachment among the young, particularly in relation to fitting in with peer groups. As the trend towards more direct marketing to children changes the family dynamic, she raises ethical questions around pester power and the changing nature of family socialization. As marketing initiatives – on the internet, mobile media, and even in schools – creates a series of new challenges and evokes calls for increased regulation and monitoring, she argues that those companies targeting children need to consider the ethical implications involved.

In the final chapter, Stephen Kline picks up on this central debate about children as competent or vulnerable consumers and develops his argument around the issue of food and childhood obesity in what is seen as an increasingly risk averse society. He explores this idea from the perspective of the moral panic that endures in contemporary public debate and discusses the role of the media in this positioning of children as vulnerable consumers in need of protection. As the industry builds its counter arguments, he illustrates how this question of children's competencies as consumers in the mediated marketplace begins to take central stage in the debate. As he notes, this question of competencies revolves around three key issues of advertising and media literacy, consumer literacy, and economic literacy. Kline looks at each of these in detail and argues for our need to remain vigilant in an increasingly sophisticated communication environment. While it is apparent that children are actively engaged in the market there remain questions over their marketplace literacy, and this chapter raises a number of important issues in relation to children as consumers.

In summary, this text offers a comprehensive and insightful overview of various aspects of children's consumption and their role as consumers. As the children's market grows in importance, we need to more fully understand their role as consumers both in terms of ensuring that they are adequately equipped to deal with the changing market and that any marketing addresses their specific needs and vulnerabilities. As the various chapters show, there is no clear answer to the question of whether children are either vulnerable or competent; the truth, if it exists, seems to lie somewhere between the two. That is not to say that we should not continue to regulate, monitor and legislate where appropriate, but it recognizes that we need to give children some credit as consumers. In looking at children as consumers it is easy to forget that we are adults and what may seem trite, fickle or unimportant to us may take on a different meaning to a young consumer. Debates around media literacy, marketplace competencies, or even specific aspects of consumption such as nutritional literacy are all attempts to address some of these issues, but from a policy perspective how we move forward depends very much on whether we start from a position of seeing children as vulnerable or competent. Hopefully this book will help readers to decide on where they stand in relation to young consumers. The title of the book, *Understanding Children as Consumers*, hints at new ideas about children as engaged and active consumers in the marketplace.

References

Acuff, D. (1997) *What Kids Buy and Why: The Psychology of Marketing to Kids*. New York: Free.

Advertising Association (2007) 'Interim review of the media landscape: food advertising changes in context'. Industry submission by the AA's Food Advertising Unit, September. Available at http://www.adassoc.org.uk/Interim_Review_of_Media_Landscape.pdf (accessed 16 June 2009).

Advertising Association (2009) 'Children's wellbeing in a commercial world'. A contribution by the Advertising Association to the DCSF enquiry, 26 January. Available at http://www.adassoc.org.uk/html/research_and_reports.html (accessed 16 June 2009).

Andersen, L.P. (2007) 'Why don't they just show the product? Tween's reception and conception of TV-advertising', in K. Ekström and B. Tufte (eds), *Children and Media Consumption: On the Front Edge*. The international Clearinghouse on Children, Youth and media, Nordicom, Göteborg University. pp. 221–234.

Bartholomew, A. and O'Donohoe, S. (2003) 'Everything under control: a child's eye view of advertising', *Journal of Marketing Management*, 19 (3–4): 433–458.

Buckingham, D. (2000) *After the Death of Childhood: Growing Up in the Age of Electronic Media*. Cambridge: Polity.

Buckingham, D. (2008) *Youth Identity and Digital Media*. Cambridge, MA: MIT Press.

Buckingham, D. and Willett, R. (eds) (2006) *Digital Generations: Children, Young People and New Media*. New Jersey: Lawrence Erlbaum.

Carauna, A. and Vasello, R. (2004) 'Children's perception of their influence over purchases: the role of parental communication patterns', *Journal of Consumer Marketing*, 20 (1): 55–66.

ChildWise (2008) *Monitor Report 2007/08*. Available at http://www.childwise.co.uk/ChildWise-monitor-survey.asp (accessed 16 June 2009).

ChildWise (2009) *Monitor Report 2008/09*. Available at http://www.childwise.co.uk/ChildWise-monitor-survey.asp (accessed 16 June 2009).

Clay, D. (2008) 'Assessment of the impact of the commercial world on childhood: a report by kids industries for the Advertising Association', (June). Available at http://www.adassoc.org.uk/ki_AA_RESPONSE_V2_30.6.08.pdf (accessed 16 June 2009).

Cook, D.T. (2004) *The Commodification of Childhood: The Children's Clothing Industry and the Rise of the Child Consumer*. London: Duke University Press.

Cross, G. (1997) *Kids' Stuff: Toys and the Changing World of American Childhood*. Cambridge, MA: Harvard University Press.

Cross, G. (2004) *The Cute and the Cool: Wondrous Innocence and Modern American Children's Culture*. New York: Oxford University Press.

Davis, J. (1990) *Youth and the Condition of Britain: Images of Adolescent Conflict*. London: Athlone.

Del Vecchio, G. (1997) *Creating Ever Cool: A Marketeer's Guide to a Kid's Heart*. Gretna: Pelican.

Ekström, K. and Tufte, B. (2007) *Children and Media Consumption: On the Front Edge*. The International Clearinghouse on Children, Youth and Media, Nordicom, Göteborg University.

Guber, S. and Berry, J. (1993) *Marketing to and through Kids*. New York: McGraw-Hill.

Gunter, B. and Furnham, A. (1998) *Children as Consumers: A Psychological Analysis of the Young People's Market*. London: Routledge.

Halifax (2008) *Pocket Money Survey* (press release). Available at http://www.lloydsbankinggroup.com/media/pdfs/halifax/2008/August/25_08_08_Halifax_pocket_money_survey_2008.pdf (see also http://www.walesonline.co.uk/business-in-wales/personal-finance/2009/02/18/children-s-pocket-money-rose-four-times-inflation-rate-91466-22953384/ or http://news.bbc.co.uk/1/hi/education/7837848.stm (accessed 16 June 2009)).

James, A., Jenks, C. and Prout, A. (1998) *Theorizing Childhood*. New York: Teachers College Press.

Kaiser Family Foundation (2006) 'It's child's play: advergaming and the online marketing of food to children'. A Kaiser Family Foundation Report (July). Available at http://www.kff.org/entmedia/7536.cfm (accessed 16 June 2009).

Kaiser Family Foundation (2007) 'Food for thought: television food advertising to children in the United States'. A Kaiser Family Foundation Report (March). Available at http://www.kff.org/entmedia/7618.cfm (accessed 16 June 2009).

Kline, S. (1993) *Out of the Garden: Toys, TV, and Children's Culture in the Age of Marketing*. New York: Verso.

Kline, S., Dyer-Witheford, N. and De Peuter, G. (2003) *Digital Play: The Interaction of Technology, Culture and Marketing*. Montreal: McGill-Queen's University Press.

Langer, B. (1994) 'Born to shop: children and consumer capitalism', in F. Briggs (ed.), *Children and Families: Australian Perspectives*. Sydney: Allen & Unwin.

Langer, B. (2005) 'Consuming anomie: children and global commercial culture', *Childhood*, 12 (2): 259–271.

Lawlor, M. and Prothero, A. (2002) 'The established and potential mediating variables in the child's understanding of advertising intent: towards a research agenda', *Journal of Marketing Management*, 18 (5/6): 481–499.

Lee, M., Choi, Y., Taylor, E. and Cole, R. (2009) 'Playing with food: content analysis of food advergames', *Journal of Consumer Affairs*, 43 (1): 129–154.

Lindstrom, M. and Seybold, P. (2003) *Brand Child: Insights into the Minds of Today's Global Kids: Understanding Their Relationship with Brands*. Sterling, VA: Kogan Page.

Linn, S. (2004) *Consuming Kids*. New York: New.

Livingstone, S. (2009) *Children and the Internet: Great Expectations and Challenging Realities*. Cambridge: Polity.

Livingstone, S. and Helsper, E. (2004) 'Advertising foods to children: understanding promotion in the context of children's daily lives'; review of the literature prepared for the Research Department of Ofcom. Available at http://www.ofcom.org.uk.

Livingstone, S. and Helsper, E. J. (2006) 'Does advertising literacy mediate the effects of advertising on children? A critical examination of two linked research literatures in relation to obesity and food choice', *Journal of Communication*, 56: 560–584.

McNeal, J. (1987) *Children as Consumers: Insights and Implications*. Lexington, MA: Lexington.

McNeal, J. (1992) *Kids as Customers: A Handbook of Marketing to Children*. New York: Lexington.

McNeal, J. (1999) *The Kids Market: Myths and Realities*. Ithaca, NY: Paramount Market Publishing.

McNeal, J. (2007) *On Becoming a Consumer: The Development of Consumer Behavior Patterns in Childhood*. New York: Elsevier Science & Technology.

Mayo, E. and Nairn, A. (2009) *Consumer Kids: How Big Business is Grooming our Children for Profit*. London: Constable.

Moore, E. (2004) 'Children and the changing world of advertising', *Journal of Business Ethics*, 52 (June): 161–167.

Moore, E.S. and Rideout, V.J. (2007) 'The online marketing of food to children: is it just fun and games?', *Journal of Public Policy & Marketing*, 26 (2): 202–220.

Nairn, A. and Fine, C. (2008) 'Who's messing with my mind? The implications of dual-process models for the ethics of advertising to children', *International Journal of Advertising*, 27 (3): 447–470.

Nairn, A., Ormrod, J. and Bottomley, P. (2007) 'Watching, Wanting and Wellbeing', National Consumer Council, London. Available at http://www.agnesnairn.co.uk/policy_reports/watching_wanting_and_wellbeing_july_2007.pdf.

Office for National Statistics (2009) *Social Trends 39*. Basingstoke: Palgrave Macmillan. Available at http://www.statistics.gov.uk/socialtrends39/

Palmer, S. (2007) *Toxic Childhood: How The Modern World Is Damaging Our Children And What We Can Do About It*. London: Orion.

Preston, C. (2004) 'Children's advertising: the ethics of economic socialisation', *International Journal of Consumer Studies*, 28 (4): 364–370.

Robertson, T.S. and Rossiter, J.R. (1974) 'Children and commercial persuasion: an attribution theory analysis', *Journal of Consumer Research*, 1 (1): 13–20.

Schor, J. (2004) *Born to Buy: The Commercialised Child and the New Consumer Culture*. New York: Scribner.

Schor, J. (2006) 'When childhood gets commercialized, can children be protected?', in U. Carlsson (ed.), *Regulation, Awareness, Empowerment Young People and Harmful Media Content in the Digital Age*, The International Clearinghouse on Children, Youth and Media, Nordicom, Göteborg University. pp. 101–122. Available at http://www.nordicom.gu.se/

Seiter, E. (1993) *Sold Separately: Children and Parents in Consumer Culture*. New Brunswick, New Jersey: Rutgers University Press.

Spungin, P. (2004) 'Parent power, not pester power', *International Journal of Advertising and Marketing to Children*, 5 (3) (April–June): 37–40.

Tufte, B., Rasmussen, J. and Christensen, L. (eds) (2005) *Frontrunners or Copycats?* Copenhagen: Copenhagen Business School Press.

Wooton, M. (2003) 'Pestering parents: how food companies market obesity to children', Report 62, Center for Science in the Public Interest. Available at www.cspinet.org/new/pdf/pesteringparentsnopictures.pdf.

Notes

1 Much of the discussion in the book centres on children under 12 and excludes infants. A number of chapters focus on tweens i.e. those between 7 and 12 years old.

2 Dan Cook (2004: 3) uses the term 'pediocularity' to describe the situation where the child's view is represented and adjudicated by commerce.

3 But with that comes some responsibility. If we are to allow children to 'choose', if we consider them as competent and capable, we have to live with the consequences. Treating them as consumers is not without risk but there are differing degrees of choice and debate around what is deemed acceptable and unacceptable consequences.

4 The advertising industry has responded and recent reports found limited evidence of a decline in children's wellbeing over the past fifteen years (Advertising Association, 2007, 2009; Clay, 2008). However, there are concerns over the measure of self-esteem and the analysis used, and for this reason the reports are not cited in the text (personal communication, Agnes Nairn).

5 This follows the procedure used by Mayo and Nairn (2009) to estimate the size of the children's market including all purchases directly related to raising children but excluding additional family purchases that children may influence. Data from the US Census Bureau, Current Population Survey, 2008 Annual Social and Economic Supplement (http://www.census.gov/population/socdemo/hh-fam/cps2008/tabC2-all.csv) show 74.014 million children under 18 in US households. Figures from the USDA Expenditure on Children by Families 2006 report (http://www.cnpp.usda.gov/Publications/CRC/crc2006.pdf#xml= http://65.216.150.153/texis/search/pdfhi.txt?query=dependent+children+numb ers&pr=CNPP&prox=page&rorder=500&rprox=500&rdfreq=500&rwfreq=500&r lead=500&rdepth=0&sufs=2&order=r&cq=&id=49a59efdd) estimate the total cost of raising a child from birth to 17 years in husband-wife families is $143,790 (Before-tax income: Less than $44,500); $197,700 (Before-tax income: $44,500 to $74,900); and $289,380 (Before-tax income: More than $74,900). In single person households this is $136,200 (Before-tax income: Less than $44,500) and $289,740 (Before-tax income: $44,500 or more). If we average these out at $211,362 this

represents an average of $12,433 per year. Using the population figures this represents a children's market of around $921bn.

6 Data from the UK ONS (2009) *Social Trends* 39, 15 April (http://www.statistics. gov.uk/downloads/theme_social/Social_Trends39/Social_Trends_39.pdf) show 13 million dependent children under 16 years old living with at least one parent in the UK. Data from the Liverpool Victoria Annual Cost of a Child Survey 2009 (http://www.lv.com/media_centre/press_releases/lv=%20cost%20of%20a%20ch ild) estimate that it costs £194,000 to raise a child from birth to 21. This represents £9,227 a year. As average annual costs vary over a child's life and costs tend to be higher from 19 to 21 years old an estimate of £9,000 was made from birth to 16, to cover the ONS definition of dependent children. This gives a figure of around £117bn. This represents an increase of 4 per cent on previous estimates with cost up almost 40 per cent over the previous five years since the survey started.

7 Halifax Bank of Scotland (HBOS) is now part of the Lloyds Banking Group plc.

8 Many thanks to Rosmary Duff of ChildWise for these latest figures. The full report can be seen at http://www.childwise.co.uk/contact-childwise.asp

9 ChildWise is an established market research and marketing strategy agency which specializes in research with children. The ChildWise Monitor is a comprehensive annual report on children's and teenagers' media consumption, brand attitudes and behaviour, now in its fifteenth year. ChildWise estimate that 82 per cent of 5–10 year olds receive £5.70 p.w. (= £4.70 each/all children) which translates to £19.4 million per week; 86 per cent of 11–16 year olds receive £14.10 p.w. (= £12.10 each/all children) which translates to £54.3 million per week.

10 Generation Y, those born between 1982 and 2000, represent around 80 million US consumers and have a major impact on family spending. They are more affluent as in many cases both their parents work and they have higher expectations. As co-purchasers in family spending they contribute to family decisions about cars, clothes, electronic equipment and family holidays (http://couponing.about. com/b/2006/10/16/youth-influences-half-of-consumer-spending.htm).

11 See also http://news.bbc.co.uk/1/hi/education/7837848.stm

Part I

Children as Consumers

2   Developing as Consumers

Valérie-Inés de la Ville and Valérie Tartas

Chapter aims

- To introduce three alternative perspectives used by marketing researchers and practitioners to explain how children develop as consumers.
- To discuss the cornerstone elements of these three models and the contrasting explanations they propose about the learning processes through which children develop as consumers.
- To delineate new research avenues in order to account for the creative capacities of children when they participate in joint consumption activities.

Introduction

Scientific articles aimed at linking the realms of childhood and economy appeared in the early 1950s and dealt mainly with the role children play when they take part in family consumption practices (Strauss, 1952). The concept of consumer socialization is a relatively recent research area having been defined for the first time in 1974 by S. Ward: 'The processes by which young people acquire skills, knowledge, and attitudes relevant to their functioning as consumers in the marketplace' (Ward, 1974: 2). This broad definition implies an interdisciplinary approach, requiring social and cultural backgrounds, language skills, psychological development, emotional and symbolic dimensions, and so on (Robertson and Feldman, 1976). Thus, this chapter aims to clarify the contributions of three established alternative perspectives to understanding the development of children's abilities as consumers.

- The first is a classic developmental-stage based perspective which focuses on the progressive acquisition of economic knowledge by children and aims at describing the transformation of children s consumption abilities.
- The second combines different process-centred models which focus on the role of social environment and aim at explaining how children are influenced by socialization agents in their acquisition of economic abilities.
- The third suggests that children are immersed in the realm of mass consumption culture and views children's consumption as a socio-historical activity that needs to be grasped in its entire complexity.

Furthermore, since consumer activities are situated within a broader context of social relationships, they serve as a means by which children learn about contemporary society and prevailing social rules (Oestergaard and Jantzen, 2000).

First perspective: cognitive development and the acquisition of economic knowledge

One branch of research draws on seminal work by the Swiss psychologist Jean Piaget (1937), applying it to the analysis of the development of economic thinking by children. This research perspective asks 'what' does the child know? It focuses on understanding what kind of economic knowledge children are able to use when they are confronted with practical problems linked to consumption activities. Using Piagetian terms, development can be defined as the process of adapting to the outside world. During this progression, individuals construct increasingly elaborate cognitive mechanisms to improve their control over their surrounding world. This developmental process unfolds in a natural way: children gradually build up skills by acting on their environment (the assimilation process), which will in turn impose its own structures on them (the accommodation process). Thus, three stages are proposed to describe and explain the cognitive development: the *sensori-motor stage*, where infants construct their knowledge through their actions on the surrounding world, which are at first quite limited; the preparation and entry into the *concrete logical operation stage* where children are able to decentrate and consider others' points of view; and the third one called the *formal thinking stage* where adolescents become able to reason on hypotheses and not only about concrete reality. The increasingly complex logical designs that characterize adult thought are regarded as the ultimate result of child developmental processes (see Young and Roland-Lévy, Chapters 7 and 9 in this book).

The American researcher Deborah Roedder-John (1999) has documented twenty five years of accumulated international research on children in relation to their role as consumers. She has incorporated the findings into a general conceptual framework that conceives of consumer socialization as progressing through a series of three sequential stages capturing major cognitive shifts from preschool to adolescence: the *perceptual stage* (3 to 7 years), the *analytical stage* (7 to 11 years), and the *reflective stage* (11 to 16 years) (see Table 2.1). These stages, essentially defined in terms of age groups, include various dimensions that characterize children's knowledge. Motivations as well as cognitive and social skills are aspects of these stages, which are also related to children's growing sophistication with regard to products, brands, advertising campaigns, shopping, pricing, decision-making strategies, and influential strategies.

Using Piaget's theory, Roedder-John's framework seeks to identify the main shifts in children's understanding of basic economic concepts. It depicts young children's skills as being limited and only based on perceptual skills, which are not enough to understand the implicit messages contained in advertising for example. Thus from 3 to 7 years old, children show an egocentric orientation, as they are not able to differentiate points of view. Therefore, they might not be able to distinguish the persuasive motivations of the advertiser from the information needed by the consumer. Moreover,

Table 2.1 Stages in children's development as consumers

Characteristics	Perceptual stage 3–7 years	Analytical stage 7–11 years	Reflective stage 11–16 years
	Knowledge structures		
Orientation	Concrete	Abstract	Abstract
Focus	Perceptual features	Functional/underlying features	Functional/ underlying features
Complexity	Unidimensional	Two or more dimensions	Multidimensional
	Simple	Contingent (if-then)	Contingent (if-then)
Perspective	Egocentric (own perspective)	Dual perspectives (own+others)	Dual perspectives in social context
	Decision-making and influence strategies		
Orientation	Expedient	Thoughtful	Strategic
Focus	Perceptual features	Functional/underlying features	Functional/ underlying features
	Salient features	Relevant features	Relevant features
Complexity	Single attribute	Two or more attributes	Multiple attributes
	Limited repertoire of strategies	Expanded repertoire of strategies	Complete repertoire of strategies
Adaptive	Emerging	Moderate	Fully developed
Perspective	Egocentric	Dual perspectives	Dual perspectives in social context

Source: Roedder-John, D. (1999) 'Consumer socialisation of children – a retrospective look at twenty-five years of research', in *Journal of Consumer Research*, 26 (3): 183–213, with permission of The University of Chicago Press. © 1999 by Journal of Consumer Research Inc.

children's ability to deal with information is limited and prevents them from making decisions based on a plurality of dimensions as adults do. This model provides descriptive information outlining how a child's intellect develops within the analytical stage – starting from fragmentary and imprecise ideas and proceeding towards a more logical understanding. In the analytical stage, children are becoming aware of the complexity of the market because their way of reasoning becomes more abstract and is no longer only driven by their own perceptions. The reflective stage allows pre-adolescents and adolescents to develop critical thinking about the marketplace and how it functions.

Drawing on this cognitive stage-based framework of child development, Roedder-John presents five areas of research, which she considers to be the effects of the process of consumer socialization. They imply an acquisition of various knowledge, skills and values, for instance advertising and persuasion knowledge, transaction knowledge, and decision-making skills and abilities, negotiation skills, values and motives of consumption.

As a managerial transposition of the cognitive developmental theory of Piaget, this framework of consumer socialization was mainly addressed to marketing managers with a two-fold aim: firstly, to describe the development of consumer socialization through three cognitive stages, and secondly, to offer a 'toolkit' to help marketing practitioners improve their targeting of children and adolescents. Roedder-John acknowledged that she focused on research from a managerial and marketing perspective, and that her concentration on consumer research published in marketing and communication journals led her to exclude other research areas dealing with child development. This might explain why her theoretical framework overlooked three important points:

- *Cognitive development is driven by biological or internal factors*   To go beyond the mere physical objects that were the main focus in Piagetian studies, Roedder-John used Selman's (1980) theory, which integrates the social dimensions of child development and documents the changes in children's way of thinking about the social world. Although it takes into account children's capacity to consider another's point of view and to behave in accordance with a conventional system of social roles, this perspective provides a very limited understanding of child consumer socialization since it conceives of socialization itself as a fundamentally solitary cognitive construction. From a Piagetian perspective, the socialization process of the child is seen only from the point of view of the endogenous factors that lead the child to pass from self-centredness to other-centredness. In such a perspective, only internal processes may explain the development of economic thinking and the transitions between the different stages.
- *The use of age as a marker of cognitive skills*   By placing 'age' – instead of the internal structure of thought – as the cornerstone of her framework, Roedder-John diverted Piagetian theory from its own foundations. She conceived of development as only a difference of degree in the understanding and use of economic knowledge, and not as a qualitative difference in the nature of reasoning involved in economic activities and market situations, whereas in Piagetian terms the idea of

stages is much more complex and relates to the internal cognitive mechanisms of assimilation, accommodation and equilibration. Jean Piaget himself stressed that what should be retained from his model was the succession of stages and not the age ranges because these could vary greatly according to cultural and social contexts (Bringuier, 1977: 57). However, some researchers do criticize stage-oriented theories of child development as, in the context of a globalizing marketplace fostering the internationalization of mass media and consumer culture, the everyday life of contemporary children is extremely different from that of former times (Gunter and Furnham, 1998).

- *The exclusive focus on logical reasoning*   By considering children as 'economic problem solvers' trying to succeed in an adult economic world (Duveen, 1994), managerial approaches promote a specific kind of knowledge and reasoning (logical) while overlooking a major mode of human thought, the narrative one. Most of the studies in economy psychology and economics were conducted to find out if children would behave as logical and rational actors in economic decision making. However children's economic activities appear not to be based on a purely rational basis. As Bruner (1986) pointed out, two major modes of thinking characterize human cognition: the 'syntagmatic' or 'narrative' mode and the 'paradigmatic' or 'logical' mode. Narrative mode of thought (see Vignette 1) does not compensate for under-developed logical abilities, as these are two different modes of thinking. In the first, events are connected to one another through a narrative frame allowing the creation of stories, whereas in a paradigmatic mode reasoning faculties pursue logical truth. If the child develops his or her narrative capacity very early on in everyday activities, the paradigmatic thought (or logico-scientific) only emerges after systematic education, for which the institutional dimension, such as the schooling system, has received little consideration within the Piagetian theory.

Vignette 1: The narrative mode of perceiving and thinking

Cultural psychology, as proposed by Bruner, deals with how individuals make sense of the world and how they engage with established systems of shared meaning, with the beliefs, values, and symbols of the culture at large. It concentrates on how individuals construct 'realities' based on common cultural narratives and symbols, and how reality is 'intersubjective' through social interaction rather than 'external' or 'objective'. The 'narrative, constructivist or interpretive' mode of perceiving and knowing about the world is more suited to our perception of people and experience, while the 'paradigmatic or logico-scientific' mode is appropriate to the natural and physical sciences. Narrative cognition is concerned with the meaning of experience.

> From infancy, most of children are immersed in the texts of popular culture. The texts and artefacts of popular culture frame children's understanding of the world and of them ... visual representation such as cinematic texts, stylised illustrations, cartoons, videos or photographs are part of the landscape of meaning that social subjects encounter in everyday life. (Luke, 1994: 289)

In short, we can conclude that the theory of cognitive development has played a dominant role in management academic circles as well as in marketing practice (Siegel et al., 2002). Nevertheless, critics have pointed out that socialization should be defined as a function of environmental influences rather than as a purely individual cognitive process, which constitutes a transition to the second perspective.

Second perspective: acquiring social skills and knowledge through interaction with socialization agents

A second course of study endeavours to overcome certain limitations of the cognitive-driven approaches by incorporating the social aspects of economic development, using various social variables, and applying the social education model elaborated by Bandura (1977). This process-oriented approach to consumer socialization has gained ground in understanding 'how' the child acquires his or her economic knowledge.

Moschis and his colleagues (Moschis and Churchill, 1978; Moschis and Moore, 1979) developed an alternative theory of child consumer socialization, which offered a more accurate definition of consumer socialization that refers to three theoretical elements: the structural antecedents, the socialization process in itself, and the behavioural outcomes. This initial definition has been enriched by successive complementary contributions that interweave three theoretical frameworks which all focus on the processes at stake in the development of economic understanding and consumer behaviours (see Figure 2.1).

The first can be found in the Piagetian theory as revisited by Berti and Bombi (1988), which suggested that children are active role-takers in the economic domain. Drawing on these studies, the authors defined economic socialization as an on-going process by which the child assimilates knowledge and reasoning about the economic world and consumption practices. The emphasis was put on children's methods of interpreting the marketplace as well as on the specificity of the cognitive operations needed to understand economic notions.

The second draws on the social role model theory (Eagly, 1987), which suggests that a child is supposed to learn how to play different roles in society such as pupil, sibling, grandson, as well as consumer. The economic education is achieved in practice owing to four main sources of information: parents and family habits, peers, advertising, and the products themselves. The inclusion of social roles emphasized the importance of the social environment on children's cognitive elaborations. It considered the influences of parents and peers as well as the effect of gender as the main factors that help

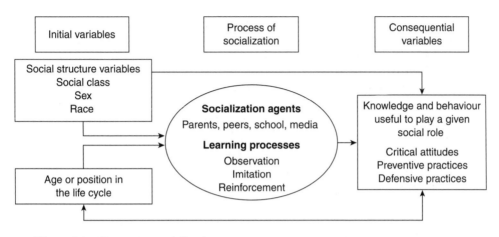

Figure 2.1   Consumer socialization process

Source: Adapted from Moschis and Churchill (1978) and complemented by several authors

children become active economic agents – able to choose a product, learn how to buy it, and understand how the marketplace is governed.

The third uses Bandura's (1977) theory of social learning which suggests that two central processes – observation and imitation (mimicry of other consumers e.g., parents, peers, brothers and sisters, etc.) – can explain both real consumer behaviour (such as comparing prices and products) and more complex and abstract notions (such as purchasing power and taxes). The role of social environment is explained through two main independent variables: the nature of the social environment in which the child is involved, and the type of reinforcement or feedback provided by the environment.

The combination of these three theoretical contributions that were considered interrelated led, for instance, to Lassare and Roland-Lévy (1989) linking four variables that derived from general socialization theories: 1) the socialization agents (peers, family, school, mass media); 2) the learning process (in particular imitation or vicarious learning); 3) the social structure variables (age, sex, social class); and 4) the learning content. Their work allowed a broader understanding of consumer socialization processes and represented a clear invitation to explore how the socialization process actually works in everyday and casual social activities as well as in more formal social contexts.

The main contributions of the theoretical frameworks elaborated within this perspective include linking cognition to social interactions and avoiding the limitations of a strictly individualistic cognitive development approach. Authors such as Berti and Bombi (1988), Lassare and Roland-Lévy (1989) or Lachance and Legault (2007) focused on the way children or young people are integrated into society through the appropriation of the roles played by various models. Thus, this body of research shows that the main socialization agents involved in children's consumer socialization are threefold: traditional (family circles, peers and school), professional (marketing managers, communication agencies), and finally virtual (web communities, social networking websites).

These process-oriented frameworks about child consumer socialization perceive social environment through two key variables: the child's social environment and the feedback and reinforcement provoked by this environment. Thus, this process approach tries to consider the individual and the cognitive operations involved in economic situations as well as the social contexts in which each child develops. However, in spite of their ambitious attempt, these frameworks leave three important issues unanswered.

- *A limited scope of exploration that ignores young children* This theoretical perspective allowed a recombination of several research results obtained through different methodologies: surveys through semi-structured interviews, face-to-face interviews in focus groups, observations and questionnaires. Nevertheless, the first shortcoming comes from the empirical studies that are mainly focused on pre-adolescents, adolescents, young adults and adults (Lachance and Legault, 2007), neglecting young children such as preschool and early school children. As a result, this process perspective only covers a limited explanatory scope since it favours pre-adolescents and adolescents.
- *Vicarious learning cannot account for children's creative capacities* The modelling exposure perspective argues that being confronted by parental economic behaviour is sufficient to trigger the development of a child's economic skills. But then a crucial question remains unanswered: how can we explain the emergence of new behaviours in children, adolescents, or adults (see Vignette 2)? It is then necessary to go beyond this second process-oriented approach to explain creative behaviours, i.e. behaviours that were not previously available in the social environment and that could not have been modelled or imitated. Focusing exclusively on observation and imitation impedes the development of an explanation for creative behaviours originating independently from those already developed within family circles or peer groups. In psychology, the modelling approach has been criticized: imitation of adults or more experienced children is neither a necessary nor a sufficient condition to explain children's cognitive progressions (Doise and Mugny, 1981).

Vignette 2: Some examples of creative behaviours

Children are immersed in new digital tools and networks which were not available to their parents. This leads them to invent collective forms of appropriation, peer-to-peer creativity and differing modes of self-expression:

- Instant text-messaging such as MSN and chatrooms or SMS on mobile phones that nurture the development and institutionalization of a new abbreviated language and its subsequent language games.

- Deviant uses of MMS image-messaging on mobiles phones such as 'Happy Slapping' videos.*
- Peer-to-peer exchanges that foster the emergence of new business models in cultural industries.
- Creation of personal websites and blogs.
- Continuously staging one's activities and friendships online through social networking sites such as Facebook.

*Children send videos via mobile phones showing a child being beaten or slapped by others.

- *Interaction does not constitute the key unit of analysis* Even though social interactions are not the central focus of their empirical analysis, the process models highlight the role of interaction with others – individuals enacting their institutional roles – as a central explanatory factor. In fact, the individual and social issues are seen as two separate entities, which certainly need to be re-entangled. However, in the end the individual remains the cornerstone of the analysis and the theoretical elaboration. Social influence approaches maintain a focus on the individual as the basic unit of analysis and examine the influence of 'outside' social forces. In the social influence perspective, since individual competence is traditionally seen as separate from environmental circumstances, individuals are considered to possess knowledge prior to being involved in a social interaction, and then to have a social experience allowing a consideration of other possible courses of action, finally absorbing them so they become a part of their personal repertoire.

Yet as Cram and Ng (1999: 301) note, 'both psychological and marketing approaches (social learning theory) have inherent faults in terms of their ability to provide a full picture of children's consumer socialization. These faults include a lack of understanding of children as active agents within a cultural context which, in turn, has resulted in a dearth of cross-cultural research and the widespread acceptance of the white, middle-class nuclear family as the "normal" context within which children are socialised'. Out of this critique these authors go on to develop their own approach, called 'scaffolding', which is based on Bruner and Haste's (1987: 1) definition of socialization as a process through which children acquire a 'framework for interpreting experience and learning how to negotiate meaning in a manner congruent with the requirements of culture'. Their 'scaffolding' approach ties three consumption-related concepts – 'ownership', 'money' (as a medium of exchange), and 'price' – which provide children with a framework for integrating an increasing variety of consumption experiences. Cram and Ng discuss how these concepts validate and support children's consumer socialization, leading to a wider perspective of consumer socialization. In this sense, they opened up avenues for socio-cultural approaches to children's consumption which lead us to the third perspective.

Third perspective: transforming children's participation in joint consumption activities

This more recent approach draws on cultural psychological theory, considering that children are immersed in the realm of mass consumption culture. In contrast with the two previous ones, this perspective goes beyond considering children as mere individuals and contends that development results from the progressive involvement of children in several *social activities* available in their environment. From a theoretical standpoint, the emphasis is on examining how children actually participate in socio-cultural activities and especially how they take part in consumption activities. To understand how children learn and develop through a participation in socio-cultural activities, it is necessary to accept that cultural significance is more than the mere addition of changes in individual thinking that result from social interaction and discussions with other participants (Rogoff, 1998: 686). A key contribution of this perspective is to underline that institutional backgrounds (family, school, religion, etc.) and their derived power structures shape both language and cultural meanings in a given society.

Within this framework, the child is clearly integrated into a social body with which he or she interacts and from which he or she receives help and reassurance when daring to participate in everyday social life. Consequently, the relevant unit of analysis is certainly not the isolated child confronted with a problem, but rather the joint activity developed within an interaction: between a child and an adult, a child and a more experienced child, or within a small group. By confronting a practical problem such as a purchase decision, or defining a socially acceptable use of an object with a more experienced partner, a child can discover the cultural significance of objects. In this perspective, the transformation of children's consumer roles is the lens through which developmental transitions are understood.

The developmental approach proposed by the Russian psychologist Vygotsky is the cornerstone of this third perspective as it considers development in relation to the cultural environment in which the child develops. Culture in itself is not seen as a merely external variable but as a constitutive element of child development. To go further, Vygotsky (1934/1985) used the concept of 'psychological' or 'semiotic' tools to account for the relationship between the individual and the external world (Wertsch, 1985). Child consumer activities constitute a social activity mediated by various cultural tools such as the language, the social standards called upon, the rhetoric evoked, and the purchased objects or products themselves. Through everyday activities, the child gradually assimilates a conventional language particular to consumption – such as concepts of brand, price, quality, comparisons of products – and a set of social standards relating to consumption in a given cultural context – such as mastered references, a search for identity, membership within a group, and feeling of belonging to a social

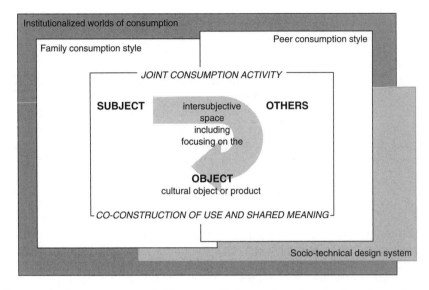

Figure 2.2   Consumption activities as mediating and mediated cultural experiences

Source: de la Ville, 2005

class (Gronow and Warde, 2001). Thus, studying the psychological tools or the systems of signs used by children during their development as economic actors enables a precise analysis of how they understand and practise consumption. To obtain what they want, children must tell an appropriate story and know how to present their actions and objectives in order to make them legitimate within specific social groups – family circles or peer groups. As the narrative capacities of the child increase in the process of economic socialization, researchers can analyse the evolution of children's accounts of their consumption practices. By 3 to 4 years of age, children can be regarded as 'experts' in the use of various narrative forms, knowing how to handle different rhetorical registers in order to evoke empathy in their close relations, which explains how children can influence family purchases.

This leads us to suggest that children develop as economic actors within a complex cultural system that combines several inter-dependent dimensions (see Figure 2.2). In the *joint consumption activity*, three elements are interwoven:

- The child is never alone but is always guided by others (adult caregivers and more experienced children) in questioning the practices of consumption and in constructing socially shared meanings.
- The term 'cultural object' covers any socially and historically created product (not only the material and physical characteristics of the object but also its symbolic and semiotic dimension).

- The cultural object on which attention is focused is a socially and historically created product that includes in its design a technical, social and commercial background. This institutional background strongly directs its potential uses.

The significance of children's consumption practices is framed by the normative requirements of both family and peer consumption styles. The child has to learn to deal with the conflicting requirements held by the different social groups to which he or she belongs (Page and Ridgway, 2001). Moreover, beyond these face-to-face relationships, children's consumption practices are also enabled and constrained by wider institutional systems including:

- The institutionalized worlds of consumption (i.e. distribution and retailing, regulatory requirements, socially permitted sales techniques, sales on the internet, cultural events like Christmas, Easter, carnival festivities, etc.).
- The on-going innovations of the socio-technical design system that bring new opportunities in designing products for children. For example 'smart toys' or interactive cuddly toys mix electronics and traditional techniques and reflect the development of the toy industry, especially in relation to technological innovation.

Among the various mediating cultural tools that are used within this system, some are developed by managers and play a major role, such as:

- *Packaging* This structures and channels children's learning experiences by constraining the categorization process used to recognize, classify and compare products (Cochoy, 2002).
- *Brand characters* This creates an effective relationship between the brand and the child and establishes brand recognition by young consumers (Lawrence, 2003).
- *Advertising* As a persuasive technique inherent to mass media (Kline, 1993; Kline et al., 2003), it contributes to the diffusion of values, social norms, symbolic languages and behaviours linked to consumption practices.

As a consequence, children's consumption practices cannot be reduced to a mere purchase decision: educational, social and institutional dimensions are at the core of the long process allowing children to take part in the consumer world. Moreover, when using an item, a child discovers and learns important information about social life and its normative requirements. Thus, child consumption practices are both a mediated and a mediating social activity through which a child learns many things far beyond consumption itself (de la Ville, 2005). For instance, when choosing a gift to take to a birthday party, the child learns that different social rules come into play depending on whether the beneficiary is a boy, a girl, or an adult and so on (Cook, 2002). If child consumption can be considered a mediated activity – through different forms of semiotic tools (such as language, advertising, packaging, etc.) and through different kinds of guidance (adult or peer) – it is also important to understand it as a mediating social activity. Indeed, by participating in joint consumption activities, children not only acquire knowledge and competences linked with consumption (for example about brands or products), they can also learn to develop their social abilities such as their persuasion skills, their vocabulary, their way of interacting with others, and their ability to divert authority requirements and play with formal and informal status.

Considering this complex system, the central focus of enquiry becomes: how do children participate in socio-cultural consumption activities and how does their position change from being *peripheral participants* (Lave and Wenger, 1991) – as the users of a product bought by their parents or the observers of buying situations – to being *central participants*, namely as decision makers? Indeed, learning to consume is not simply a matter of socialization: it supposes that the child is able to adjust his level of participation in the activity depending on varied socio-cultural rules (Rogoff et al., 2006). Accordingly, research should focus on deciphering the variety of consumption activities in which children are involved and on understanding the social and cultural conditions that make them adjust their participation by different degrees:

- First degree: *a peripheral participation*   Meaning that young children are mainly in a position of observers, when discovering the items brought home by their parents or older siblings, when accompanying their parents to shop in traditional markets and retail outlets, or even when observing shopping online at home.
- Second degree: *a more focused and active participation*   Meaning children now prescribe consumer items, which are legitimized by caregivers, peers or siblings.
- Third degree: *a central participation*   Meaning children now act as active and competent consumers, able to legitimately decide how to spend their own pocket money in some consumption areas that are culturally defined as specific spaces for children within a cultural community.

This cultural perspective shows that children are able to create their own social rules and modify words and objects belonging to adulthood. In so doing, they generate their own socially shared meanings and cultures. The heroes and celebrities they admire, the new forms of narratives they explore, the games and playing activities in which they are involved, the possibilities offered by the technologies they use and so. on, are constituent elements of children's culture that differ from their parents' (Buckingham, 2000; Cook, 2008). Birthday celebrations are a very emblematic form of children's socialization where the correct social rules to be followed are not only defined by parents but also by children themselves (Sirota, 1999).

Conclusion

We have contrasted and clarified the potential contributions of three perspectives of consumer socialization to the understanding of how children gradually enter the realm of consumption practice and learn to take part in varied consumption activities. In the first perspective, by considering socialization to be a fundamentally solitary cognitive construction by an individual developing through a succession of stages, academic researchers in management and marketing tend to perpetuate a quite restricted under-standing of children's consumer socialization. They favour the logical-mathematical dimension of thought and overlook the narrative, socio-cultural, institutional and historical dimensions that also constitute consumption. But even if the second perspective attempts to integrate the social environment as a constitutive part of the process of economic socialization, it often reduces it to a matter of influence on the choices made by an individual child. That is why it appears necessary to develop a broader approach that takes into account two important points:

- Contemporary children develop within different cultural backgrounds (a dominant mass consumption culture in western societies versus other cultural systems in developing countries for instance).
- Political, religious and social institutions provide different mediating tools and relationships that shape children's cultural activities – including consumption activities.

Nevertheless, gaps still exist in our understanding of the various interrelated factors shaping the process of consumer socialization: 'Cultural changes, such as the growth of single-parent families, and technological change, such as the internet, suggest the need to revisit existing findings about socialization and address new concerns' (Roedder-John, 2002: 79).

Future research directions

For a more comprehensive understanding of how children develop their consumption activities, marketing research should focus on the language children practise in their everyday life. The consumption activities in which children are involved constitute a 'permanent re-creation', an on-going invention through which children renew cultural assets. Children adapt products, toys, and the like to particular circumstances, re-combining them according to the perceived objective, and inventing meanings that remain temporary (depending on technological and media advances, in particular through websites dedicated to information and commerce). Thus, from a methodological standpoint, this inventive dimension of child consumption practices should encourage us not to consider children as mere respondents, but as co-researchers who actively participate in the interpretation of their own experiences as apprentice consumers (Woodhead and Faulkner, 2003; Greene and Hogan, 2005).

A second line of investigation could tackle the issue of risks linked to con-sumption and determine to what extent a child's desires shape his or her daily activities. As a consequence, another key research perspective could be aimed at understanding the modes of informal education – within retail stores, at home, among siblings or in peer groups – that contribute to shaping children's knowledge about consumption practices in relation to specific cultural contexts. It should lead us to reflect on the status of children in the consumer society and the methods available for education aimed at increasing the degree of vigilance and reflexivity of young consumers. Furthermore, this line of study could specify the consumption situations in which children may be considered as vulnerable consumers in need of protection. Conversely, a complementary research perspective could question the social construction of specific areas where children are conceived as actually empowered consumers, as even more competent or expert than adults in the marketplace.

A third line of improvement includes an analysis of the historical, institutional and cultural aspects of the joint problem-solving activities that are observed in consumption practices. Socio-cultural approaches pay special attention to how both participants and institutions determine the goals, means, situation, and definition of consumption activities. A reflection on the evolution of the institutional elements that enable and justify the child's position right at the heart of commercial situations is essential. Children's economic socialization takes place within a broader historical trend in western cultures that has been apparent since the beginning of the twentieth century in the USA. The 'empowerment' of children as consumers in their own right provides contemporary young consumers with the institutional, cultural, and ideological resources to legitimate their active participation in the marketplace (Cross, 2002; Cook, 2004).

Note

This research project is funded by a French national research grant awarded by the Programme National de Recherche sur l'Alimentation (PNRA).

Discussion questions

1 Trace three contrasting definitions of the consumer socialization of children.
2 Do the three perspectives on consumer socialization differ when relating to children or adults?
3 How do the three approaches to consumer socialization define children's agency?
4 What arguments can these three perspectives on consumer socialization offer to determine whether a child is 'competent' or 'vulnerable' in everyday consumption activities?

Further reading

Eagly, A. and Chaiken, S. (1993) *The Psychology of Attitudes*. Fort Worth, TX: Harcourt Brace Jovanovich.

Ricoeur, P. (1991) *From Text to Action: Essays in Hermeneutics II* (translated by Kathleen Blamey and John B. Thompson). Evanston, IL: Northwestern University Press.

Valsiner, J. (2000) *Culture and Human Development*. London: Sage.

Vygotsky, L.S. (1978) *Mind in Society: The Development of Higher Psychological Processes*. Cambridge, MA: Harvard University Press.

References

Bandura, A. (1977) *Social Learning Theory*. Englewood Cliffs, NJ: Prentice-Hall.

Berti, A. and Bombi, A.S. (1988) *The Child's Construction of Economics*. Cambridge: Cambridge University Press.

Bringuier, J.C. (1977) *Conversations Libres Avec Jean Piaget*. Paris: Laffont.

Bruner, J.S. (1986) *Actual Minds, Possible Worlds*. Cambridge, MA: Harvard University Press.

Bruner, J.S. and Haste, H. (1987) 'Introduction', in J.S. Bruner and H. Haste (eds), *Making Sense: The Child's Construction of the World*. London: Methuen. pp. 1–25.

Buckingham, D. (2000) *After the Death of Childhood*. London: Polity.

Cochoy, F. (2002) *Une Sociologie du Packaging ou L'âne de Buridan Face au Marché*. Paris: Presses Universitaires de France.

Cook, D.T. (ed.) (2002) *Symbolic Childhood*. New York: Peter Lang.

Cook, D.T. (2004) *The Commodification of Childhood: The Children's Clothing Industry and the Rise of the Child Consumer*. London: Duke University Press.

Cook, D.T. (2008) 'The missing child in consumption theory', *Journal of Consumer Culture*, 8 (2): 219–243.

Cram, F. and Ng, S.H. (1999) 'Consumer socialization', *Applied Psychology: An International Review*, 48 (3): 297–312.

Cross, G. (2002) 'Valves of desire: a historian's perspective on parents, children, and marketing', *Journal of Consumer Research*, 29 (December): 441–447.

de la Ville, V.I. (2005) 'The invention of the child consumer: what is at stake for marketing practice and research?', in B. Tufte, J. Rasmussen and L.B. Christensen (eds), *Fontrunners or Copycats?* Copenhagen: Copenhagen Business School Press. pp. 135–158.

Doise, W. and Mugny, G. (1981) *Le Développement Social de L'intelligence*. Paris: Interéditions.

Duveen, G. (1994) 'Children's savings: a study of development of economic behaviour', *Journal of Economic Psychology*, 15 (2): 375–378.

Eagly, A. (1987) *Sex Differences in Social Behavior: A Social-Role Interpretation*. Hillsdale, NJ: Erlbaum.

Greene, S. and Hogan, D. (eds) (2005) *Researching Children's Experience: Methods and Approaches*. London: Sage.

Gronow, J. and Warde, A. (2001) *Ordinary Consumption*. London: Routledge.

Gunter, B. and Furnham, A. (1998) *Children as Consumers: A Psychological Analysis of the Young People's Market*. London: Routledge

Kline, S. (1993) *Out of the Garden: Toys and Children's Culture in the Age of TV Marketing*. Toronto: Garamond.

Kline, S., Dyer-Witheford, N. and De Peuter, G. (2003) *Digital Play: The Interaction of Technology, Culture and Marketing*. Montreal: McGill-Queen's University Press.

Lachance, M. and Legault, F. (2007) 'College student's competence: identifying the socialization sources', *Journal of Research for Consumers*, 13: 1–21.

Lassare, D. and Roland-Lévy, C. (1989) 'Understanding children's economic socialization', in K.G. Grünert and F. Olander (eds), *Understanding Economic Behaviour*. Dordrecht: Kluwer Academic. pp. 347–368.

Lave, J. and Wenger, E. (1991) *Situated Learning, Legitimate Peripheral Participation*. Cambridge, MA: Cambridge University Press.

Lawrence, D. (2003) 'The role of characters in kids marketing', *Journal of Advertising and Marketing to Children*, 4 (3): 43–48.

Luke, C. (1994) 'Childhood and parenting in popular-culture', *Australian and New Zealand Journal of Sociology*, 30 (3): 289–302.

Moschis, G. and Churchill, G. (1978) 'Consumer socialization: a theoretical and empirical analysis', *Journal of Marketing Research*, 15 (4): 599–609.

Moschis, G. and Moore, R.L. (1979) 'Decision making among the young: a socialization perspective', *Journal of Consumer Research*, 6 (September): 101–112.

Oestergaard, P. and Jantzen, C. (2000) 'Shifting perspectives in consumer research: from buyer behaviour to consumption studies', in S.C. Beckmann and R. Elliot (eds), *Interpretive Consumer Research: Paradigms, Methodologies and Applications*. Copenhagen: Copenhagen Business School Press.

Page, C. and Ridgway, N. (2001) 'The impact of consumer environments on consumption patterns of children from disparate socioeconomic backgrounds', *Journal of Consumer Marketing*, 18 (1): 21–41.

Piaget, J. (1937) *La construction du réel chez l'enfant*. Neuchâtel: Delachaux et Niestlé.

Robertson, T.S. and Feldman, S. (1976) 'Children as consumers: the need for multi-theoretical perspectives', *Advances in Consumer Research*, 3 (1): 508–512.

Roedder-John, D. (1999) 'Consumer socialization of children: a retrospective look at twenty-five years of research', *Journal of Consumer Research*, 26 (3): 183–213.

Roedder-John, D. (2002) 'Consumer socialization of children: a retrospective look at twenty-five years of research', in F. Hansen, J. Rasmussen, A. Martensen and B. Tufte (eds), *Children: Consumption, Advertising and Media*. Copenhagen: Copenhagen Business School Press. pp. 25–89.

Rogoff, B. (1998) 'Cognition as a collaborative process', in D. Kuhn and R.S. Siegler (eds), *Cognition and Language* (vol. 2), *Handbook of Child Psychology* (5th edition). New York: Wiley. pp. 679–738.

Rogoff, B., Moore, L., Najafi, B., Dexter, A., Correa-Chavez, M. and Solis, J. (2006) 'Children's development of cultural repertoires through participation in everyday routines and practices', in J. Grusec and P. Hasting (eds), *Handbook of Socialization*. New York: Guilford.

Selman, R.L. (1980) *The Growth of Interpersonal Understanding*. New York: Academic.

Siegel, D.L., Coffey, T.J. and Livingstone, G. (2002) *The Great Tween Buying Machine: Capturing Your Share of the Multibillion Dollar Tween Market*. Chicago, IL: Dearborn.

Sirota, R. (1999) 'Les civilités de l'enfance contemporaine: l'anniversaire ou le déchiffrage d'une configuration', Dossier Sociologie de l'enfance 2, *Education et Sociétés*, 1: 31–54.

Strauss, A. (1952) 'The development and transformation of monetary meanings in the child', *American Sociological Review*, 17 (June): 275–286.

Vygotsky, L.S. (1934/1985) *Pensée et langage*. Paris: Editions Sociales.

Vygotsky, L. (1934/1986) *Thought and Language*. Cambridge, MA: MIT Press.

Ward, S. (1974) 'Consumer socialization', *Journal of Consumer Research*, 1 (September): 1–14.

Wertsch, J.V. (1985) *Vygotsky and the Social Formation of Mind*. Cambridge, MA: Harvard University Press.

Woodhead, M. and Faulkner, D. (2003) 'Subjects, objects or participants? Dilemmas of psychological research with children', in P. Christensen and A. James (eds), *Research with Children: Perspectives and Practices*. London: Routledge Falmer (first edition 2000). pp. 9–35.

Consumer Socialization in Families

Karin M. Ekström

Karin M. Ekström

Chapter aims

- To define socialization and discuss how it has been viewed at different times in history.
- To explore socialization as a reciprocal process.
- To discuss socialization occurring in families.
- To give examples of various family types allowing for different influence patterns and socialization practices.

Vignette 1: Family decisions

Living in consumer culture involves an abundance of different products to choose between. For example, a family deciding to go skiing has a variety of skis and snowboards to choose between. Downhill, cross-country and telemark skis represent different ski styles and require different equipment, in particular skibindings. There are also freestyle, freeride and all-mountain snowboards to choose between. In addition, there is a variety of equipment, such as ski boots, boat liners, poles, clothes, goggles, helmets, ski wax, bags, sport watches, etc. Navigating the consumer culture requires time spent searching for information to compare the alternatives and sometimes also technological competence. While much of this comes from retailers, media and peers, children and parents influence and learn from each other about consumption since they often have different experiences and interests.

Introduction

This chapter deals with consumer socialization in families, in other words, how family members learn to become competent as consumers. Children encounter consumer culture at an early age. It first involves the child's own consumption experiences (e.g., toys, clothes, watching TV, seeing advertising in the store), but also purchases and consumption experiences made by parents and siblings (e.g., family cars, MP3 players, internet advertising) and interactions with peers and family friends. Many different socialization agents, (for example, parents, siblings, peers, retailers, media, advertising agencies and educators) affect a child's consumption experiences and the learning associated with the role as a consumer (see Vignette 1). The family is often considered the most important agent due to the frequency of interaction and close relations between the family members, at least during the early years. Also, peers are considered important socialization agents, in particular during adolescence. Parents are also socialized as consumers by their children.

This chapter focuses specifically on socialization in families. A discussion of the definition and meaning of socialization is followed by examples of different family types. These family types are ideal types representing stereotypical images of families' consumption experiences, different degrees of child influence involving yielding, consumer learning or socialization. They are based on an earlier empirical study and have previously been reported in Ekström (1995). The chapter ends with a further discussion on socialization in postmodern families.

Children as consumers

The development of a consumer culture has led to children encountering commerce at an earlier age than ever before in history. Also, an increase in consumer welfare in the western world has provided more opportunities for consumption. There are several reasons for marketers' interest in children as consumers. Children have purchasing power and influence products for themselves. Moreover, the brand preferences developed as children are likely to be carried into adult life so many companies are interested in achieving 'brand loyal' child consumers. Olsen (1995) discussed that consumers often use the same brands as their parents once used, suggesting an important link between the consumption behaviour of parents and their children. But children also influence the consumption of products for the family as well as their parents' (see McNeal and Yeh, 1993; also Tinson and Nancarrow, Chapter 8 in this book). Their consumption experiences often differ from their parents' since they interact in different technological and social spheres. As a result, children are frequently aware of trends, technology and environmental issues which their parents may not always be aware of.

This can lead to children sometimes influencing their parents by contributing knowledge in these areas (e.g., Ekström 1995; 2007a).

Mead (1970) discusses the development of our society into a prefigurative culture; a culture in which adults learn not only from adults, but also from their children. White-Riley et al. (1971: 961) argue that 'as the parent socializes the child, he almost certainly as a consequence both teaches certain things to himself and also learns from the growing child'. It is more realistic to view family influence and consumer socialization in families as reciprocal processes rather than uni-directional. Influence is, however, not always noticeable and direct. A family member may consider another family member's needs without being told to do so explicitly, for example a mother purchasing food which her child likes. Another example of indirect influence is learning by observing, for example parents becoming more fashion conscious by watching their children's consumption of clothes. This may not always be a conscious process.

Consumer socialization

Consumer socialization is defined by Ward (1974: 2) as: 'the process by which young people acquire skills, knowledge, and attitudes relevant to their functioning as consumers in the marketplace'. Consumer socialization is important for understanding how consumers relate to culturally determined societal norms and how they adapt to transformations in society (Ekström, 2006). There are different opinions on whether living in a consumer culture leads to desirable or undesirable consumer socialization of children. For example, Ward et al. (1990) argue that children who become consumers early on can learn positive aspects about consumption but can also become materialistic and this can lead to conflicts between parents and children. Over time, the two prevailing attitudes on children as consumers have been that they are either seen as competent, or at least capable of learning to become consumers, or as victims who need protection from marketing dangers. This dualistic view is problematic in that it ignores the contextual differences encompassing the role of child consumer (Ekström, 2010). It results in a too narrow picture of what it means to be a child in today's society. A child can be competent in one situation, but not in another. Therefore, the consumer role needs to be studied in specific contexts without generalizing from one another.

Over the years, there have been many studies on the consumer socialization of children and adolescents (e.g., Churchill and Moschis, 1979; Moschis, 1985; Carlson and Grossbart, 1988). A comprehensive review of consumer socialization was conducted by Roedder-John (1999: 207) who concluded that 'there can be no doubt that children are avid consumers and become socialized into this role from an early age' (see also de la Ville and Tartas, Chapter 2 in this book). A recent example of research is

Grønhøj's (2007) study focusing on environmental consumer socialization among children. One reason for the focus on childhood is that consumer socialization is assumed to be strongest in childhood. Berger and Luckmann distinguish between primary and secondary socialization. Their definition of primary socialization is 'the first socialization an individual undergoes in childhood, through which he becomes a member of society' (1967: 150). Secondary socialization is defined as 'any subsequent process that inducts an already socialized individual into new sectors of the objective world of his society' (ibid.). They assert that biological limitations are less and less important in secondary socialization, instead secondary socialization integrates different bodies of knowledge which often build upon learning sequences. For example, in order to be able to find the best bargains as a consumer, one must first learn how to handle money (see Roland-Lévy, Chapter 9 in this book) and then how to search for information. In a continuously changing society, it can be assumed that secondary socialization plays an important role. The development of many technological skills builds on existing technological competence. For example, it is easier to operate a new model of a mobile telephone if one already has the experience of using one.

In fact, a criticism of earlier socialization research is the tendency to look upon childhood as a journey towards adulthood and stability, not recognizing that adulthood also represents a period of flexibility (Lee, 2001). In a continuously changing society, adults as well as children are exposed to new roles and situations. Socialization is a life-long process (Brim, 1966; Ward, 1974; Ekström, 2006). Another critique of earlier socialization work is Parsons' (1956) view that society has a consensus over values, norms and conventions, and that it determines the values and norms children internalize (Lee, 2001). Instead, we are today noticing the mediated character of society and the diminished central control of the state (Lee, 2001). There exists a divergence of values illustrated by different individuals giving each other different consumption advice, communicating on the internet by personal blogs, chat groups, Facebook, MySpace, etc. Also, another criticism of earlier socialization theory is that it includes universalistic ideas of child development and sees children as passive (James and James, 2004). Socialization is then seen as being the same for all children and the individuality of the child and the social environment is not considered (James and James, 2004). Rather than talking about childhood it is more appropriate to talk about childhoods, since each childhood is unique (James and Prout, 1997). This discussion could also be applied to parenthood, that there are parenthoods rather than parenthood (Ekström, 2007b).

Yet, another criticism is that a majority of consumer socialization studies have had a uni-directional view focusing on children learning consumption-related matters from their parents (e.g., Moschis and Churchill, 1978; Carlson and Grossbart, 1988). It represents a one-sided view of influence in families and neglects the fact that parents also learn from their children. Bell (1968, 1971) argues that parents and children can be viewed as a social system in which each participant's responses constitute stimuli for the other. Only a few studies have considered parental consumer socialization (e.g., Foxman et al., 1989; Ekström, 1995). It should be recognized that influence also occurs across generations, between children, parents, grandparents, aunts, uncles, cousins and so on. Martens et al. (2004) discuss the importance of understanding how Bourdieu's (1984) capital is transferred between generations. They write: 'parents provide economic capital (which may prove critical in gaining access to social networks), but as children grow older, it may well be their social capital (their friends, family, parents' friends and institutional contacts such as schools) that most influences their consumption orientations. In such a case, how cultural capital is accumulated is not simply a process of transfer between parents and children, but between a host of social networks and institutional relationships' (Martens et al., 2004: 166). Dotson and Hyatt (2000, 2005) question the pre-eminent role of parents in children's lives today due to societal developments. They argue that peers and the mass media, primarily television, are key socialization agents and suggest that as parental influence diminishes when children reach adolescence there is a steady increase in the influence of peers and media. As children spend more time with peers and are exposed to more commercial 'hype' in their daily lives this has implications for childhood socialization.

Furthermore, even unborn children can influence and socialize their parents in their upcoming parental role. For example, people often think about their future role as parents when purchasing a new home or a safer car before a child is born. The celebration enacted in baby showers represents the tendency among adults to cater for the needs of the unborn as well as their parental role in the consumer culture. Also, people from the past can influence consumption patterns and do not need to still be present to apply such influence. Consumer socialization is often more subtle than purposive (Ward, 1974). Tallman et al. (1983: 25) have suggested that in most cases 'socialization takes place indirectly as an unintended, or at least, implicit consequence of an ongoing relationship'.

Consumer learning has been the common denominator for studying consumer socialization processes. Direct learning can imply that the socialized person learns something by being told something. Indirect learning can imply that the socialized person learns something by observing someone (see Vignette 2). In studying consumer socialization, cognitive developmental theories (e.g., Piaget, 1970) have often been used (e.g., Roedder-John and Whitney, 1986). It is then assumed that a child has to reach a certain stage of cognitive growth before learning can occur. Also, social learning theories (e.g., Bandura, 1977) have been used (e.g., Moschis, 1987) in socialization studies, emphasizing learning in relation to the social environment (see de la Ville and Tartas, Chapter 2 in this book).

Vignette 2: Children's indirect influence

The children may not influence verbally, but people adapt when they have children. We adapt automatically, maybe faster than we would if we had not had any children. Then we would have continued in our old ways. (father)

I think that I dress more fashionably now because I have them and also see their clothes. I maybe would not keep up with the trends otherwise. Now I know through my children what is fashionable ... (mother)

Source: Ekström (1995, 2007b)

Furthermore, a combination of theories, such as modeling, reinforcement, and social interaction, has also been proposed by consumer socialization researchers (e.g., Churchill and Moschis, 1979). Interaction as communication as communication has specifically been studied by using McLeod's and Chaffee's (1972) communication typology (e.g., Moschis et al., 1984). McLeod and Chaffee (1972) define a concept-oriented communication structure as an environment where the child is encouraged to develop his/her own ideas. They define a socio-oriented communication structure as an environment where the child avoids controversy and does not argue, since he or she does not want to risk offending others. Studies have found children in families with pluralistic communication styles (high concept-orientation and low socio-orientation) to know more about consumption matters (Moore and Moschis, 1981). In the future, it is recommended to employ socio-cultural theories in socialization studies in order to better grasp the influence of external processes on our lives and to understand how socialization differs between classes, ethnicity, and genders (Ekström, 2006).

Family types

Ten different family types were developed in order to illustrate different consumption experiences, different degrees of child influence and socialization occurring in families. These are ideal types representing stereotypical images of families based on an earlier empirical study. The results have previously been reported in Ekström (1995). Babbie (1983: 302) expresses that 'an ideal type is a conceptual model comprised of the essential qualities of a social phenomenon'. Weber is considered to be the founder of ideal types and an example of this analytical technique is found in his study of characteristics of bureaucracies. An ideal type is no actual picture of reality, but abstracts of reality (Weber, 1983/1922). They are often exaggerated or simplified. When developing ideal types, it is important to look for contradictions between ideal types, but not within the ideal types (Weber, 1983/1922).

The ten family types were developed based on the author's interpretation of the characteristics among 36 Swedish families interviewed in Sweden's second largest city, Göteborg. One half of the families lived in an affluent area and the other half lived in a less affluent area, thereby representing differences in socio-economic variables. In each case parent(s) and one of the children were interviewed separately, but the interviewer asked about all the children in the family and the interviewees sometimes referred to other children in the family during the interview. The sample was based on the children's age and consisted of children in 7th, 8th, and 9th year of junior school (one third); children in high school (one third), and 'children' between 20 and 30 years old (one third). Children were randomly selected from class lists and personal registers. Adolescent and adult children were especially interesting to study since the focus was on consumer socialization. It was not uncommon for 'children' between 20 and 30 years old to live at home, due to a housing shortage in the bigger cities. Five of the families interviewed had no children living at home. For children, an equal number from each gender was selected.

The family types were developed based on the researcher's interpretation of the characteristics among the families. The analysis of the interviews and the interview descriptions written immediately after each interview were important tools for the development of the family types. Five pairs of family types were developed distinguishing between modern and traditional families, as illustrated in Figure 3.1.

Figure 3.1 shows the basis for identification, in other words, the main characteristics upon which the family types[1] are based. All the families interviewed were classified as belonging to either one of the two extreme family types. The reason for classifying each family according to the five dimensions was that it made it possible to relate the family types to different degrees of influence (categorized as high, medium, and low family influence groups depending on how much influence children had). This made it possible to determine that for some family types children's influence was stronger than in other family types. The distinction between high and low influence was mainly based on frequency of influence (i.e. children had influenced their parents several times), but for durable goods a high influence indicated participating in the decision-making stage (for a more detailed description of the classification see Ekström, 1995). The family types are described in more detail below.

BASIS FOR IDENTIFICATION	FAMILY TYPES	
	Modern families	*Traditional families*
1. Decision-making mode, parent–child relations communication structure	Friendship	Authoritarian
2. Innovativeness	Trendy	Conservative
3. Orientation towards purchasing, purchasing power	Heavy spenders	Restricted
4. Degree of planning, organization	Spontaneous	Structured
5. Purchasing roles	Intermingled	Role-specialized

Figure 3.1   Ten different Swedish family types

The friendship versus the authoritarian family

As illustrated in Figure 3.1, the basis for identification in the friendship versus the authoritarian family is the decision-making mode, the parents–child relation, and the communication structure.

The *friendship family* is characterized by family members treating each other like friends. Parental roles do not appear as distinct and there seems to be a lack of parental authority. This is reflected in the family trying to decide democratically about purchasing and consumption. Dialogue and open communication are encouraged by the parents who think it is important for their children to learn by discussing and contributing to family decisions. A concept-oriented communication structure (where the child is encouraged to develop his/her ideas) is prevalent. Also, parents will often think that they can benefit by learning from their children. They seem to appreciate their children's advice and knowledge when available. When shopping together they give each other advice. A parent who shops by him/herself often asks for the children's opinions later at home. Parents and children also borrow things from each other (e.g., clothes, books). Cohesion between family members appears to be strong and they often do things together because they enjoy being together.

The *authoritarian family* exhibits more traditional parent–child roles. It is the parents who decide about purchasing and consumption for the family, even though they may also at times be willing to listen to and be influenced by their children. The degree of parental authority differs depending on the type of decision. The generation gap between parents and children appears much greater in this family type than in the friendship family. Parents seem to discuss purchasing and consumption decisions with each other more frequently than with their children and they do not always encourage the children to become involved. This happens mainly when the parents ask for the children's advice. Also, a parent will sometimes make independent decisions without considering his/her spouse. The fact that this family does not always make democratic decisions regarding purchasing and consumption is reflected in the children's tendency to avoid interfering with their parents' decisions. Instead, they will wait for the parents to ask. Also, the children may have little interest in influencing independent parents because they know that they are hard to influence. A socio-economic communication structure (with the child avoiding controversy and not arguing in order not to risk offending others) is prevalent.

The trendy versus the conservative family

As illustrated in Figure 3.1, the basis for identification in the trendy versus the conservative family is innovativeness, in other words, being among the first to purchase a product after it is launched.

The *trendy family* differs from other families by being more inclined to adopt new products/services (e.g., fashion consciousness), and lifestyle changes (e.g., environmental concern). The family members are often innovators or early adopters for certain product groups, in other words, among the first to buy a newly launched product. If not among the first, the family is part of an early majority in adopting new products. The trendy family is more adventurous and prone to take risks by being open to discovering novelties. The need for variety is also reflected in that the family is more likely to switch brands and shops instead of remaining loyal for a long time. It varies between families and for products whether it is the parents, the children, or both parties, who initiate the adoption of certain trends.

The *conservative family* are in contrast to the trendy family, as neither the parents nor the children show an interest in trends. They do not think that it is important to follow changes in society regarding purchasing and consumption and are late in adopting new products by belonging to the laggards or the late majority in doing so. The family questions the idea of buying new products with new functions when they already have something similar that works well. The trigger for purchasing is often that an old product no longer works or that the family after some time realizes the need for a new product. The family appears to be somewhat risk averse and is less prone to discover novelties. The family members also often remain loyal to brands and shops that they are already familiar with.

The heavy spenders family versus the restricted family

As illustrated in Figure 3.1, the basis for identification in the heavy spenders family versus the restricted family is an orientation towards purchasing and purchasing power.

The *heavy spenders family* loves purchasing and consumption. Besides this orientation, the family also has the purchasing power allowing the family members to be heavy spenders. As a result, the family owns many products. Also, the joy of purchasing is reflected in the fact that the family often replaces things that break instead of trying to repair them. New things are also sometimes bought even though there is nothing wrong with the old ones (for example, a coffee-maker in a new colour). Furthermore, items which normally are considered high involvement purchases (i.e., requiring time and effort for searching for information and evaluating products) such as durable goods are sometimes regarded as low involvement purchases for parents in this family. As a consequence, parents sometimes involve their children by asking them to go out and purchase such items.

The *restricted family* is not oriented towards purchasing and consumption. The main reason is often a lack of purchasing power depending on a lower income. Another reason is that the restricted family sometimes has many children in combination with a lower income, which restrains the family finances even more. There are fewer opportunities for children who are interested in purchasing and consumption to influence their parents when purchasing power is lacking. Yet, another reason could be a lack of interest in purchasing and consumption. As a result of the above, the family owns a limited number of products. They do not purchase unnecessary or trendy things. Furthermore, the family tries to repair broken items instead of buying new things. The parents are always involved in the purchases of durable goods and would never delegate such purchases to their children.

The spontaneous versus the structured family

As indicated in Figure 3.1, the basis for identification in the spontaneous versus the structured family is the degree of planning and organization.

The *spontaneous family* does not plan their purchases, because they do not see the need for planning and sometimes lack the time to structure their purchasing. When there is a need for a product, the family goes out and purchases it. This implies that the family members do not usually collect information and make comparisons before entering the store. Instead, they are more willing to let the purchasing situation influence their purchase behaviour and are open for suggestions at the moment of shopping and purchase based on impulsiveness. It is possible that this gives children more opportunities to influence family purchases. Also, this family is more inclined to take risks and likes variety and novelty. Such spontaneity can lead to the family buying goods on credit rather than saving for items. The degree of involvement varies for each product and family member, but the amount of involvement is usually higher for durable goods than convenience goods. As a result, the family is more likely to compare durable goods than convenience goods while in the store.

The *structured family* usually plans purchases as soon as a family member realizes the need for a product. They get involved in the purchasing process long before entering the store, for example by collecting information prior to purchasing. The degree of involvement varies, however, for each product and family member. For durable goods, collecting information and making comparisons are always done before entering the store, and also when in the store. Purchases of convenience goods are planned, but any comparison mainly takes place in the store. It seems as if the purchasing behaviour follows some type of agenda. For convenience goods, the family usually follows a shopping list, compares the unit pricing, uses coupons, purchases economy packages for the best deals, and so on. For durable goods it is important to find the different alternatives and compare them. Careful planning indicates a lack of spontaneity and impulse purchases. As a result, there may be fewer opportunities for children to influence family purchases. When these parents are influenced by their children, they are not thus influenced on the spot, but instead think about their children's suggestion for some time and plan the purchase. The structured family is not necessarily risk averse. Instead, careful planning is based on a willingness to do things the right way or in the best way possible. In some extreme cases, there seems to be some type of perfectionism regarding purchasing. Also, the structured family's careful planning is reflected by money often being saved before purchasing something.

The intermingled versus the role specialized family

As indicated in Figure 3.1, the basis for identification in the intermingled versus the role specialized family is purchasing roles.

The *intermingled family* contains members who have more non-traditional roles. It is possible to find the father grocery shopping or the mother purchasing durable items. Also, the children are responsible for purchases for which they have not been traditionally responsible, for example durable goods or parents' clothing. The parents will consider the children as important contributors of information when making decisions. It is likely that they will turn to their children for advice if the product area is unfamiliar or if they are unfamiliar with the roles, and they may then need advice and encourage the children to take part in making decisions. As a result, they may be more open for influence from their children. In a one-parent family, it is possible that children will take the missing spouse's role, and in a two-parent family, that the child may take the uninvolved spouse's role.

The *role specialized family* exhibits a traditional role specialization, with the mother or the father dominating certain purchase decisions. For example, the mother purchases convenience goods and the father purchases durable goods.

Also, the roles played by children regarding purchasing are somewhat traditional. They are not given responsibility for purchasing products which they have not been traditionally responsible for purchasing. For some decisions, parents will rely more on each other for advice instead of asking the children.

Children's influence in the different family types

Children's influence (involving yielding, consumer learning or socialization) was high in a majority of the friendship families, the trendy families, and the heavy spenders families. Also, influence was high in half of the spontaneous families. All these family types seem to have characteristics which allow children to exert their influence on family purchases and their parents' consumption. The friendship family encourages dialogue and democracy, and hence a willingness to listen to the children. The trendy family is open to trying new things and therefore also likely to consider the children's ideas. In the heavy spenders family, family finances as well as the frequency of shopping may lead to more opportunities for children to exercise their influence. Also, the spontaneous family is more open for suggestions at the moment of shopping rather than by planning ahead. If children happen to be present when the purchase decision is made, they may have a say and exert a possible influence.

Furthermore, the results show that influence from children was low in a majority of the authoritarian families. Children's influence was also low or moderate in a majority of the conservative, the restricted, and the structured families. These family types seem to have characteristics which limit children's influence.

Different degrees of influence were found in the role specialized family, but high and low influence from children was somewhat more common. Apparently this family type has characteristics which both allow and limit children to exert influence. Furthermore, different degrees of child influence were found in the intermingled families, but it was somewhat more common with high and moderate influence from children. This family type seems to have characteristics which allow children to exert influence. Also, all the one-parent families interviewed (six of the 36 families) were intermingled families. The interviews showed that parents and children in one-parent families seemed to have more of a friendship relationship. They seemed to discuss purchases and consumption together and it sometimes appeared as if the children took parental roles in family decisions. It is also possible that one-parent families experience more time pressure and task overload and therefore allow their children to have more influence. A majority of the one-parent families interviewed had limited financial resources which probably restricted children's potential to influence. Children's influence on family purchases and their parents' consumption was high in one of the one-parent families (an affluent family), while for the rest it was moderate or low (the less affluent families). With limited financial resources, there may be less purchases and less opportunities to influence. This indicates the importance of considering the context. Also, there is a need to question the postmodern freedom of choice (e.g., Lodziak, 2002) since opportunities to consume will differ for various consumers.

Half of the families lived in an affluent area and half of the families lived in a less affluent area. Children's influence in earlier studies has been found to vary with socio-economic factors (e.g., Moschis and Mitchell, 1986). In this study, affluence has been used as a measure of the family's purchasing power, defined as an index composed of variables such as income, standard of living, perceived amount of durable goods (perceived by the author when interviewing the families, as all but four interviews took place in the family home). Another variable – perceived overall impression of affluence – was used when a discrepancy was found between the three purchasing power variables mentioned above. About half of the interviewed families were affluent, the rest of the families were equally medium affluent or less affluent. Children's influence on family purchases and their parents' consumption was high in a majority of the affluent families. Influence was moderate in half of the medium affluent families. Influence was low in a majority of the less affluent families. Furthermore, in a majority of the families interviewed, the parents had a high education. Influence was high in about half of the families with a high education. In families with a medium education, both low, moderate and high influence was found. Influence was low in a majority of the families with a low education. Apparently, children's influence on family purchases and their parents' consumption varied with socio-economic factors also in this study. Also, socio-economic variables are often correlated. Examples of an affluent and a less affluent one-parent family interviewed are presented in Vignette 3. The affluent family represents the trendy family type and the less affluent family represents the restricted family type.

Vignette 3: An affluent and a less affluent one-parent family interviewed

The affluent trendy one-parent family

There are no signs of mass produced durable items in the family's home. The father emphasizes during the interview that he raises his children to be individuals and not to follow group pressure. He encourages his children

(Cont'd)

to dare to wear clothes which no one else has. Also, he dislikes it when the children come and ask about something they want to purchase because everybody else has it. The father is a trendsetter and strives to have new things before anyone else has them. He wants his children to be curious and try different things. When travelling, he always books scheduled flights. Charter flights imply conformity which he dislikes. During the interview, he wears jeans and a T-shirt, which his children have influenced him to purchase.

The less affluent restricted one-parent family

Both the interviewed mother and her son emphasize that the family has limited resources and do not purchase much. Children's influence seems moderate and a reason may be the limited resources which restrict purchases. The mother has asked her children for advice when thinking of buying a coffee table. The son mentions the table during the interview, but in the context of encouraging the mother to travel instead of purchasing a table. He thinks the table can wait. Actually, he emphasizes that the children think that their mother should allow herself to have some fun. Furthermore, the interview showed that the mother is influenced regarding the use of products. Her children show her how to buy durable goods and help her with practical things, such as electrical switches. The oldest son has purchased a fire alarm for her.

It is noticeable that the lifestyles are different for the two families in Vignette 3. While limitations to consume are of no concern for the affluent family, the less affluent family has restrictions. However, the children in the less affluent family want the mother to enjoy herself and to travel rather than buying a coffee table. Earlier studies (Hjort, 2004; Pugh, 2004) have shown that parents in families with financial restrictions sometimes sacrifice things for themselves in order to allow their children possibilities to consume. The importance of keeping up with other consumers' consumption increases in a consumer culture where consumption is often perceived as a social marker and this is usually noticeable among young consumers.

A majority of the families interviewed had a concept-oriented communication strategy (the child is encouraged to develop his/her ideas). It is possible that such families are more willing to participate in this type of study. All the friendship families had a concept-oriented communication structure. The authoritarian families had mainly a socio-oriented communication structure (where the child avoids controversy and does not argue, since he or she does not want to risk offending others), even though a few had a concept-oriented communication structure.

There are different degrees of strength in influence. Children's influence can imply parents yielding to their children's wishes, parents learning from their children and ultimately parents becoming socialized as consumers. Consumer socialization represents the strongest influence, implying functioning better as a consumer in society. In family types where children are listened to and allowed to influence, it is likely that parents will yield and in particular will learn and become socialized when compared to family types limiting children's influence.

Socialization in postmodern families

Family structures have changed over time. The extended family has, since the Industrial Revolution, been replaced by two-parent families and one-parent families. Increased geographical mobility and different living conditions (e.g., retirement homes) have led to less interaction among the generations. The family of today is more receptive to outside influences such as peer groups, the mass media, day-care centres and formal education than before. Relations between parents and children are of continued importance even though the forms of interaction may have changed. Discussions at the dinner table and negotiations about consumption are sometimes replaced by conversations on the mobile phone, text-messages (SMS) and e-mails.

The definition of family has also changed over time. Traditionally, the family is referred to in terms of blood or legal relations. A postmodern definition of the family considers the family as a locus, not of residence, but of meaning and relationships (Stacey, 1990). This means that the family encompasses a social network that includes members from the formal and/or informal family. Family members will also have relations to each other after separations and when social networks are continuously formed and redefined. Family life, childhood and parenthood should not be described in the singular, but in the plural, thereby avoiding uniformity and recognizing the diverse meanings in today's society.

De Vault (1991: 54) defines a family as 'a socially constructed group, continually brought into being through the activities of individuals. Repeated activities – and especially routines and rituals like those of family mealtimes – sustain the reality of a family'. Social construction means that the meaning of the family should not be taken for granted, but the family is given meaning in a flux of transformations in a continuously changing society. Family life can be better understood by focusing on family activities and consumption practices (Ekström, 2004). Influence and socialization studies would benefit from studying families' everyday consumption practices in a more in-depth fashion. Different contexts where family consumption is negotiated (for example, interaction with media and retailers) should be considered, as well as structural factors allowing and limiting consumption (e.g., income, class, area of living, etc.).

Conclusion

Living in a consumer culture involves an increased focus on the role of consumers. Competence as a consumer is acquired though experience and by interaction with family, peers, media, retailers, educators, etc. This chapter has focused specifically on influence and socialization in families. It has been argued that consumer socialization is a reciprocal process since parents and children learn from each other about consumption. This is often a subtle process. Different examples of family types were presented with different influences involving yielding, consumer learning or socialization. Family types representing modern families seemed to allow their children more influence than traditional families. It is likely that a stronger influence such as socialization is more common in families where children have more opportunities to influence their parents' consumption. The results show that children's influence on family purchases and their parents' consumption varies with socio-economic factors.

Future research directions

Since families change over time, it is necessary for future research to continue to consider relations and interactions between parents and children. The family types presented in the chapter represent traditional and modern Swedish families based on an earlier empirical study (Ekström, 1995). Relations between parents and children are likely to differ in postmodern families of today and there is a need to investigate how influence involving yielding, or learning, or socialization takes place between family members. The multiplicity of childhoods and parenthoods and the different contexts in which negotiations about consumption take place need to be recognized, as do cultural differences. There is also a need to study family relations encompassing a broader social network.

The family is not an isolated hegemonic entity, but there exists a plurality of different families. Also, power in families has changed over time as a result of more full- and part-time employment outside the home. Migration has led to many families being dispersed all over the world and keeping in touch by communicating via the internet and SMS. Global media have led to that children's role as consumers are changing. We need to understand more about the relations and negotiations in families and how the family is constructed through practices. Again, we need to understand how the family is related to other social networks in a society characterized by a flux of transformations.

Discussion questions

1 What roles do marketers play in the consumer socialization of children?
2 How important is the family in the consumer socialization of children compared to other socialization agents?
3 The chapter has focused on socialization in families, but there are also other socialization agents operating. Which responsibilities do you think media and advertising agencies have in the consumer socialization of children?
4 Describe the reciprocity between parents and children in terms of consumption.

Further reading

Chankon Kim, C., Yang, Z. and Lee, H. (2009) 'Cultural differences in consumer socialization: a comparison of Chinese–Canadian and Caucasian–Canadian children', *Journal of Business Research*, 62 (10): 955–962.

Handel, G., Cahill, S. and Elkin, F. (2006) *Children and Society: The Sociology of Children and Childhood Socialization*. Oxford: Oxford University Press.

Lueg, J.E., Ponder, N., Beatty, S.E. and Capella, M. (2006) 'Teenagers' use of alternative shopping channels: a consumer socialization perspective', *Journal of Retailing*, 82 (2): 137–153.

Miller, D. (1998) *A Theory of Shopping*. Oxford: Polity.

O'Guinn, T.C. and Faber, R.J. (1991) 'Mass communication and consumer behavior', in T.S. Robertson and H.H. Kassarjian (eds), *Handbook of Consumer Behavior*. Englewood Cliffs, NJ: Prentice-Hall.

References

Babbie, E. (1983) *The Practice of Social Research*. Belmont, CA: Wadsworth.

Bandura, A. (1977) *Social Learning Theory*. Englewood Cliffs, NJ: Prentice-Hall.

Bell, R.Q. (1968) 'A reinterpretation of the direction of effects in studies of socialization', *Psychological Review*, 75: 81–95.

Bell, R.Q. (1971) 'Stimulus control of parent or caretaker behavior by offspring', *Developmental Psychology*, 4: 63–72.

Berger, P.L. and Luckmann, T. (1967) *The Social Construction of Reality*. Harmondsworth: Penguin.

Bourdieu, P. (1984) *Distinction: A Social Critique of the Judgement of Taste*. London: Routledge & Kegan Paul.

Brim, O.G. (1966) 'Socialization through the life cycle', in O. Brim and S. Wheeler (eds), *Socialization After Childhood: Two Essays*. New York: Wiley. pp. 1–50.

Carlson, L. and Grossbart, S. (1988) 'Parental style and consumer socialization of children', *Journal of Consumer Research*, 15 (June).

Churchill, G.A. Jr. and Moschis, G.P. (1979) 'Television and interpersonal influences on adolescent consumer learning', *Journal of Consumer Research*, 6 (June): 23–25.

DeVault, M.L. (1991) *Feeding the Family: The Social Organization of Caring as Gendered Work*. Chicago: The University of Chicago Press.

Dotson, M.J. and Hyatt, E.M. (2000) 'A comparison of parents' and children's knowledge of brands and advertising slogans in the United States: implications for consumer socialization', *Journal of Marketing Communications*, 6 (4): 219–230.

Dotson, M.J. and Hyatt, E.M. (2005) 'Major influence factors in children's consumer socialization', *Journal of Consumer Marketing*, 22 (1): 35–42.

Ekström, K.M. (1995) *Children's Influence in Family Decision Making: A Study of Yielding, Consumer Learning and Consumer Socialization*. Göteborg: Bas ek.för.

Ekström, K.M. (2004) 'Guest editor's introduction: family consumption', *Consumption, Markets and Culture*, 7 (3) (September): 185–190.

Ekström, K.M. (2006) 'Consumer socialization revisited', *Research in Consumer Behavior*, vol. 10, R.W. Belk (ed.). Oxford: Elsevier Science.

Ekström, K.M. (2007a) 'Parental consumer learning or "keeping up with the children"', *Journal of Consumer Behavior*, 6: 203–217.

Ekström, K.M. (2007b) 'Participating in the catwalk of consumption', in K.M. Ekström and B. Tufte (eds), *Children, Media and Consumption: On the Front Edge*. Yearbook at The International Clearinghouse on Children, Youth and Media, Nordicom, Göteborg University.

Ekström, K.M. (2010) 'Keeping up with the children–changing consumer roles in families', in K.M. Ekström and K. Glans (eds), *Beyond the Consumption Bubble*? London: Routledge.

Foxman, E.R., Tansuhaj, P.S. and Ekström, K.M. (1989) 'Adolescents' influence in family purchase decisions: a socialization perspective', *Journal of Business Research*, Spring.

Grønhøj, A. (2007) 'Green girls and bored boys? Adolescents' environmental consumer socialization', in K.M. Ekström and B. Tufte (eds), *Children, Media and Consumption: On the Front Edge*. Yearbook at The International Clearinghouse on Children, Youth and Media, Nordicom, Göteborg University.

Hjort, T. (2004) *Nödvändighetens pris: Konsumtion och knapphet bland barnfamiljer* [The price of necessity – consumption and scarcity among families with children]. Lund University, Lund dissertations in social work.

James, A. and James, A.L. (2004) *Constructing Childhood: Theory, Policy and Social Practice*. New York: Palgrave Macmillan.

James, A. and Prout, A. (eds) (1997) *Constructing and Reconstructing Childhood: Contemporary Issues in the Sociological Study of Childhood*. London: Falmer.

Lee, N. (2001) *Childhood and Society: Growing Up in an Age of Uncertainty*. Buckingham: Open University Press.

Lodziak, C. (2002) *The Myth of Consumerism*. London: Pluto.

McLeod, J.M. and Chaffee, S.H. (1972) 'The construction of social reality', in J.T. Tedeschi (ed.), *The Social Influence Process*. Chicago: Aldine-Atherton. pp. 50–59.

McNeal, J.U. and Yeh, C.-H. (1993) 'Born to shop', *American Demographics*, June: 34–39.

Martens, L., Southerton, D. and Scott, S. (2004) 'Bringing children (and parents) into the sociology of consumption', *Journal of Consumer Culture*, 4 (2): 155–182.

Mead, M. (1970) *Culture and Commitment: A Study of the Generation Gap*. New York: Natural History Press/Doubleday.

Moore, R.L. and Moschis, G.P. (1981) 'The effects of family communication and mass media use on adolescent consumer learning', *Journal of Communication*, 31 (Fall): 42–51.

Moschis, G.P. (1985) 'The role of family communication in consumer socialization of children and adolescents', *Journal of Consumer Research*, 11 (March): 898–913.

Moschis, G.P. (1987) *Consumer Socialization: A Life Cycle Perspective*. Lexington, MS: Lexington Books.

Moschis, G.P. and Churchill Jr., G.A. (1978) 'Consumer socialization: a theoretical and empirical analysis', *Journal of Marketing Research*, 15 (November): 599–609.

Moschis, G.P. and Mitchell, L.G. (1986) 'Television advertising and interpersonal influences on teenagers' participation in family consumer decisions', in *Advances in Consumer Research*, vol. 13 (ed. R.J. Lutz). Provo, UT: Association for Consumer Research. pp. 181–186.

Moschis, G.P., Moore, R.L. and Smith, R.B. (1984) 'The impact of family communication on adolescent consumer socialization', in *Advances in Consumer Research*, vol. 11 (ed. T.C. Kinnear), Ann Arbor, MI: Association for Consumer Research. pp. 314–319.

Olsen, B. (1995) 'Brand loyalty and consumption patterns: the lineage factor', in J.F. Sherry Jr. (ed.), *Contemporary Marketing and Consumer Behavior: An Anthropological Sourcebook*. Thousand Oaks, CA: Sage.

Parsons, T. (1956) 'The American family: its relation to personality and the social structure', in T. Parsons and R.F. Bales (eds), *Family, Socialisation and Interaction Process*. London: Routledge and Kegan Paul.

Piaget, J. (1970) 'The stages of intellectual development of the child and Piaget's theory', in P.H. Mussen, J.J. Conger and J. Kagan (eds), *Readings of Child Development and Personality*. New York: Harper and Row.

Pugh, A. (2004) 'Windfall child rearing: low-income care and consumption', *Journal of Consumer Culture*, 42 (2): 229–249.

Roedder-John, D. (1999) 'Consumer socialization of children: a retrospective look at twenty-five years of research', *Journal of Consumer Research*, 26 (December): 183–213.

Roedder-John, D. and Whitney Jr., J.C. (1986) 'The development of consumer knowledge in children: a cognitive structure approach', *Journal of Consumer Research*, 12 (March).

Stacey, J. (1990) *Brave New Families: Stories of Domestic Upheaval in Late Twentieth Century America*. New York: Basic.

Tallman, I., Marotz-Baden, R. and Pindas, P. (1983) *Adolescent Socialization in Cross-Cultural Perspective: Planning for Social Change*. New York: Academic.

Ward, S. (1974) 'Consumer socialization', *Journal of Consumer Research*, 1: 1–16.

Ward, S., Klees, D.M. and Wackman, D.B. (1990) 'Consumer socialization research: content analysis of post-1980 studies and some implications for future work', in *Advances in Consumer Research*, vol. 17, (eds. M.E. Goldberg, G. Gorn and R.W. Pollay), Ann Arbor, MI: Association for Consumer Research. pp. 798–803.

Weber, M. (1983/1922) *Ekonomi och samhälle, Föreståendesociologins grunder 1.* Lund, Sweden: Agos.
White-Riley, M., Foner, A., Hess, B. and Toby, M.L. (1971) 'Socialization for the middle and later years', in D.A. Goslin (ed.), *Handbook of Socialization Theory and Research.* Chicago, IL: Rand McNally.

Note

1   As a result of being ideal types, the characteristics of a particular family type were found to exist to different extents among the families interviewed. Hence, a family belonging to a certain family type does not necessarily have all the characteristics associated with that particular family type. In other words, even though each family was classified according to the five dimensions, it is important to note that some families are better representatives of the family types than others.

4   Methodological and Design Issues in Research with Children

Teresa Davis

Chapter aims

- To examine current practice in doing research with children.
- To identify some of the design and methodological issues of working with child subjects.
- To identify some of the emerging new design and methodological approaches to research with children.

Introduction

Why are there relatively few studies that examine children as consumers? Consumer research studies using child samples are infrequent, at least partly because of methodological and design issues. It is difficult as a researcher to gain access to child subjects. In some countries (such as Australia) in order to carry out research amongst children permission in written form must be gained at a number if different levels from the relevant state Department of Education, the principal of the public school concerned, parents of the children and each individual child (if the child is 8 years and over), as well as having police clearance before they can begin to collect data. The ethics of dealing with child informants is complex and necessary; however it also means that fewer research studies with children are published. Commercial market research with children, where children are recompensed for their participation, yields many more studies, but most are client/product specific and rarely help in our overall understanding of children as consumers.

This chapter will look at some of the ethical issues around doing such research with children and will then move on to consider the methodological and design issues particular to studies that utilize a child sample. The chapter will also introduce some innovative techniques employed by researchers working in this area.

Ways of 'seeing children' and ethical considerations

Ethical considerations, processes and dilemmas are frequently encountered in doing research with children. This is more the case than when doing research with adults, because of the issues of minority status, of informed consent, and anxiety about the cognitive competencies of children. The ethical view of doing research with children is often driven by the underlying philosophical underpinnings of the research. Apart from the institutional requirement of ethics, the researcher's perspective on how the child is perceived affects how the design, method, and ethics of the study are framed. Christensen and Prout (2002) suggest that social researchers who work with children have their 'ethical view' of children formed by social theory. That is to say, their paradigmatic perspective tends to shape not only their research questions, methods and theoretical perspectives, but also their ethical view of children as individuals (see Vignette 1).

Following Jenks's (1982) and Bauman's (1993) argument that social science researchers tend to see children as 'the other' in modernity and often adopt a 'paternalistic' view of children as individuals who are dependent and not fully able to participate as adults in social roles, Christensen and Prout (2002) identify four main perspectives:

1   The child as the object of research.
2   The child as the subject of research.
3   The child as a social actor within the study context.
4   Children as participants in the research and actively co-producing the phenomenon and the study.

Each of these perspectives in based on the researchers' stance on social theory – their way of 'seeing' the child's position in society (see Vignette 1).

Vignette 1: Ethical dilemmas in children's research

When working within the school system, a group of 8 year olds were enlisted for individual interviews on their 'brand experiences'. One of these children was a child with Down's Syndrome, who was keen to participate because all

---

her classmates were participating. The class teacher suggested to this child that she could read a book instead. The teacher then turned to the researcher and explained 'an interview with her would not be very useful' (from the author's own research experiences, 2004).

What could the interviewer's response be? A useful reflexive task would be to ask 'How do I as a researcher see the child?' Your response would depend on whether you see the child as a object, a subject, or a participant in the research.

In the *first perspective*, which draws its view of the child in research from the traditional objective paradigms, children are seen as objects to be researched. Their lives are studied from the outside by adult researchers objectively, recognize the dependency of each child as an 'unformed being', and take a paternalistic view. This tends to translate into methods that rely more on the accounts of 'adults' around the child. Thus in studying children's experiences, these research accounts are always weighed up and tempered by the accounts of parents, teachers, social workers or other 'gatekeepers'. This is seen as 'protective' of children as a vulnerable group because of their cognitive status and inherent 'unreliability' when it comes to sourcing factual information. The ethical perspective therefore follows assumptions of the unequal power, ability and procedures which involve the adult researchers and 'significant adults' in the child subject's life – parents, teachers, law makers, regulators. In practical terms, this translates into a great deal of focus on 'protecting the child'. For example, regular police checks are required by the ethics committees of Australasian universities for researchers who will have direct contact with children. Many also insist on a third person being present when children are being interviewed.

Challenging this view is a *second perspective*, that is a somewhat more 'child-centred' view which sees children in research as not merely 'objects' to be acted upon but as subjects. Developmental psychologists have used this approach as a recognition of the child's cognitive faculties as 'becoming' and not completely 'adult' in their understanding. This is strongly reflected in the 'age/cognitive developmentally appropriate' task and methods designed to cater to these developing abilities (Davis, 2000). The ethical focus here is on the ability of the child to give informed consent. Written consent is usually given only by children of 8 years old and above. Following the cognitive developmental models, the assumption that children below the age of 7 years old (Inhelder and Piaget, 1964) cannot give such consent is made and parental/guardian consent is required. Children in this pre-operational (Inhelder and Paiget, 1964) stage are seen as unable to understand the abstract notion of giving consent, and are therefore unable to give 'informed consent'. This subject position of the young child is produced and reinforced both by the ethical institution and the gatekeepers around the child.

In the *third perspective*, children are recognized as social actors who are changed by and effect change in the social context within which they live. Researchers who approach research through this lens see children as having independent experiences of their social world. Thus their 'voice' is foregrounded and attempts are made in terms of data collection methods and interpretation to stay 'true' to the child's experiences. Ethics in this research perspective is driven by the need to keep the 'authenticity' of the child's voice. Davis (1998) and James et al. (1998) call this the 'tribal child' perspective. Children are seen as belonging to a culture that is different from that of adults. Here ethnographic methods are often employed to carefully channel the voice of children, with researchers spending extended periods in the 'field' which allow the children to become familiar with them and build trust (Christensen, 2004). However, Christensen describes how the children she studied explained to her long after the research was completed that they resented 'all your silly questions' (2004: 169). She was initially seen as another adult who was intrusive and just the same as other 'powerful' adults in their lives. After a long time in the field and learning to negotiate the ethical dilemmas of non-disclosure between the teachers and the children, Christensen felt she had gained their trust. But she points out that unless the children are convinced that the researcher is a 'non-interfering' and 'acceptable' adult, they will tend to classify them with other authoritative adults in their everyday life (teachers, parents, etc.). Grover (2004) also points to this lack of trust that appears to be inherent in many children. She reports on a Norwegian study (by Donnestad and Sanner, 2001) where a 16 year old boy, when asked about researchers and welfare support people working within the child welfare services, replied 'Many people in the support system pretend to be our friends. But you can't rely on them. They tell our stories to other adults. They can destroy us by using power and force us into an institution'.

In the *fourth perspective*, ethics is concerned with ensuring children are participants in the research, that they do not merely voice their experiences using researchers as the conduits of such accounts but are 'co-creators' in the design and methods of collecting information. This perspective is largely driven by the 1989 UN Convention on the Rights of the Child, particularly Article 12 which enshrines the child's right to express their views freely and participate as a human and a citizen. There is also the recognition that the 'culture' of childhood is not a single grouping, rather that there are a variety of 'childhoods and cultures of communication' within these groupings (Davis, 1998).

Thus ethics of research in this perspective adheres to giving children a voice not simply in terms of their own experiences, but also in the design, conduct and methodology of the research – in short shaping the research itself. Here, in addition to the 'formal' ethical requirements of ethics committees, the researcher seeks to involve children in all stages of the research. Understanding how children within a particular 'context of childhood' see themselves, their experiences and their relationships, is key. Qvortrup makes the case for using multiple paradigmatic perspectives in choosing methods for research with children: 'If we seriously mean to improve the life conditions for children we must, as a minimum precondition, establish reporting systems in which they are heard themselves as well as reported on by others' (1997: 101; see also Todd, Chapter 13 in this book). In the following sections these perspectives are examined and various methodological approaches detailed.

Different approaches to studying child consumers

From both ends of the research methodology continuum there exists a paradigmatic divide between researchers about the complexity of doing research with children. The following two sections will examine some of the current understandings about doing research with children from both paradigmatic perspectives.

Positivist research with children

At the 'mainstream' positivist end of the spectrum, we can see researchers describing the need to tailor measurement scales for child samples and customizing experimental stimuli to suit the cognitive abilities of each child subject. Concerns translate into the innovative creation of experimental design and stimuli and a simplification of complex verbal or measurement tasks into visual/pictorial material. Thus an adaptation is made of the 'adult version' of scales to make them 'cognitive age appropriate' e.g., using a 'smiley face' scale for Likert strongly agree–disagree scales. This is primarily based on the principles of cognitive development theory, especially the idea that children can be categorized into hierarchical stages of cognitive ability (Roedder-John, 1999: see also Chapters 2, 9 and 7 respectively, by de la Ville and Tartas, Roland-Lévy and Young in this book, for a further discussion of cognitive development).

Perrachio and Mita (1991) developed seven rules to avoid common pitfalls when doing research with child participants:

1 *Making sure the   knowledge domain   is familiar to the child* As Chi (1977) suggests, children process information best when they are asked to access information they use frequently. For example, in trying to identify children's decision-making steps ask them to tell you how they would choose a video game or make a selection between three kinds of sweets in the supermarket. Any example that they may have experienced in everyday life would make the task easier to complete.
2 *Provide them with rich contextual and retrieval cues* Do this in order to allow participants to access the information you are trying to obtain by using familiar

objects i.e. everyday items. For example, Perrachio (1992) used a familiar sequence of purchase exchange events narrated by a child to aid the child informants.

3 *Ensure you include only elements that are absolutely necessary to your task and use minimal stimuli for experiments.*

4 *Minimize the complexity of the task presented*   If you are asking them to engage in a choice task, include only two or three objects, as more than that could pose a cognitive challenge in terms of comparing and evaluating multiple options.[1]

5 *Employ language that the child uses in everyday life*   Local and regional colloquial uses of object names and places are an example here. If the child has to spend too much time understanding the language used, s/he may not perform as s/he normally would, thereby skewing the data. For example, Sellers (1989) cites the example of the child (interpreting questions quite literally) when asked 'Do you wish your family were bigger?' giving the response No, my family are all quite tall already.

6 *Highlight the few key elements of the task and get the child to focus on those.*

7 *Employ clear and achievable goals for the child to follow*   If a cumulative task is required ask her/him to complete intermediate goals in a sequential manner. For example, if the child has to choose between two brands and do this for three different product categories, present them with one product category at a time; at each point ask them to complete the choice between the two brands in a single product category before moving on to the next category.

Source: Perrachio, L. (1992) 'How do children learn to be consumers? A script-processing approach', *Journal of Consumer Research*, 18 (March): 425–440. With permission of The University of Chicago Press. © 1992 by Journal of Consumer Research Inc.

Some examples of how these principles have been applied in published consumption research are presented below.

- *Visual and concrete stimuli*   Chaplin and Roedder-John (2005) simplified the task of self-brand connections for their young subjects by modifying the way questions were framed in their experimental design study – for example, by using 'Who am I?' instead of the 'I am ...' open-ended question. They also adopted a collage assembly board for the children to use to express visually what brand they felt they could connect to. The children could pick out pictures of the brand logos and stick these onto a pin board. Thus the harder cognitive tasks of recalling brand names or reading them (and the reading skills of very young children may not be up to this) were made non-verbal and the task completion was simplified. In another study Otto et al. (2006) used 'tokens' to concretize the idea of saving money to explore children s savings strategies.
- *Sequencing categorization and choice tasks*   Markman (1989) suggests children should use 'thematic' rather than 'taxonomic' categorization in identifying acceptable brand extensions, which means they can view these in a different way to adults. In exploring brand meaning amongst children, a 'sorting task' was devised to see if in the identification of core brand attribute/associations children could indeed make such thematic rather than taxonomic brand associations (Davis, 2007). Each informant was first presented with a set of 18 cards in total, with two of these bearing the brand names and logo of 'Sanitarium'[2] and 'Billabong'[3]. The other 16 cards had pictures of generic products on them with the names of the product also written on these (e.g., a picture of a loaf of bread with the word 'bread' printed below it). They were asked to use the first card (for example the 'Sanitarium' brand cue card) to

categorize the remaining 16 product picture cards (generic product pictures with no brand cues) into two equal piles of 'best fit' (ranked 1–8 in order of degree of fit) and 'worst fit' (ranked as with the best fit). The verbal instructions given to the children were to look at each of the 16 product cards in turn and choose to place them in either of two piles 'one which went well with Sanitarium' and one pile that 'did not go well with Sanitarium'.[4] The study found that children had a 'thematic' (complementarity) approach to understanding which extensions were suitable for what brands unlike the adult 'taxonomic' (similarity-based) approach. This meant that brand managers using 'adult'-type reasoning for children's brand extension decisions might look at the 'brand meaning' more thematically. Thus while a cereal brand, such as 'Sanitarium', would, in adult terms, make other cereal products such as cereal bars (taxonomic-similar category), children associated the brand 'Sanitaruim' with breakfast, so bread or toast is appropriate for the brand as toast 'went with' cereal (thematic-complementarity).

- *Creating a relevant experimental context*   Perrachio (1992) used retail encounter scripts to examine if children learnt consumer skills in ways that were comparable to those of adults. She used a 'script' or a shopping story to contextualize the learning stimuli (see Vignette 2). Using this engaging stimuli in a visual (video sequence) format, she reported that even 5 year old children were able to complete the experimental task. The study yielded significant results, suggesting that children need cued retrieval, audiovisual reinforcement and contextual response formats to learn complex consumption skills, but importantly, that they were capable of doing so. The study showed the importance of the format in which the information was presented made a great deal of difference to the way children processed it, coded it, and later retrieved it from memory.

Vignette 2: Story scripts as narrated by a child

Hi, my name is Billy. I am going to tell you a story, ready? Yesterday was my birthday. I got lots of presents. All of them were great except one. It was the one from my Grandpa. It was a shirt. When I tried it on it was too big. So, I decided to return to the store and get a smaller one. The tags on the shirt said it was from a store near my house. So, my Mom, sister and I decided to got to the store.

   When we got to the store, we looked for a sales clerk. We saw one behind the counter and walked over to her. I put my bag down on the counter. I told the sales clerk that I needed a smaller one.

   The clerk checked the tags to make sure it was from her store. Then she went to the back and got another shirt. The clerk gave me the shirt. It was just my size. I was very happy. My mom, my sister and I left the store and went home.

Source: Perrachio (1992)

- *Task demands on outcomes*   Macklin and Machleit (1990) examined how children performed on the recall and recognition of brands as well as their memory for brand and product attributes. The results showed quite clearly that the young sample performed surprisingly well when the task was simplified and non-verbal responses were used. In the study 4 year old children performed significantly better when responding non-verbally (pointing to the recognized/recalled brand rather than naming it). The researchers therefore advocated strongly for ensuring the task demands of a study were carefully examined. Children may not display actual perfor- mance and cognitive abilities because of the complexity of the task design used rather than this being due to Piagetian cognitive developmental limitations.

Among the positivists therefore we see that researchers focus on task design and stimuli simplification as ways of making the research easier for the child sub- jects to complete. Very careful use of language and instruction is employed to overcome issues of varying language, literacy and numeracy competencies among children of various cognitive ages.

Interpretivist research with children

Coming from the other end of the paradigmatic continuum, interpretivist researchers find themselves using multiple methods to understand how child consumers see, understand and experience consumption. Concerns are largely about children as research subjects and the need to engage with them in a manner different from those used with adults. Traditionally, these research studies use in-depth interviews and some projective techniques. Newer and more innovative ways of engaging with child 'subjects' call for rethinking the role of the child in research as the 'subject' (Pole et al., 1999). It is not as easy to interview a child as it is an adult, nor is it a simple matter to put a child at ease when as a stranger you are trying to gain insights into a young child's consumption life. Among interpretivists, multiple forms of interviewing (phenomenological or ethnographic) are used, as are a number of 'projective techniques'. In carrying out an ethnographic or phenomeno- logical interview, the rules about how to establish rapport and trust and how to listen to informants are similar.

Vignette 3: Unambiguous questions

Interviewer: Would you use the Mongoose brand in the future – like when you are in big school?

9 year old   No, in big school I have to wear my uniform so I cannot wear
(Year Four   my Mongoose shirts.
primary school)
informant:

Source: from an interview transcript of a study of 26 Australian school children and their favourite brands (Davis, 2004, researcher's reflective log)

- *Interviews*   The need to avoid unambiguous questions, a common pitfall when interviewing children, is illustrated in Vignette 3. The interviewer has been speaking to the child about his favourite brand 'Mongoose' which includes branded clothing, bikes and skateboards. Her final question is an attempt to find out how long- or short-lived a 'favoured' brand status is with children. Knowing that for a child of 9 years old, it would perhaps makes sense to 'concretize' an abstract notion such as 'the future' by explaining it as 'like when you are in big school' (i.e., in two or three years' time). However, the child has no hesitation in interpreting the question as 'Will you wear Mongoose shirts in school when you are in big school?'. He responds by pointing out that when he is in big school he will still be in school and will therefore be required to wear a school uniform.

  With young informants, the interview has to begin with some reassurance of the confidentiality of the information conveyed in the interview. This should be done in a simple and careful manner. Children value the 'promises' of confidentiality, privacy and choice that adult interviewers make. In fact these children may see these unfulfilled promises as lies (Maas and Abbeduto, 2001) rather than as broken promises in their everyday experiences. Thus, promises made need to be carefully followed through. In most cases, children will respond positively to such information. However, as Bassett et al. (2008) found, this sometimes inadvertently 'formalised' the interview setting. The adolescents they were interviewing became less relaxed and more constrained. Yet, this did also depend on how the informants viewed the interviewer. But it does still alert us to the importance of the opening as the point when the tone of the interview is set and the relationship of interviewee and interviewer in terms of rapport, trust, power and so on are established. As Moore et al. (2008) found, children appreciated those interviewers who gave them a choice about how they could respond to particular questions. For example, as one of their young informants explained 'If people didn't want to do something and you were mean and said that they had to do it, that would be mean, so it was good that you weren't mean. [The researcher] asked me to draw my house and I didn't want to (because it is hard to draw it because of the shape) so I didn't do that 'we just talked about it. That was good. I didn't have to do anything I didn't want [to]' (Moore et al., 2008: 87).

  While most adult interviewees are not daunted by audio-taping an interview, children tend to be far more conscious/distracted by it. Often the relaxed introductory chitchat takes on a different tone once a recorder is switched on. As Bassett et al. (2008: 122) suggest 'it was as though the recorder formalized our roles' the teen suddenly became the informant and I became the interviewer'. Children are also sometimes very conscious of what they say when they know this is being recorded in an audio or visual form. Anxiety to say the 'right thing' is sometimes manifested as a result, as are 'playing up to the camera' effects. In either case the interview becomes difficult. However, the obtrusiveness of recorders has become less of an issue with the advent of the tiny recordable MP3 players and children can become used to this quickly and not be distracted by it in interviews. This is a technology children are familiar with: 74 per cent of American teens have an MP3 player (Pew Internet Project, 2009).

  Complete quiet and privacy in interviewing children are sometimes not possible for practical and ethical reasons. This can make interviews with children particularly difficult. They will often take place in a 'public space', such as the library in a school or in the living room of a family home. The presence of other children/siblings, parents/teachers and so on makes it difficult to get a young child to give truly 'independent' responses. Very young children for example will constantly look to their mothers before they respond, or if in a school context will look at their teacher and respond only when that teacher encourages them or gives them permission to speak. This therefore can make it very difficult to allow the conversation to flow naturally or even to build up a rapport.

Across these three sections discussed, runs a common thread – the issue of the 'power differential'. In doing research with children, particularly those who are vulnerable, this (natural) power imbalance can be exaggerated through the process, where the researcher is considered the expert (Jones, 2000). Moore et al. (2008) suggest several ways to empower children in terms of the location, the technology or spatial control. For example, sitting on the floor to talk to school-children figuratively reduces the power differential – making the adult a little uncomfortable, while the child becomes very comfortable. Another way they suggest is to allow the children to choose where to meet or talk. In a similar vein, they also suggest making the child 'the boss of the tape recorder'. When the child is allowed to be in charge of the technology, for example, choosing to decide when s/he presses the record button on or off, this helps in making them feel they are in control of what is happening and therefore they are more likely to be relaxed and engaged in the interviewing process.

It helps to speak to parents/teachers before interviewing the child to gain some insights into his/her life. Initial demographic information from consent forms and the like could be used to begin the conversation. It could also give the interviewer an idea of what topics can be discussed with the child and what should be avoided. Disclosing some information about oneself to the child can help to build that critical component of trust between the interviewer and the child. In opening a discussion about children's favourite brands the author always began by telling the child what her favourite chocolate brand is. To avoid influencing the child's own preferences, the researcher could use chocolates as an example while the child spoke of their favourite brands of 'daily toiletries' and 'lunchbox snacks'. Sharing information about likes and dislikes helps establish a connection and a sense of trust (Davis, 2004). Likewise, identifying common ground or 'belonging' to some group the child belongs to can be used as part of the process of gaining trust and establishing a rapport with the child. This may be as simple as talking about common dislikes – 'I don't like Brussel sprouts either'. It helps to allow the child to feel there is enough common ground between her/him and the interviewer as to be able to speak freely especially if the conversation is about sensitive issues.

- *Projective techniques* These are used widely in research with child consumers because they help interviewers to get closer to the meanings that lie below the surface but which young children may have trouble articulating. Drawing has been used as an effective 'non-verbal' means of getting children to articulate their thoughts and feelings. For example, Marshall and Aitken (2007: 274) used free form drawings by New Zealand children to examine the notion of how children relate to possessions. They found 'that the drawing exercise provides a rich data source and an interesting approach to researching children's preferences'. They suggested that drawing as a 'natural' everyday activity that children are used to engaging in at home and at school they are relaxed about it and the pictures then form a natural 'talking point' to explore complex feelings and emotions. McNeal and Ji (2003) advocate drawing as a 'rich data', and suggest that it is a useful way to 'tap into young consumers' minds'. It almost serves as an 'autodriving' technique to allow children to reflect upon and articulate their relationships with the objects.

Likewise Chan (2006) used a drawing task with children in China to ask them to depict children with a 'few' and then 'many' toys as a starting point to a discussion on wealth, materialism and happiness. She reported that such a drawing task was a great way to begin an otherwise complex discussion about abstract ideas. However, she suggested that the task be sequenced and in retrospect that she should have asked them to complete the picture of the child with few toys and to discuss it before asking them to draw the picture of the child with 'many' toys. This she feels may have made it easier for the younger children in terms of task comprehension.

New approaches to researching children

Morrow and Richards (1996: 96) suggested children and childhood research needed to move away from 'the narrow focus of socialization and child development' towards an approach that takes seriously children's own experiences of their lives as children. The assumption of seeing the child as a vulnerable, unformed being may overlook the meanings and unique perspective and 'lived' experience of the life phenomenon. More recently Cook (2008: 230) suggested that some of this new perspective on the child consumer as 'active social beings living in the here and the now' uses the same language as that of commercial market research which suggests political reasons for 'empowering' the child in this way in order to view them as independent, competent consumers. Moore et al. (2008) suggest that shifting the focus from the child as a 'subject' to one of a child who is an active participant of the research and who shapes it involves addressing 'power imbalances' and using 'child reference groups' as a kind of 'advisory' panel in research design. Some of the new approaches to doing research with children embrace these ideas.

- *Online methods* Online blogs have been used to examine the ways in which teenagers exchange information about brands in a process of 'passive socialization' covering issues of a sensitive nature such as eating behaviours, welfare and family dynamics (Muratore, 2008). Online environments are another 'natural' environment for the informants where they can remain anonymous and in control. However, the ethics of online data collection should be negotiated carefully (see Kozinets, 2002). While Kozinets speaks of the methodology used with adult samples, the ethics of disclosure while being a participant online can be extremely fraught and will need careful consideration (see Tufte and Rasmussen, Chapter 11 in this book, for more on this issue).

- *Photography* Bannister and Booth (2005) use a 'child centric' approach with interviews and projective techniques based around photographs that the young informants have taken of their everyday lives. Likewise Bartholomew and O'Donohoe (2003) used cameras to allow children to take pictures of their bedrooms. This empowered children to decide what parts of their rooms they wanted to reveal to the researchers. The pictures were used to initiate discussions about their possessions and allowed the children to be much more 'engaged' in the research than if a researcher had merely talked to them about their possessions. Chitakunye and Maclaren (2008) asked teenagers to carry a disposable camera around for a week to record any eating-related event, thereby providing (quite literally) a fuller picture of their eating events and rituals. This approach allowed the researchers to 'go where the children went and see what the children did', overcoming a number of issues surrounding ethics and access, as it was controlled by the informant, was unobtrusive, and engaged the teenagers in the study.
- *Comic books and documentary narrative* In a wonderfully innovative example of customizing data collection methods to suit the participating child informant, Kirova and Emme (2008) used the notion of the 'fotonovella' to examine the lives of immigrant children in a Canadian school setting. This is a popular narrative medium in Latin American countries, as well as amongst the Chicano and Latino communities in the USA, and consists of using photographs or 'comic book' style drawings with 'speech balloons'. After running workshops on how to produce photographs and the format of the fotonovella, young informants were asked to create narratives of their school life. The richness of the imagery and resultant data demonstrated how the simplified verbal yet visually rich method helped the immigrant children to communicate powerfully by using images. The researchers suggested that as the 'fotonovella as a research method not only acknowledges the interplay of language and visual image but also addresses the fundamental epistemological question, how can the language of inquiry correspond to the expression of the phenomena being studied?' (Kirova and Emme, 2008: 38).

In an academic research field such as consumer research, children are often seen as 'difficult' subjects because of access (issues of ethics and the levels of permission involved) and because of the need to use complex methods and approaches. There is clearly a paucity of such studies, especially those that employ innovative methods and techniques to address the issues of imbalance between child informants and adult researchers. Imbalances of maturity, of power, of cognitive competencies of meaning and language exist and need to be resolved in new ways to fill the gap that also exists in our knowledge and understanding of children as consumers.

Conclusion

In an era where the 'paternalism' towards groups seen as vulnerable in the community (and in this we can include children) has shifted towards a more sensitive and empowering perspective, giving children a voice in research appears to be appropriate. The construction of the 'child subject' in most of these research methodologies makes assumptions about the 'incompetent' child which some of present-day perspectives belie. While children remain vulnerable to ethical and other exploitation in research, they should be allowed to speak in their 'own voice'.

Cognitive equality apart, a child's voice is a legitimate and important one to listen to by all those who engage in research with children if we claim to want to hear what they have to say. The key driver, therefore, should be to engage with children in a participatory way, listening to their voices in ways that allow them to speak as directly and openly as possible without making them passive 'subjects' in the process. This growing school of thought on participatory research with children calls for a reworking of existing fundamental views about children and their place in the social order. Finally, research with children as with all other research depends on a good sound understanding of the particular research context and the participants. Thus not all groups of children are alike, so the dangers of assuming all children are competent social actors or equal partners in research should be recognized.

Future research directions

There is a growing interest in these new approaches to conducting research with young consumers. Thomson (2008) suggests that that visual and online methods (photographs and visual narratives) are a simple way of giving 'control' to children to use their own voices. However, she also points to a need to rethink how these new methods may create new ethical issues around privacy and consent. The methods that appear to yield the most useful outcomes in terms of reflecting the voices of children are visual ethnographic methods. Pink (2007) talks about the 'ethnographicness of photography' that allows the researcher to capture a lot more than just textual data. More powerfully, visual narrative methods such as the ones that Thomson (2008) and Kirova and Emme (2008) suggest combine the power of photographs and pictures with a child's own voice narrative. Yet, as Johansson et al. (2009) show, giving Nordic children disposable cameras and asking them to record their individual 'foodscapes' can turn children into artists. In their innovative study the composition of food on a plate or backgrounds was often carefully thought out and arranged for the camera, yet the visual data helped to explain a great deal of nuance about the children's attitudes to, knowledge of, and perspectives on what constituted 'healthy' and 'unhealthy' food, what was a 'good meal', etc.

One must of course acknowledge that not all research questions will lend themselves to the use of 'visual' data. Alternatives do exist – letting children audio-tape their own discussions with peers, construct collages of their feelings or emotions, use verbal narratives or oral story telling and projective techniques all can be applied in a variety of research contexts and to answer a number of different research phenomena involving children. Using multiple methods to 'triangulate' and confirm meaning and the authenticity of the data is strongly recommended. This may take the form of simply asking a question and having the response confirmed by engaging the child in a choice task a little later (see Vignette 4). Direct questions could be confirmed by using projective techniques as well. The idea here is to combine complementary techniques to add nuance and depth to the data and the subsequent analysis.

Vignette 4: Confirming meaning

In a task that examined children's understanding of healthy eating, food choices and television food advertising, children were asked in individual interviews how much television they watched and how much unhealthy food they ate. One informant told the interviewer that her parents did not allow her to watch any 'commercial television' (only public channels which carried no advertising). She also emphasized how much fruit she ate and how her mother would make all her school snacks herself to ensure the food was natural and organic and free of pesticides, etc.

A little later in the interview she was asked what she would choose to eat for lunch if she were offered either a grilled sandwich (chicken, lettuce and tomato) or a hotdog and for a snack either ice cream or yogurt. She replied that she would not eat a hotdog ever because it was full of bad meat and that ice cream was unhealthy, and even yogurt was full of additives. The interviewer was impressed by the 9 year old's understanding of food manufacturing and standards of healthy eating.

In the final task the child was asked to select (real choice) a heavily advertised unhealthy snack, a healthy piece of fruit, an advertised healthier option, and an unadvertised unhealthy snack. She picked the highly advertised, unhealthy option. When asked why she chose it, she responded by saying 'My mother would never let me try anything like this'.

Source: author's own research experiences (White and Davis, 2007)

Discussion questions

1   Explain why it is important to carry out research that enhances our understanding of children as consumers.
2   'Commercial consumer research is plentiful, while academic research of the child consumer is significantly less frequent'. Discuss this statement and identify possible reasons why this may be so.
3   List and discuss some of the ethical issues in carrying out research with children.

4 Discuss the ways in which the perspective of the researcher in seeing the child consumer as a 'subject' may pose issues with the interpretation and outcomes of the research undertaken.
5 Is the view of the child consumer as a research participant/partner, non-controversial? Examine how this view of the child as a 'being in their own right' could pose ethical issues.

Further reading

Archaud, D. (1993) *Children: Rights and Childhood*. London: Routledge.

Christensen, P.M. and James, A. (2000) *Research with Children: Perspectives and Practices*. London: Routledge.

Croghan, R., Griffin, C., Hunter, J. and Phoenix, A. (2008) 'Young people's constructions of self: notes on the use and analysis of the photo-elicitation method', *International Journal of Social Research Methodology*, 11 (1): 1–12.

Mauthner, M. (1997) 'Methodological aspects of collecting data from children: lessons from three research projects', *Children and Society*, 2: 16–28.

Morrow, V. and Richards, M. (1996) 'The ethics of social research with children: an overview', *Children and Society*, 10: 90–105.

Graue, M.E., Walsh, D.J., Ceglowski, D.A., Fernie, D., Kantor, R., Leavitt, R.L., Miller, P.J. and Ting, H.Y. (1998) *Studying Children in Context: Theories, Methods, and Ethics*. Thousand Oaks, CA: Sage.

Tinson, J. (2009) *Conducting Research with Children and Adolescents: Design, Methods and Empirical Cases*. Oxford, UK: Goodfellow.

References

Bannister, E.N. and Booth, G. (2005) 'Exploring innovative methodologies for child centric consumer research', *Qualitative Market Research: An International Journal*, 8 (2): 157–175.

Bartholomew, A. and O'Donohoe, S. (2003) 'Everything under control: a child's eye view of advertising', *Journal of Marketing Management*, 19: 433–457.

Bassett, R., Beagan, B., Ristovski-Slijepcevic, S. and Chapman, G.E. (2008) 'Tough teens: the methodological challenges of interviewing teenagers as research participants', *Journal of Adolescent Research*, 23 (2): 119–131.

Bauman, Z. (1993) *Postmodern Ethics*. Oxford: Blackwell.

Chan, K. (2006) 'Exploring children's perceptions of material possessions: a drawing study', *Qualitative Market Research: An International Journal*, 9.

Chaplin, L. and Roedder-John, D. (2005) 'The development of self: brand connections in children and adolescents', *Journal of Consumer Research*, 32 (1): 119–129.

Chi, M. T. (1977) 'Age differences in memory span', *Journal of Experimental Child Psychology*, 23: 255–281.

Chitakunye, D.P. and Maclaren, P. (2008) 'Everyday practices surrounding young people's food consumption, *Advances in Consumer Research*, 35: 918–919.

Christensen, P.H. (2004) 'Children's participation in ethnographic research: issues of power and representation', *Children and Society,* 18: 165–176.

Christensen, P.H. and Prout, A. (2002) 'Working with ethical symmetry in social research with children', *Childhood,* 9 (4): 477–497.

Cook, D. (2008) 'The missing child in consumption theory', *Journal of Consumer Culture*, 8 (2): 219–243.

Davis, J. (1998) 'Understanding the meaning of children: a reflexive process', *Children and Society*, 2: 325–335.

Davis, T. (2000) 'What children understand about consumption constellations: differences across three age groups', *Advances in Consumer Research*, 27 (S.J. Hoch and R.J. Meyer (eds), Provo, UT: Association for Consumer Research). pp. 72–78.

Davis, T. (2004) 'The secret life of brands: Australian children and their brands: implications for advertisers', in P. Neijens, C. Hess, B. van den Putte and E. Smit (eds), *Content and Media Factors in Advertising*. Amsterdam: Het Spinhuis.

Davis, T. (2007) 'Children and brand meaning: a thematic categorization task', *Journal of Brand Management*, 14 (3): 255–266.

Donnestad, E. and Sanner, M. (eds) (2001) *Hello is Anyone There? Young Messages from Another Reality*. Report to the United Nations General Assembly Special Session on Children. New York, September 2001, *Kristiansand Forum for the Convention on the Rights of the Child*.

Grover, S. (2004) 'Why won't they listen to us? On giving power and voice to children participating in social research', *Childhood,* 11: 81–93.

Inhelder, B. and Piaget, J. (1964) *The Early Growth of Logic in the Child: Classification and Seriation*. London: Routledge and Kegan Paul.

James, A., Jenks, C. and Prout, A. (1998) *Theorizing Childhood*. Teachers College Press, P.O. Box 20, Williston, VT 05495-0020.

Jenks, C. (ed.) (1982) *The Sociology of Childhood: Essential Readings*. London: Batsfors (reprinted Aldershot, Greg, 1992).

Johansson, B., Makela, J., Roos, G., Hillen, S., Jensen, T.M. and Houtilainen, A. (2009) 'Nordic children's foodscapes: images and reflections', *Food Culture and Society,* 12/1: 25–51.

Jones, A. (2000) 'Exploring young people's experience of immigration controls: the search for an appropriate methodology', in B. Humphries (ed.), *Research in Social Care and Social Welfare*. London: Jessica Kingsley. pp. 31–47.

Kirova, A. and Emme, M. (2008) 'Fotonovela as a research tool in image-based participatory research with immigrant children', *International Journal of Qualitative Methods*, 7 (2): 35–57.

Kozinets, R. (2002) 'The field behind the screen: using netnography for marketing research in online communities', *Journal of Marketing Research*, 39 (February): 61–72.

Maas, F.K. and Abbeduto, L. (2001) 'Children's judgements about intentionally and unintentionally broken promises', *Journal of Child Language*, 28: 517–529.

Macklin, M.C. and Machleit, K.A. (1990) 'Measuring preschool children's attitude', *Marketing Letters*, 1 (3): 253–265.

Markman, E.M. (1989*) Categorization and Naming in Children: Problems of Induction*. Cambridge, MA: MIT Press.

Marshall, D. and Aitken, R. (2007) 'Putting brands in the picture: children's drawings of their favourite things', *Asia Pacific Advances in Consumer Research*, 7: 268–276.

McNeal, J.U. and Ji, M.F. (2003) 'Children's visual memory of packaging', *Journal of Consumer Marketing*, 20 (5): 400–427.

Moore, T., McArthur, M. and Noble-Carr, D. (2008) 'Little voices and big ideas: lessons learned from children about research', *International Journal of Qualitative Research*, 7 (2): 77–91.

Morrow, V. and Richards, M. (1996) 'The ethics of social research with children: an overview', *Children and Society*, 10: 90–105.

Muratore, I. (2008) 'Teenagers, blogs and socialization', *Young Consumers*, 9 (2): 131–142.

Otto, A., Schotts, P., Westerman, J. and Webley, P. (2006) 'Children's use of saving strategies: an experimental approach', *Journal of Economic Psychology*, 27 (1): 57–72.

Perrachio, L. (1990) 'Designing research to reveal the young child's emerging competence', *Psychology and Marketing*, 7 (4): 257–276.

Perrachio, L. (1992) 'How do children learn to be consumers? A script–processing approach', *Journal of Consumer Research*, 18 (March): 425–440.

Perrachio, L. and Mita, C. (1991) 'Designing research to assess children's comprehension of marketing messages', *Advances in Consumer Research*, 18, (23).

Pew Internet Project (2009) Available at http://www.pewinternet.org/Reports/2009/12-Wireless-Internet-Use.aspx (last accessed 11 August 2009).

Pink, S. (2007) *Doing Visual Ethnography: Images, Media and Representation in Research* (2nd edition). London: Sage.

Pole, C., Mizen, P. and Bolton, A. (1999) 'Realising children's agency in research: partners and participants', *International Journal of Social Research Methodology*, 2 (1): 39–54.

Qvortrup, J. (1997) 'A voice for children in statistical and social accounting: a plea for children's right to be heard', in A. James and A. Prout (eds), *Constructing and Reconstructing Childhood: Contemporary Issues in the Sociological Study of Childhood* (2nd edition). London: Routledge Falmer.

Roedder-John, D.R. (1999) 'Consumer socialization of children: a retrospective look at twenty-five years of research', *Journal of Consumer Research*, 26 (December): 183–213.

Sellers, P. (1989) 'The ABCs of marketing to kids in *Fortune*', May 8, pp. 113–120.

Solberg, A. (1996) 'The challenge in child research: from, "being" to "doing"', in J. Brannen and M. O'Brien (eds), *Children in Families: Research and Policy*. London: Falmer.

Thomson, P. (2008) *Doing Visual Research with Children and Young People*. London: Routledge.

White, L. and Davis, T. (2007) 'Children and snack foods: is there a relationship between television viewing habits and nutritional knowledge and product choice?', *Advances In Consumer Research – Asia Pacific* (Vol. VII).

Notes

1 Schatz (1973, as cited in Perrachio, 1990) showed how young children can easily complete choice tasks which involved choosing from four objects, but when this was increased to six objects to choose from, the 4 and 5 year old informants were unable to complete the task successfully.

2 The Sanitarium Health Food Company was established in 1898 and was the first company in Australia to promote cereals as a breakfast alternative to bread. Its

flagship products include 'Weetbix', granola and 'So good'. Sanitarium is a wholly Australian-owned company best known for its wide range of cereals and cereal bars. It holds the largest market share for the dairy alternatives product category.

3   Selling in over 60 countries, Billabong Australia was established as a producer of surf boards and surf gear. Its main business still remains in surf wear, but it has expanded to include skate wear, extreme sport accessories of all kinds. Founder Merchant Gordon owns 20 per cent of the company. It is closely associated with the strong 'surfie' subculture in Australian coastal towns.

4   After this task was completed by the children, the first pile was examined by them and the cards were placed in a sequence of 'went with (brand) best' to 'went with (brand) least'. Most of the children chose to arrange them in a line on one side of the Sanitarium brand cue card, putting the ones that 'went best' closest to and the ones that 'went least' furthest away. The act of physically placing the brands in a sequence 'closer to' and 'farther away from' the brand helps the children concretize the (otherwise abstract) idea of 'distance' and 'closeness' to the brand.

Part II

Encountering Marketing

5 Children and the Market: An American Historical Perspective

Gary Cross

Chapter aims

- To discover when and how children's desires were expressed in the marketing of children's goods.
- To identify the claims and problems of marketing specialists in attributing agency to child consumers.
- To explore how changing understandings of childhood and parenting impacted the marketing of children's goods and to children in the twentieth century.
- To reveal how children's rebellion from adult expectations shaped their desires and attempts by advertisers to reach them.
- To discuss the implications of the recurrent tension over marketing to children within and beyond the family.

Vignette 1: Childhood memories

A Christmas Story is a 1983 film, based on the humorist Jean Shepherd's nostalgic memory of his childhood in 1940s Midwestern America, that revolves around a 9 year old boy's obsession with receiving a 'Daisy Red Ryder carbine-action 200-shot range model air rifle' for Christmas. Despite heroic efforts to win over his mother, his teacher, and even a department store Santa, they all dismiss his wish with 'No, you'll shoot your eye out'. Finally, on Christmas morning, after having to endure wearing pink rabbit pajamas, a gift of a well-meaning but clueless aunt, he finds a final hidden present, the longed-for air rifle commonly known as a BB gun that his father has bought for him. Dad justifies this to his wife with a sheepish admission that he had received a Daisy when he was a boy.

Introduction

With humour, the film in Vignette 1 reveals a common issue of children and the market: the resistance of parents to children's desires. Left unsaid was the fact that the makers of the Red Rider BB gun not only cultivated boys' longings by identifying the toy with a famous radio cowboy character of the era, but Daisy also used advertising to tutor boys on winning over reluctant parents who controlled the purse strings. These ads advised kids to put a Daisy ad under the milk bottles on their doorstep or even within a magazine that Mom or Dad was bound to read. In the end, another feature of Daisy's ad campaigns that date from the 1910s won out – the appeal to Dad and his memory of receiving his Christmas BB gun.

While such appealing to cross-generational male bonding in ads was common (especially so for electric train sets from the 1910s to the 1960s), this crude attempt to manipulate a parent through a child was not. In fact, most advertising for children's goods, even playthings, was directed toward parents and not children in the USA until the advent of television and especially via the revolution of the direct-to-child marketing of Mattel toys on the *Mickey Mouse Club* in 1955. As we can see from our story, this did not mean that children had no say in family purchases even before massive direct marketing was aimed at them, but until relatively recently manufacturers got to the kids and kids got to the goods through parents.

When, how, and to what effect has the children's market become an expression of kids' desires? As a twentieth-century historian of childhood and consumption this question is central – but it is not easy to answer. Ellen Seiter (1993) found in TV advertising in the 1980s an appeal to the 'noisy, and thrilling' in a fantasy world where 'kids rule' and Allison James (1998) noted how young children embrace adult-defying candy. From a more commercial perspective, marketing literature has abandoned the old view that children lack either the capacity or the right to make consumer decisions and instead have increasingly argued that children naturally have a will and desires apart from parental demands, have needs that are biological rather than induced by social contact, and have the free speech right to learn about products through advertising (Cook, 2000; Schor, 2004). The problem is that the quest for autonomy in children is more complex. As a historian of children's consumption, I would argue that it is neither 'natural' nor simply 'rebellious'.

It is very difficult to know when children became agents or how and when the age of children's consumer decision making changed. This is not only a matter of a lack of data, but also a problem of sorting out the relative roles of parents and offspring in consumer choice. Some might say that oral history or memoirs are good sources of children's viewpoint, but I find them nostalgic (coming from an adult perspective), highly unrepresentative, and thus suspect. The kids' viewpoint, however, can be gleaned indirectly from changes in the toy (and plaything) market. At the beginning of the twentieth century, these products reflected adult perspectives – designed to instruct the young to assume later economic and sexual roles (think of didactic stories, dolls intended to teach sewing, or even construction toys). Soon thereafter, this market began to be governed by adult memories of their childhoods and ideas about the delightful and delighted child (the cute), as well as by hopes and expectations of what their offspring will become when they grow up. Finally, about a generation later, changes in commercial playthings and narratives showed that kids over the age of parental control (and that age drops continually in the twentieth century) broke from parental toy preferences. While children embraced or abided adult preferences in playthings and media (books, movies, radio and TV), they also rebelled against them in what I've called the 'cool' (Cross, 2004). Using a historical approach to advertising and changing children's products, we can find out when and how this ambiguous relationship between children and their elders shaped the emergence of a child-focused marketing.

The 'cute' and consumer markets for children

Marketing children's goods is barely a century old. Children's playthings were long the afterthoughts of manufacturing adult goods (often made with the scraps of wood and other materials left over from producing furniture or tools) or even made by kids themselves. Many toys originated as fads (like balloons) or the ritual objects (like dolls and miniature playsets) of adults (Cross, 1997). Even the amusement parks appearing in the 1890s at Coney Island catered not to children but primarily to young adults seeking to escape the culture and control of the older generation of parents and ethnic and neighbourhood communities. The mechanical thrill rides attracted adults while children were confined to the beach. Only in the 1920s were miniature coasters and ferris wheels offered to young children (Mangels, 1952; Register, 2001).

The child's market emerged with new attitudes toward the young appearing about 1900 among the middle class. With decreased child mortality, smaller families and greater affluence children became 'priceless', plucked from labour markets and valued as affective consumer goods. Increasingly, parents ceased seeing their children as burdens or assets to train and exploit (Zelizer, 1985). Rather, they found children to be natural recipients of delightful things as 'wondrous innocents'. A key change was parents' embrace of the 'cute'. No longer meaning too clever (as in the admonition, 'Don't be cute'), the 'cute' – defined as particular ways that children interact with adults, suggesting at once dependence and vulnerability as well as the vitality, innocent charm and impishness that adults encouraged – became central to modern American child rearing. Although wonder could be evoked by the child's discovery of nature, in the twentieth century it was sparked primarily through commercialized fantasy and novelty. This spending on the child went beyond offering adults status and display through the child. At the core of this change was the adult's acceptance of children's desire as natural, especially when it was expressed as wonder – as, for example, in the ritual of the Christmas morning opening of presents from 'Santa Claus'. This embrace of the 'cute' may have led to permissive parenting or the jaded child, expressed often in the 'excesses' of Christmas gifts or in the bratty children in Roald Dahl's (1964) novel made into a movie, *Willy Wonka and the Chocolate Factory*. But it also became the core appeal in marketing children's goods in the twentieth century, as evidenced by everything from Kodak's cheap Brownie Camera (featuring popular children's storybook characters in 1898) and the Shirley Temple doll of the 1930s to more recent fads like Cabbage Patch dolls and Beanie Babies.

The 'cute' and the commercialized childhood came together around a trend toward the child-centred holiday. Traditions of gifting the child at Christmas, a custom that replaced communal celebrations, became progressively elaborate from the 1820s on and had accelerated by the end of the nineteenth century with the department store toy department and the annual ritual of children visiting Santa Claus there. Chanachak became a child-centred Jewish response to the success of Christmas in the 1910s. Likewise, children's birthday parties and gifts emerged from a new stress on the individual and the significance of calendar age. Writer Linda Lewis suggested: 'A birthday gives a child a curtain raiser for his personal drama … [B]y licensing egocentric behavior, a birthday suggests the suspension of limits' (Lewis, 1976: 24). The simple, repetitive, and child-like song, *Happy Birthday to You* (1893), became the anthem of the child's party, focusing attention on the birthday boy or girl just before the rite of making a wish and blowing out the candles. Still, this was a slow progression. Early twentieth-century birthday parties focused on the parents and their friends with the child being expected to dress up and be respectful. By the 1950s, child-rearing books offered advice on 'theme' parties and activities focusing on the wishes and attention spans of children. All this has culminated in catered birthday parties and commercialized fun centres designed to accommodate large parties (Pleck, 2000).

Markets certainly nurtured and expanded the cult of the wondrous child, so central to the idea of the 'cute', giving permission to spend on children and affirming children's desires. This was not necessarily manipulative, however. The commercial effort to encourage gift-giving to children had picked a bud already there. Adults longed to connect to childhood emotions through gifting the young. In a larger sense the cute child eased adults' coping with complex and contradictory feelings about consumer culture and the economic changes behind it. From the beginning of the twentieth century, toys and other children's goods offered adults as well as children an escape through fantasy from uncontrolled change. At the same time, these products allowed both generations to embrace the excitement of novelty. Even more, through the gifting of the wondrous child and enjoying the delight in the child's eye, adults renewed feelings of discovery in a consumer culture that by its sheer repetition of consuming had led many to feel sated and bored. The pleasure of the 'innocent' consumption in the child brought adults back to their own Edenic state as consumers (Cross, 1997, 2004).

We find evidence of all this in toys that no longer just prepared the young for adulthood (as did Victorian-era dolls) or kept toddlers quiet (teething rings) but offered children the props for fantasy play. The Teddy Bear began at the New Jersey seashore as a fad in 1906 but it quickly became a tradition that parents embraced in nostalgia. These playthings quickly became associated with new media (cheap storybooks, magazine illustrations and ads as well as comic strips and movies) that featured delightful, lively and playful, but often 'naughty' (if ultimately 'nice') characters (Cross, 2004). The most successful of these 'cross-over' products came from Walt Disney whose Mickey Mouse was licensed for many toys and dolls soon after his première in a 1928 cartoon. Disney's success was rooted in his cross-generational appeal to the 'cute', to begin with in the form of the delightful image of the childlike animal (that suggested play to the child and innocence to the adult) (Lorenz, 1981).

Disneyland (1955) and later Walt Disney World (1971) were successful initially because they encouraged children to 'act out' the 'cute' in wide-eyed enchantment on rides and in attractions based on Disney's cartoons and movies. The fact that most Disney stories and buildings took the perspective of a child allowed a cross-generational bonding insofar as grandparent, mother, father, and child entered into a shared family fantasy (Marling, 1997). Absent from Disneyland was any encounter with the fears and fascinations of adult life – the disasters, death, and the hereafter that were common themes in earlier amusement parks. Not only had such dark ideas become taboo for children, but adults also now preferred to shift their gaze toward the fresh imaginings of young life. This was more than a bowdlerization of the carnival. Disney exploited the growing appeal of wonder expressed through the aesthetic of the 'cute' child. The core reason for Disney's success may be in the bonding of nostalgia and 'timeless' cuteness across the generations. Disneyland did not get 'old' simply because oldsters expected to return to their pasts at Disneyland. At the same time, adults passed on to the next generation these same sites and experiences, which, for the very young, were truly new. This may explain why core attractions in Fantasyland remained for decades: Peter Pan's Flight, Mr. Toad's Wild Ride, Dumbo's Flying Elephants, and the Mad Hatter's Tea Party, staples from the mid-1950s, remained into the twenty-first century.

In the 1950s, fantasy was no longer just or even particularly for the young, but also for the old waxing nostalgic about the worlds of their youth. Main Street USA, a fantasy miniature reconstruction of the central business district of a 1900-era American small town, was the route into Disney's Magic Kingdom, a site designed for parents and grandparents to 'remember' their childhoods and to 'teach' their offspring about it. For Disney, 'helping' adults return to the place of their childhoods was, at least, as important as appealing to children – indeed even more so (Cross and Walton, 2005).

The 'cool' and children's consumer agency: origins in new media

Marketing child goods to adults continued to emphasize 'improvement' and training motifs throughout the twentieth century especially in women's and child-rearing magazines, but marketing of the 'cute' to parents of the 'cute' has been a dominant theme. And for our purposes of discovering the time and place of child consumer agency, the selling of the 'cute' muddles our objective. It is hard to disentangle the parent's motive from the child's (with the latter seeking parental approval).

This problem vanishes with the appearance of new products that suggest a rejection of the 'cute' by the child. This is obvious in the older child's cult of the 'cool', a look and behavioural set that are mirror opposites of the 'cute' and understood by older children as expressions of freedom from adults' possessive needs. To be 'cool', a posture, attitude, or response has to be the opposite of wondrous, sweet and dependent; it has to be jaded, emotionally reserved, independent, and – in some cases – deliberately unattractive. The attraction of the 'cool' may be an inevitable rebellion from a parent's imposition of the 'cute' (made perhaps more urgent and extreme by the increasing enthusiasm of parents for cuteness). The 'cool' became the child's marker of growing up. More subtly the 'cool' emerged from the 'cute' itself. After 1900, adults met deep-seated needs by giving their children unexpected excitement and relief from today's reality and tomorrow's uncertainty. By their very nature, these gifts of fun did not prepare children for adult roles. The 'cute' provided no cues for growing up. At the same time, because the cult of the 'cute' required parents' acceptance of children's self-expressiveness, and even a measure of naughtiness, children quite naturally transformed adult-imposed fantasies into dream worlds of their own that became the 'cool'. In effect, kids took over the secret garden and, with the help of fantasy merchants, largely locked their parents out. What had been the 'cute' – ultimately controlled by parents – became the 'cool' seemingly ruled by the kids.

The first clear signs of the 'cool' appeared among older boys in the 1930s and 1940s in products and media characters like Buck Rogers and Dick Tracy and in the 1950s with the dark and violent worlds of horror and crime comics. At first, the 'cool' was primarily the domain of boys. In the 1960s and 1970s, rebellious fantasy extended to girls and small children when the 'cool' look of Barbie and grimacing action-figure toys partially displaced Tiny Tears baby dolls and electric trains. What ties all of these examples together is the absence of the bond between parent and child. The science fiction hero

Buck Rogers is a hero who has no father and is no son. The 'cool' is often adapted from the world of the working class or minority, allowing the middle-class child to break away from the parent's domesticating cult of the 'cute'.

Media and fantasy toy makers provided the substance of the 'cool' by marketing directly to children from the late 1920s. What made this possible was the appearance of new venues of childhood autonomy in the form of Saturday film matinees, late afternoon children's radio, and the comic book. From the mid-1950s, Saturday morning cartoons and ads designed specifically for children greatly accelerated this process and, of course, a new genre of movies and videos (beginning with *Star Wars* in 1977) and video games from the mid-1970s produced the autonomous culture of the cool that we know today (see Nairn, Chapter 6 in this book).

In the late 1920s, new outlets for a unique children's commercial culture emerged that liberated children from parents by challenging middle-class sensibilities in new entertainments. With their roots in cheap working-class magazines, short chapter movies (or serials) appeared in 1913. Respectable middle-class critique condemned these 'cliffhangers' (often built around beautiful women pursued by bad guys and usually featuring veiled sadistic sexuality or futuristic and supernatural fantasy) as unsuitable for children. However, by 1930, with the coming of the talkies or sound motion pictures and more sophisticated adult audiences, the serials were more or less 'passed on' to the young. They became a staple of Saturday afternoon matinees when theatres became the domain of kids. Cowboy, detective, and science fiction themes dominated these serials in the 1930s, borrowing stories and characters from the comic strips, pulp magazines, and radio programmes (Zinman, 1973).

Network radio (from 1926) offered another children's venue. NBC pioneered the national programming of popular entertainment that split audiences not by region, class, or ethnicity, but by sex and especially age. Though many children's programmes were educational and uplifting (often with no advertising), by 1930 advertisers had learned that children were extremely attentive and loyal listeners. Kids were eager for afterschool adventure programmes. These were often sponsored by food companies who offered toys and trinkets to listeners who then pestered parents into buying a certain coffee or cereal for the packaging that had to be mailed in for the 'premiums' (like Sergeant Preston's 'Yukon dog cards' and Little Orphan Annie's 'decoder' rings) (Boemer, 1989; Harmon, 1992).

Comic books provided the young with a third site of autonomy. Unlike the newspaper comic strips from the 1890s that reached a mostly adult audience, comic books were directed toward and purchased by children. In 1935 Disney characters appeared in comic books and soon Warner Brother characters (Bugs Bunny and Daffy Duck) were available featuring feisty characters who outwitted their adult-like adversaries. The comic book took on a more disturbing tone for middle-class parents when the stories from cheap detective and adventure magazines for adults also began to appear as comic books. A rather new concept appeared when Detective Comics (DC) published *Superman*, the first superhero comic book, in 1938. The key ingredient to these comic books was the 'cool', the appeal of the world of the rough and tough adult in crime, superhero, jungle, and eventually horror stories (Goulart, 2000; Wright, 2001).

New toys: fantasy play apart from parents

These new venues of children's entertainment paralleled changes in marketing to children, especially of playthings. During the Depression, toy and novelty companies realized that they had to appeal to the wishes and wealth of children if they wanted to stay in business. Early changes came in the marketing of boys' toys. Before the 1930s, expensive sets of toy cars and military figures were sold to adults (who, in turn, gave them to children on special occasions). Adapting to the bad economic times, manufacturers learned to market single vehicles or military figures, often in new cheaper materials (like rubber and tin) directly to children. Key to the success of this sales strategy was to adapt these commercial collectibles to children's new media heroes. For Christmas 1934, for example, Daisy – longtime producer of relatively expensive air rifles – offered a Buck Rogers Space Pistol at 25 cents, a price within the reach of many kids. Soon a vast array of figures and toy weapons based on radio and comic book characters appeared in cheap dime-store sales bins. These collectible toys and figures then accelerated the trend of taking the fantasy story away from the parents or doting uncles without any adult knowledge of the fantasy back story to the playthings (O'Brien, 1990).

Commercial television adopted the same strategy with Saturday morning cartoons that advertised toys and sugared foods in terms that leaned toward the 'cool' rather than the 'cute' (even though early kids' shows often featured adult hosts, parent-pleasing themes, and entertainment that parents had seen when they were children in the 1930s). TV became more of a venue for children's autonomy when new and often more edgy cartoons began to appear in the late 1950s. Hanna-Barbera introduced limited animation in 1958 (greatly reducing the number of figure drawings necessary). The result was a large amount of highly repetitive cartoons (*Huckleberry Hound*, *Yogi Bear*, and *The Flintstones*). By the mid-1960s Marvel Comic Book superheroes had also appeared as TV cartoons (*Incredible Hulk* and *Spider-Man*). The percentage of children's programming devoted to cartoons rose from 23 per cent to 80 per cent in the 1960s (Turow, 1981; Erickson, 1995). These cartoons were the opposite of the tone and character of 'improving' programming like *Mr. Rogers' Neighborhood* and the commercials that sponsored them treated the child as a 'blend of potential anarchist and hyperactive maniac' (Young, 1990: 15).

Like the 'cool' characters in children's movies, radio, and comic books, children's TV generated markets for licensed character dolls, toys, and play-sets. But again, most of these were directed toward boys. These included cowboy figures (Gene Autry, Roy Rogers, and Hopalong Cassidy, for example), especially in the 1950s, but a new type of play figure appeared in the 1960s with Hasbro's G.I. Joe miniature soldiers. Though not on children's TV to begin with, G.I. Joe (1964) picked up on the 1930s' break from adults' expectations of children's play. Costumed in the uniforms of American military services, G.I. Joe taught boys to identify with the experience of fathers (Second World War veterans) and their older brothers or uncles (drafted or enlisted into the US armed services). This was conventional. However, rather than encouraging boys to play the general's role of deploying a set of toy soldiers as was the point of war play in the past, G.I. Joe figures were large and jointed to allow children to fantasize one-on-one fighting with them. This appeal to boys was strengthened in 1975. After a five year respite from military action (during the most controversial days of the Vietnam War), Hasbro redesigned G.I. Joe for an ahistorical fantasy world with an array of allies and enemies to fight. This set the stage for the action figures generated first by George Lucas's *Star Wars* trilogy (1977–1983). An avalanche of action TV cartoons that served as 'programme-length commercials' created a demand for sets of action figures (*He-Man*, *Transformers*, *Dino-Riders* and even *G.I. Joe*). With these figures and play sets, the child was invited to stage scenes from the movies and cartoons. Adults had no role in the set-up of the scene as in their past play with toy soldiers and electric trains. They didn't even know the 'back story' of the movie or cartoon. The child was the convener, the creator, and director. While these toys might have encouraged children to simply mimic the story lines and characters of the movie or cartoon, this did not necessarily stifle creativity (for children deviated from those scripts). The indisputable fact is that these playthings took children into a fantasy world that was alien to parents (Stern and Schoenhaus, 1990; Cross, 1997).

From the 1930s through to the 1950s, most of this marketing was directed towards boys, a sign not only of the relative freedom enjoyed by male children as compared to their sisters, but also an indication of the 'threat' of the 'cool' in girls – which tended to suggest sexuality. This point is made clear by Mattel's introduction of the Barbie doll in 1959. First, we need a bit of context. Since the 1900s, girls' dolls had encouraged companion (as in dolls that looked like children) and nurturing play (as in baby dolls). These dolls mirrored adult fantasies about the ideal child – fresh faced, healthy and even a little impish – but bound to grow into motherhood. After the Second World War, this tradition continued with the Ginny dolls. Ginny had fashions, but she still had the chubby, short legs, round face, and bright eyes of the idealized 'cute' child, very similar to the dolls that mothers of that era had played with. Ginny was complemented with baby dolls like Betsy Wetsy. Barbie broke this pattern with her cold stare and grown up self-assured posture. Barbie's developer, Ruth Handler of Mattel, offered a doll that did not encourage girls to remain in a world of child companions or to imitate their mothers by pretending to be mothers. Instead, Barbie was the carefree, single, sensuous, and somehow forever young female. She reflected the teenage culture that had burst forth so strongly in 1954 with the coming of rock 'n' roll. A large crop of teenagers were just emerging from the front wedge of the Baby Boom; these adolescent girls had more choices and were freer of adult control than their parents had experienced as teens. To an 8 year old girl in 1959, Barbie represented this freedom. This doll, however, seemed to rush girls into the sexually charged world of adolescence long before they, or their mothers, were ready. Barbie even challenged the expectation that girls would grow up to be caregivers like their mothers. Parents were also appalled by Barbie's adult female body (exaggerated as it was), especially when they saw their daughters dressing her. Barbie divorced sexuality from motherhood and instead associated it with a carefree world of consumption. Not surprisingly, early market testing found mothers often disliked the Barbie look and concept. A real testament to the acceptance of children's desire is that parents conceded to their daughters' wishes (Mandeville, 1993; Handler, 1995).

Not all of the kids' toys and media were 'cool' however. TV cartoons and movies generated a wide range of cutified characters for young children in the 1980s (*Care Bears* and *My Little Pony*), but even with preschool children signs of the 'cool' crept in. As early as the 1960s monster figures, miniature hot-rods driven by crazed beatniks, and even toy guillotines delighted children even as they distressed their parents. And even more extreme was the Pain Parlour (including a half-dressed female torture victim), evidently satisfying the sadistic sexual urges of young boys. In 1967, Incredible Edibles let kids mould candy into horrible insects that they could dramatically eat in front of a horrified mom or little sister. Though these toys attracted only short-term interest, the principle kept reappearing. In 2002, Hasbro introduced the Queasy Bake Oven, a parody of its widely successful and conventional Easy Bake Oven dating from 1963. Instead of the conventional cakes and cookies baked in its pink predecessor, the Queasy Bake Oven, coloured garish purple and decorated with a yellow brain and a spider, let little boys mock their sisters while baking batter from 'Bugs 'n' Worms Mix' and 'Mud and Crud Cake' (Cross, 2004).

In the 1960s, toy makers adopted the theory that child's play 'takes a very unreal tone' because the child is 'looking for excitement that only comes from the unreal'. How did toy companies know what excited kids? From the 1960s onward, leading manufacturers began to base new toy designs on children's fantasies, abandoning the traditional toys that imitated adult life. Researchers asked kids to send 'letters to Santa' to find out about their deepest desires. Even more revealing, they observed how children played away from their parents – seeking to find their spontaneous, undirected fantasies, which could be developed into new toys (Kline, 1993).

A final example of the rise of the 'cool' is the rise of new thrill rides in amusement parks. Since 1955, Disney's cross-generational appeal had prevailed while old-fashioned parks dating from the turn of the twentieth century, with their rollercoasters and other unthemed 'iron rides', declined and closed. In the 1960s and especially the 1970s, however, there was a revival of the traditional amusement park and renewed interest in coasters. New parks included Six Flags (various locations), Magic Mountain (Southern California), King's Island (Cincinnati), and Great America (near Chicago). Even old parks like Cedar Point in Ohio and Kennywood in Pennsylvania were spruced up with new coasters. By 2000, most successful parks had a dozen or more monster coasters. Even Disney World adapted in 1977 with Space Mountain, an indoor roller coaster, disguising itself as an educational experience in a space capsule. Since the late 1970s, however, Disney's parks have abandoned quasi-educational exhibits and have instead built gut-wrenching rides. This did not mean abandoning the 'cute', but relegating it to a very young audience and their parents (Trogmorton, 1993; Coker, 2002; Cross, 2008).

So what had happened? Disney had had to adapt to the decline of the 'cute' and the rise of the 'cool'. The decrease in births in the 1970s translated into smaller numbers of young families in the 1980s. Probably more important, the child's (especially boys') attraction to the mystic of the frontier, global adventure and science upon which Disney had built three of his 'lands' was in decline. The Star Wars trilogy and its licensed products (1977–83), along with a more cynical popular culture that had bled into children's culture, challenged these older ideals. Part of that change was the downward push of the 'cool' when children abandoned the 'cute' culture imposed by their parents at younger ages. The striking manifestation of this was a youthful attraction to the thrill rides that their parents and grandparents had rejected decades before in the old amusement parks (Cross and Walton, 2005).

The trend toward a child's market of the cool and the child's agency that it implies is strong, but it is not without its complexity and surprises. A second example will illustrate this (see Vignette 2).

Vignette 2: New doll on the block

Visiting a large Toys R Us store near Times Square in New York City in 2004, I noticed something that surprised me though it should not have: toy and doll lines adapted from kids' TV and movie fantasies in the 1980s were again on the shelves. Back were *Care Bears, Strawberry Shortcake, Transformers*, and *Star Wars* figures and play sets that had appealed to children but not necessarily their parents a generation earlier. I had a little free time so I watched the customers. I noticed a young father with his 3 year old son near the *Star Wars* shelves and

(Cont'd)

it was obvious that the dad was trying to get his boy interested in these figures. I concluded that this was a case of a father trying to connect to his child via his nostalgia for his own childhood. The scene was 'cute'. But I also noticed something else: there were rows and rows of Barbie dolls, many dressed as 'fairy princesses' and by no means as haughty-looking as they had been in the early Sixties. Moreover, there was a new doll on the block – Bratz that had a vaguely 'ethnic' look about them, with big, almond-shaped eyes displaying heavy shadow and lips painted with red gloss. Bratz dolls offered the same array of fashion and consumer themes as Barbie had done for decades, but to many adults they also looked rebellious and an inappropriate role model. Doubtless, Bratz would be abhorrent to most mothers, especially in the white middle-class. I asked the salesperson (in a bit of spontaneous market research) who bought Barbies and who bought Bratz. Well, she said, mothers in both cases, but that often the Barbies were bought for toddlers (and often without the child present) while the Bratz were often bought following obvious pressure from a somewhat older girl.

This little story in Vignette 2 suggests the following:

- Children who had once pestered parents into buying them new and daring child-as-insider, adult-defying toys grow up and become parents who want to 'impose' on their offspring the opposite – the toy that might create a bond between child and adult.
- Children's goods that had once been 'cool' like Barbie or even *Star Wars* can become 'cute' in the next generation. Barbie is no longer the symbol of childhood independence, but a marker of parental memory and cutesified in the process. Indeed, Barbie began to lose her haughty look a few years after her launch evidently to please parents: her eyes widened and her mouth lost the pursed pose, looking more, well, 'cute'.
- Finally, new 'cool' products emerge to challenge the once 'cool' as in the emergence of the adult-defying Bratz. First offered in 2001, Bratz was invented by a former employee of Mattel and manufactured by MCA, a company that had previously specialized in electronic games. By 2005, Bratz doll sales were catching up with Barbie (at sales of two billion dollars to Barbie's three). In 2008, Mattel won a lawsuit claiming ownership of the Bratz image with still uncertain results. MCA admitted that Bratz dolls are 'sassy' (i.e. sexy) and market analysts note that 'girls seem to be growing out of their toys earlier than boys are'. All this has led to the phenonomon of 'KGOY' 'Kids Getting Older Younger (although why this has happened or what the role of merchandisers is in encouraging this trend to maximize sales is not explained in the promotional marketing literature). In fact, the authors of *The Great Tween Buying Machine* (2004) assert that companies should have no qualms about 'going around moms', by advertising parent-displeasing dolls and other products directly to children who can easily win their way with pester power (Siegel et al. 2004; see also Talbot, 2006; Casey, 2009). These highly sexualized dolls suggest also the downward shift of the 'cool' from teen to 'tween' culture (7 to 12

year olds). The dynamic of the 'cute' and the 'cool' continues to shape parent' child relations and with it children's consumer agency.

Conclusion

In this chapter, I have explored the historical origins of the modern children's market through the lens of the concepts of the 'cute' and the 'cool' as well as historical changes in toy and story lines developed for children. It suggests the need to go beyond abstract theory, contemporary market research, and play observation. These approaches are often biased in favour of viewing children as emerging free agents in isolation from their complex interactions with parents.

Future research directions

My analysis suggests a need to explore further what motivates adults as well as children. Future research might consider when and how children adapt to the adult imposition of the 'cute' and rebel from it. Likewise an investigation of adult responses to the emergence of new 'cool' lines (like Bratz) and when and how these responses change (or adapt) is needed. Further investigation of new product lines will also yield an insight on the processes described in the above historical survey. More study of the pressure on children to embrace the 'cool' at younger ages is needed (as in the recent phenomenon of 'tweens'). Finally, an exploration of the new and shifting venues of children's autonomy in fantasy-commercialized play would be fruitful as would be a study of the shift from non-commercial settings (streets and playgrounds) to consumer-based venues (video parlours, etc.). Such studies could focus on how this change affected play and the market (e.g., the shift from 'traditional' games like marbles and hopscotch to action figure collection and video games).

Discussion questions

1 Why and when did a market for children's goods emerge?
2 Why were manufacturers in the past reluctant to advertise directly to children and when and why did this change?
3 How did new attitudes toward children (as embodied in the idea of the 'cute') shape the market?

(Cont'd)

4 When, where, and why did children reject the 'cute' and embrace the 'cool'?
5 How and why were markets for 'cool' boys' products earlier to appear than girls'?
6 Why does the once 'cool' become the 'cute' and a new 'cool' emerge?

Further reading

Adler, P. and Adler, P. (1998) *Peer Power: Preadolescent Culture and Identity*. New Brunswick, NJ: Rutgers University Press.

Banet-Weiser, S. (2007) *Kids' Rule! Nickelodeon and Consumer Citizenship*. Durham, NC: Duke University Press.

Jacobson, L. (ed.) (2008) *Children and Consumer Culture in American Society: A Historical Handbook and Guide*. Westport, CT: Praeger.

Kinder, M. (1991) *Playing with Power in Movies, Television and Video Games*. Berkeley: University of California Press.

Mitchell, C. and Reid Walsh, J. (eds) (2005) *Seven Going on Seventeen*. Oxford: Peter Lang.

Quart, A. (2004) *Branded: The Buying and Selling of Teenagers*. New York: Basic.

Ravitch, D. (ed.) (2003) *Kid Stuff: Marketing Sex and Violence to America's Children*. Baltimore, MD: Johns Hopkins University Press.

References

Boemer, M. (1989) *The Children's Hour: Radio Programs for Children, 1929–1956*. Metuchen, NJ: Scarecrow.

Casey, N. (2009) 'MGA wins ruling to sell Bratz dolls through "09"', *Wall Street Journal*, 9 January: B5.

Coker, R. (2002) *Roller Coasters*. New York: MetroBooks.

Cook, D. (2000) '"The other child study": figuring children as consumers in market research, 1910s–1990s', *Sociological Quarterly*, 14 (3): 487–507.

Cross, G. (1997) *Kids' Stuff: Toys and the Changing World of American Childhood*. Cambridge, MA: Harvard University Press.

Cross, G. (2004) *The Cute and the Cool: Wondrous Innocence and Modern American Children's Culture*. New York: Oxford University Press.

Cross, G. (2008) *Men to Boys: The Making of Modern Immaturity*. New York: Columbia University Press.

Cross, G. and Walton, J. (2005) *The Playful Crowd*. New York: Columbia University Press.

Dahl, R. (1964) *Charlie and the Chocolate Factory*. New York: Knopf.

Erickson, H. (1995) *Television Cartoon Shows*. Jefferson, NC: McFarland.

Goulart, R. (2000) *Comic Book Culture*. Portland, OR: Collectors.

Handler, R. (1995) *Dream Doll*. New York: Longmeadow.

Harmon, J. (1992) *Radio Mystery and Adventure*. Jefferson, NC: McFarland.
James, A. (1998) 'Confections, concoctions and conceptions', in H. Jenkins (ed.), *The Children's Culture Reader*. New York: New York University Press. pp. 394–405.
Kline, S. (1993) *Out of the Garden: Toys, TV, and Children's Culture in the Age of Marketing*. New York: Verso.
Lewis, L. (1976) *Birthdays*. Boston, MA: Little, Brown.
Lorenz, K. (1981) *Foundations of Ethnography*. New York: Simon and Schuster.
Mandeville, G. (1993) *Doll Fashion Anthology and Price Guide*. Cumberland, MD: Hobby House.
Mangels, W. (1952) *The Outdoor Amusement Industry*. New York: Vintage.
Marling, K.A. (ed.) (1997) *Designing Disney's Theme Parks: The Architecture of Reassurance*. New York: Flammarion.
O'Brien, R. (1990) *Collecting Toys*. Florence, AL: Americana.
Pleck, L. (2000) *Celebrating the Family: Ethnicity, Consumer Culture, and Family Rituals*. Cambridge: Harvard University Press.
Register, W. (2001) *Kid of Coney Island: Fred Thompson and the Rise of American Amusements*. New York: Oxford University Press.
Schor, J. (2004) *Born to Buy: The Commercialized Child and the New Consumer Culture*. New York: Scribner.
Seiter, E. (1993) *Sold Separately: Children and Parents in Consumer Culture*. New Brunswick, NJ: Rutgers University Press.
Siegel, D., Coffey, T. and Livingston, G. (2004) *The Great Tween Buying Machine: Capturing Your Share of the Multi-Billion-Dollar Tween Market*. New York: Kaplan Business.
Stern, S. and Schoenhaus, T. (1990) *Toyland: The High-Stakes Game of the Toy Industry*. Chicago, IL: Contemporary Books.
Talbot, M. (2006) 'Little hotties: Barbie's new rivals', *The New Yorker*, 82, 40 (5 December): 74.
Trogmorton, T. (1993) *Roller Coasters*. Jefferson, NC: McFarland.
Turow, J. (1981) *Entertainment, Education, and the Hard Sell: Three Decades of Network Children's Television*. New York: Praeger.
Wright, B. (2001) *Comic Book: The Transformation of Youth Culture in America*. Baltimore, MD: Johns Hopkins University Press.
Young, B. (1990) *Television Advertising and Children*. Oxford: Clarendon.
Zelizer, V. (1985) *Pricing the Priceless Child: The Changing Social Value of Children*. New York: Basic.
Zinman, D. (1973) *Saturday Afternoon at the Bijou*. New Rochelle, NY: Arlington House.

6 Children and Brands

Agnes Nairn

Chapter aims

- To trace our understanding of children's relationships with brands.
- To examine how contemporary children use brands in their everyday lives.
- To explore the notion of 'cool' brands.
- To look at how children use brands in forging their identity.
- To identify some of the dark sides of brand activity.
- To highlight emerging issues for researchers and brand marketers.

Vignette 1: Toddler brand awareness

The Jones family were waving good-bye to friends who had come to stay for the weekend. Mr Jones helped load up their car with cases, toys and pushchairs. When the friends' car had disappeared round the corner, Alfie Jones (age 3) turned to his dad and said with puzzlement, 'Dad, why did they buy their car at Boots?' The car in question was a Ford Mondeo. Mr Jones at first didn't know what his son meant, but then he thought about the logos of the two companies. Take a look. You can see that they are remarkably similar.

Introduction

Brands are an integral part of contemporary childhood and the children's market in the UK is estimated at £99.12bn (Mayo and Nairn, 2009). Of their own money (pocket money and Saturday jobs) they spend £1.53bn on fashion; £860m on sweets, soft drinks, crisps and snacks; £440m on music; and £340m on software.

Perhaps not surprisingly given the size of the advertising budgets, children's brand awareness is highest for food and drink. Over three quarters of all children can name a favourite brand of crisps and snack (61 per cent of 5 to 10 year olds and 91 per cent of 11 to 16 year olds). Walkers is far and away the UK's favourite with 54 per cent of kids naming it spontaneously; 76 per cent can name a chocolate or sweets brand; and a much higher percentage of 5 and 6 year olds can name a brand in this category than in any other (56 per cent). Cadbury is the most popular confectionary brand (aided by the iconic 'Drumming Gorilla' advert featuring Phil Collins' music in 2008). Although children spend a large amount of money on clothes, brand names are not as salient as for food. Only 40 per cent of 5 to 10 year olds can name a clothing brand, rising to 76 per cent for 11 to 16 year olds (ChildWise, 2008).

As can be seen from the opening vignette, brands start to become interesting to children at a very young age. Alfie (age 3) had not only internalized the Boots logo (a shop he visited frequently with his mother) but he had also realized that buying a car in a retail chemist was a strange thing to do. In fact, children understand the basic notion of brand symbols long before they can read. Children in the USA will start asking for products by brand name at around 18 months old and can list 200 brands when they start school (Schor, 2004: 19). A very recent study shows that 5 year olds will use brands to categorize people into social roles (Chaplin and Lowrey, 2010). In the film *Supersize Me*, Morgan Spurlock finds that all the children he talks to can recognize a picture of Ronald McDonald but only a tiny handful can recognize Jesus or George Bush. Another study suggests that UK 10 year olds can name around 400 brands, 20 times the number of wild birds they can recognize (Mayo, 2005).

This chapter traces the ways in which researchers have tried to understand younger children's relationships with brands. As a framework the long-established cognitive development approach is compared with the more recent consumer culture theory. The diverse roles which brands play in the everyday lives of junior school children (aged 7 to 11) are then explored, with a special look at how groups of children come to accept brands as 'cool' or reject them as 'minging'. How children use brands to forge their own identity within the peer group forms the focus of the next part of the chapter before the darker or greyer sides of branding such as brand-bullying amongst children and the business practice of using children as 'brand ambassadors' are highlighted. The chapter ends by identifying emerging issues for both researchers and brand marketers.

The cognitive development approach to children and brands

The mainstream marketing literature on children's understanding of brands has been underpinned for several decades by psychological theories of cognitive development, in particular the work of Jean Piaget (1960). This research has tended to concentrate on age-stages and how children's relationship with brands correlates with their biological age. Children's developing use of the symbolic function of brands to form and reinforce social stereotypes has been a site of particular interest within this paradigm. One of the earliest pieces of research on brand or product symbolism was Belk et al.'s (1982) study comparing the abilities of US children in four age categories (preschool, 7–8, 11–12, 13–14) to match up a range of houses and cars (varied by size, style, age and cost) with different types of people (e.g., a doctor, someone who has a lot of friends, smart, a mailman, mean, the kind of person I would like to be). The researchers concluded that over time children gradually develop the cognitive ability to understand how products and brands operate symbolically, with a particularly intense period of learning occurring between the ages of 7 and 12. The experiments in this research were based on measuring children's ability to demonstrate the 'correct' use of consumption symbolism (e.g., matching a doctor with a big house and an expensive car). The benchmarks for this 'right' use of symbolism were the matches made by the adults in the sample.

However, other researchers pointed out that children (certainly in 1982) would have had little involvement with the purchase of houses or cars and that more relevant products should be researched. So a couple of years later, in a second study with children aged 9–10 and 11–12, Belk et al. (1984) conducted a similar experiment using branded jeans (Calvin Klein, Levis, and Sears), bicycles (Schwinn), shoes (Vans and Topsiders) and video games (Atari and Sears) and types of people rather than job functions. The strongest finding was that the older group of children held much stronger stereotypes than the younger group, showing once again that their understanding of the brand world increases with both cognitive development and with experience.

More recently Achereiner and John (2003) examined children's use of brand symbolism in another experimental study where groups of American children aged 8, 12 and 16 assessed the type of people likely to own K-Mart versus Levis jeans and K-Mart versus Nike trainers. This study demonstrated that whilst the youngest age group related to products and brands on a perceptual level, by age 12 children also related to brands on a conceptual level. Marshall and Aitken (2006) report similar findings in New Zealand where in discussions of special possessions 7 and 8 year olds related mainly to products (i.e. perceptual features) whilst 10 and 11 year olds had begun to relate more to brands (i.e. a more conceptual symbolic significance). The exceptions to this rule were brands synonymous with products such as PlayStation 2 or Xbox and licensed character toys such as Bratz, Noddy and Winnie the Pooh which were often highly important to the younger children. My own study (Nairn et al., 2006) found exactly the same with UK primary school children: the 7 and 8 year olds had difficulty naming specific brands whilst the abstract connections made with brands were beginning to develop with the 10 to 11 year olds. The most recent work in this area (Chaplin and Lowrey, 2010) shows that 5 year olds can infer social status from sets of brands and that by early adolescence brand-related social stereotyping has become rather rigid. Taken together these studies have established that Piaget's age-stage categories (see de la Ville and Tartas, and Young, Chapters 2 and 7 respectively in this book) are useful for showing how children progress from a feature-based appreciation of logos and product features to a full adult understanding of how brand symbols function to mark out social stereotypes.

However, whilst this individual psychological approach has undeniable benefits, it cannot shed much light on how children learn to use brands within the specific social and cultural contexts of their own everyday lives. The cognitive development approach tells us how children become adult users of brand symbols but little about how it is to be a child in the branded world. Over the past few years, therefore, researchers have sought new ways to broaden the research framework. Some researchers have tried to go beyond age differences in brand understanding to explore in much more detail differences by gender, ethnicity and social class which are, of course, also likely to influence how children interact with the symbolic realm of consumption (e.g., Swain, 2002; Elliott and Leonard, 2004). Others have explored the social dynamics of interpretation, emotions and peer group influences. In doing so many have moved away from quantitative experimental methods where the unit of analysis is the individual child to using qualitative methods including group discussions, accompanied shopping and wardrobe or bedroom audits (see for example, Russell and Tyler, 2002; Griffin, 2007; Pole, 2007).

Another part of the (1960) Piagetian approach which has been challenged is its tendency to conceptualize childhood as a universal, ahistorical phenomenon. Given the great changes in marketing to children since the time of Piaget, and indeed since Belk and his colleagues conducted their studies in the 1980s, the very nature of what it means to be a child consumer has undoubtedly changed. Thus the cognitive development framework cannot easily house some recent consumption phenomena. For example, KGOY (Kids Getting Older Younger) does not fit easily within a universal age-stage view of childhood. Moreover this paradigm tends to reinforce a picture of brands as symbolic of established stereotypes, which means it can't really keep up with the rapidly changing, fickle marketing and branding in the cyberworld currently inhabited by children. Beyond this, work by scientists such as Susan Greenfield (2006) is beginning to show that new media (such as internet and video games) not only change how children perceive their social world but may also even shape the structure of their brains. She would argue that children are not recipients of marketing messages or simply processors of brand symbolism but that the very act of engaging with the new technologies used by brands affects their thinking and feeling mechanisms. In short, there has been growing feeling that a complementary paradigm is needed to study how children relate to brands.

The consumer culture theory approach to children and brands

One such alternative approach is consumer culture theory. Arnould and Thompson coined the term (or CCT) to refer to 'a family of theoretical perspectives that address the dynamic relationships between consumer actions, the marketplace, and cultural meanings' (2005: 868). CCT views consumption as being continually shaped by on-going interactions within a dynamic socio-cultural context, and is concerned with the factors that shape the experiences and identities of consumers 'in the myriad messy contexts of everyday life' (ibid.: 875). The CCT approach has an interest in the operation and influence of 'consumer culture', as denoted by 'a social arrangement in which the relations between lived culture and social resources, and between meaningful ways of life and the symbolic and material resources on which they depend, are mediated through markets' (ibid.: 869).

CCT has emerged from a different epistemological perspective to the Piagetian model, generating a different set of research foci and methodological practices. CCT does not view individual consumers as making rational choices in the context of 'free' markets. Instead, it has drawn on the work of Bourdieu (1984), Foucault (1974, 1978), and others to examine the ideological context in which consumption takes place. CCT is proving particularly useful for helping us understand how we develop consumer identities; how marketplace cultures emerge; how consumption develops in a socio-historic context; and how consumers interpret and use mass media messages.

Given the recent arrival of CCT the body of research underpinned by its tenets is still relatively small, particularly as applied to children. The next part of this chapter therefore describes in some detail a recent two-part study by myself and colleagues which used CCT to examine how children, adopt, adapt and assign meanings to brands in the messy context of their everyday lives (Nairn et al. 2008).

Children's use of brands in everyday life

The overriding objective of the first part of the study was to identify those brands which really were meaningful to children (rather than those that we, as adults, thought would be meaningful). We therefore began by asking a range of children (all aged between 7 and 11) to tell us 'what things kids are into'. Three product categories emerged consistently across all groups. Games Consoles (Xbox, Game Cube and PlayStation), non-electronic interactive games (Top Trumps, Pokemon cards, Yu-Gi-Oh cards and Beyblades spinning tops) and dolls/action figures (Barbie, Bratz and Action Man). Children also suggested TV programmes (*Simpsons, Ant and Dec, Dic and Dom in da Bungalow, EastEnders* and *Coronation Street*), celebrity sports stars (David Beckham, Wayne Rooney, Johnny Wilkinson) and celebrity pop singers (Busted, McFly, Peter Andre, Britney Spears and Michael Jackson). The consistency with which both these categories and the brands within them were mentioned and discussed across groups allowed us to feel confident that these brands really were meaningful to children of this age and we therefore used these in the second part of the study (see Table 6.1 for the final selection).

It is perhaps no surprise that all of these brands are heavily marketed, often using highly developed and integrated marketing communications strategies. *The Simpsons* appear not just on TV but on Top Trumps cards, duvet covers, Xbox games and children's clothes. David Beckham is present not just on the football pitch but also in sports magazines, video games and endorsing his range of kidswear in Marks and Spencer. Children today inhabit a seamless world of brands which allows games, people, music, toys and commercial messages to fulfil parallel, interlinked and complementary functions.

Children engage with these brands on a direct and personal basis by watching and reading about celebrities and by buying or asking their parents to buy the toys, games and music. In line with the research by ChildWise mentioned at the beginning of the chapter, no clothes brands featured for this age of child and – although we know that these children have a strong brand awareness of food and drink products – these are clearly not considered 'things that kids are into' or interesting enough for discussion.

The purpose of the second part of the study was to explore the meaning of these brands in greater depth. We wanted to understand how the children themselves constructed meaning from consumption objects and how they negotiated this process with their peers in a group context. We therefore invited groups of three or four children to take part in a sorting game. We seated them comfortably around a cork board labelled 'Cool' on one side and 'Not Cool' on the other, and gave them a picture of each of the 14 brands identified in Table 6.1. The children were asked to talk amongst themselves and

Table 6.1 The top mentioned brands for UK 7–11 year olds in 2004/5

Busted	A boy band marketed at children (split up in 2005)
McFly	Another boy band marketed at children (launched after Busted and still going)
Britney Spears	Twenty something singer, popular with children (before her 'problems')
David Beckham	Celebrity captain of the England football team at the time of the study
The Simpsons	Popular American cartoon TV show
Barbie	Fashion doll which has been marketed to girls for over 40 years
Bratz	Series of fashion dolls marketed specifically at female 'tweens', new in 2004
Action Man	Action figure which has been marketed to boys for several decades
Beyblades	Small spinning tops used to fight against other children's tops
Pokemon	Japanese trading card game
PlayStation, Xbox, Game Cube	Three competing brands of games console
Yu-Gi-Oh	Japanese trading card game, produced after Pokemon

agree where to pin each picture. The exercises were videoed with a view to analysing the discussions, actions and body language of each group. We were not particularly interested in which brands were 'Cool' and which were 'Not Cool' but in the processes by which children negotiated the symbolic value of brands within their own peer group (see Cross's historical account of this in relation to the toy market, Chapter 5 in this book).

We worked with children who attended two junior schools (age 7–11) in the same UK city. In both schools, half the groups were drawn from a Year 3 class (ages 7 and 8) and half from a Year 6 class (ages 10 and 11). Given that this is a period of great change in how children relate to brand symbols (Belk et al., 1982, 1984; Achereiner and John, 2003; Chaplin and Lowrey, 2010), we were interested to see if there were differences in the nature of the discussions between the youngest and the oldest children. We worked both in a fee-paying private school and a more deprived state school in order to ascertain if there were any socio-economic differences and we also selected both single and mixed sex groups to control for gender divergence in how the children discussed brands. There were substantial differences by age and gender (noted below where relevant), but the socio-economic group played little part in the interactions in these groups of children.

'Cool' brands

Bourdieu's (1984) influential study of consumption practices amongst the French working class and bourgeoisie, and the disciplines involved in learning what constitutes (good) 'taste', provided a useful framework against which to interpret children's relationship with the slippery concept of 'cool' brands. Rather like (good) 'taste', 'cool' can only be understood in the context of the dynamic complexity of social interactions. Marketers (and academic researchers) frequently misunderstand this as they struggle to identify the newest object or cultural practice that is presumed to epitomize 'cool' (Nancarrow et al., 2002; Moore, 2005). Our study indicates that the more you search for 'cool', the more it dissolves into air. Like 'taste', the whole point about 'cool' is that knowledge about what is (and is not) 'cool' serves to separate a discerning elite from the uninformed masses. Interestingly, in each group the children asked if they could include a 'middle side' which provided a protection from committing a social gaffe by 'wrongly' identifying iconic branded commodities as 'cool' or 'not cool'. The groups also acknowledged that 'cool' was to some extent a reflection of the tastes of the 'cool' kids in the class – the dominant elite (see Cross, Chapter 5 in this book).

The ephemeral nature of 'cool' brands was also reflected in how children saw brands within the fast moving world of fashion and style. An uneasy relationship exists between 'coolness' and popularity. The discussions shown below about Pokemon, PlayStations and Britney Spears illustrate this highly contested terrain.

Boy 1:	Pokemon's not bad.
Interviewer:	Uh-huh.
Boy 2:	It's sort of, well, coz ...
Boy 3:	Peekachuu.
Boy 2:	Um, loads of people have got them so it's not really cool anymore. (Year 3, state school, boys group)
Boy 1:	PlayStation cool.
Boy 2:	Coz so many people have got it, and so many people love it. (Year 6, private school, boys group)
Girl 1:	Britney Spears I think in the middle.
Girl 2:	In the middle yeah.
Girl 3:	She's on the verge of going.
Interviewer:	So down in the middle, why?
Girl 1:	Because she's, she's good but she's bad coz she's going out.
Girl 1:	But she's good.
Girl 2:	She's going out but she hasn't gone yet. (Year 6, private school, girls group)

Some brands stop being 'cool' when too many people have them (Pokemon) because they have lost their cachet of exclusivity, whilst others are 'cool' precisely because, through heavy marketing, they have become 'must-haves' (PlayStation). The conversation about Britney Spears (before her more recent troubles)[1] reveals a more complex picture of how communities of children evaluate brands. This conversation shows how children make attempts to resolve this tension between in and out, exclusivity and popularity, by mobilizing the notion of the fashion cycle. They acknowledge that she's actually good at what she became famous for (i.e., singing) but that she is part of an almost ineluctable fashion spiral. This can be a slow process as discussed by a similar age girl at another school: 'she was really cool when she first started but as the year's gone on she just got like really sort of desperate and always advertises, she tries to bring herself back up but she just can't do it'.

Yet the children also know that the process can be reversible and that what's not 'cool' today may revert to 'cool' in the future. The discursive construction of 'cool' as linked to fashion cycles is, of course, highly profitable, and is traded on and encouraged by marketers (Thompson and Haytko, 1997; Klein, 2000). Some of the older children recognized the commercial potential of the relationship between 'cool' and the fashion cycle.

Interviewer:	Yeah. So do you think there's actually quite a lot of this sort of thing, like things coming in and out of fashion now?
Boy:	Yeah. Like a couple of years later you can take them to a shop or something and get lots of money for it.
Interviewer:	Uh-huh.
Boy:	I keep like, coz with the Yu-Gi-Oh cards, I've kept them all so like I was thinking about selling them on, but they wouldn't sell for that much, so I'm just going to keep them so that when they go back in fashion and stuff
	(Year 6, state school, boys group)

In other words, coolness has a shelf life, which it then lays onto branded commodities which are likely to move out of fashion and lose economic value, yet might one day come back 'in' and once again be worth some money.

We can see from the findings above that a consumer culture perspective allows us to recognize the way in which children interact actively and creatively with brands. This perspective also allows us to gain an insight into the game played between marketers and children. Marketers know that they can create 'must-haves' by heavy advertising as can be seen by the high brand awareness from a very young age of Walkers' crisps and Cadbury's chocolates. However they can overstep the mark and children are sensitive to brands ripping them off. One 10 year old boy pointed this out to us in his discussions about Beyblades: 'and they used to sell them at far too expensive cause they knew that everyone wanted to buy them so they were like £6 for one thing … so they make them extremely expensive cause they knew it'd go out of fashion soon so if they could quickly sell them now for lots of money they would get loads'. Another was equally cynical: 'It's an awful lot for just some bits of plastic and metal'. Other children were scornful of marketers 'going over the top'. Talking about Action Man one 10 year old told us, 'It's a toy that doesn't need a television show as well, they haven't got to have a TV show and stupid movies'. A girl of the same age was equally dismissive: 'I don't think anything much of things when they are on TV, it's showing they're trying to get people's attention and I think the sort of things that are good are the sort of things that don't normally get on TV. If it gets in TV, I normally wouldn't buy it'.

Brands and identity projects

Beyond the deconstruction of cool, some brands provoked highly charged emotions which were bound up with the children's identity projects. The iconic Barbie doll – a children's brand for fifty years – incited the most violent reactions by far. 'They're sickly, they're horrible! I hate them, I've always, always hated Barbies!' cried one 11 year old girl. 'I'm going to puke' said an 8 year old boy. Many children went further: 'I still have loads of them so I can torture them' one Year 6 girl told us. Her friend agreed: 'So I think I'll torture them and pull their heads off. Coz they're not particularly cool unless you torture them'. Acts of Barbie barbarism ranged from decapitation and microwaving to burning and dismembering. This rejection of the doll was closely bound up with how the children were learning to see themselves in relation to others. To disavow Barbie in particular represented a rite of passage away from 'babyishness'. As Barbies are now targeted at preschool children, the 7 to 11 year olds by rejecting the doll signalled that they had left this stage of childhood far behind. As one 7 year old put it, with perhaps some exaggeration, 'I used to like it when I was younger … a lot younger … I gave it til I was 3 and then I was like getting too old and I kept having to squish their heads off'.

In other discussions, boys accounted for their vehement rejection of Barbie in terms of the doll's association with girls and femininity: 'I think it's all about little girls, princesses' (Year 6, private school, boys group) and 'I'll tell you why it's sick. It's for girls' (Year 3, private school, boys group). The children's talk about the mass destruction of Barbies can also be read (especially for girls) as a rejection of hyper-femininity, as epitomized by 'girly girls'. In the extract below, a group of Year 3 girls try to disentangle the concepts of femininity ('sissies') and the infantile ('babies'), and Girl 3 draws on the notion of the hyper-feminine 'girly girl' to denote a typical Barbie fan.

Interviewer:	What kind of people like Barbie?
Girl 1:	Babies.
Girl 2:	Sissies.
Girl 3:	Girls, um, not babies, but really girly girls.
	(Year 3, private school, girls group)

It was apparent across all the discussions in both schools that gender played a significant role in how children evaluated brands, in particular for the Year 3 children. The gender effect extended across celebrities, TV shows and toys, as can be seen in the conversations below.

Interviewer:	OK what about Britney Spears? (…)
Boy 1:	No, no, no!

Girl 2:   Yeah, yeah, yeah!
Boy 1:   To the boys it would be oh no, to the girls it would be oh yeah.
Girl 1:   One of the girls in our class, she's a tomboy, she might not like her.
                 (Year 3, private school, mixed group)

Interviewer: And you girls, you don't like them? (Action Man)
Girl 1:   No cos they're for boys.
Interviewer: They're for boys?
Girl 1:   Unless girls can really, are really really tough tomboys just like a
                 boy and have hair exactly like a boy, um, they probably will like
                 them. But apart from that no girl likes them.
                 (Year 3, private school, mixed group)

Interviewer: OK and do you think other people in your class like *The Simpsons*?
Girl 1:   Yes.
Girl 2:   Definitely the boys, some of the girls, I don't think they would like
                 it, cause they're kind of more girly than we are (Girl 3: Yeah, all
                 the other three girls um, the boys like).
Interviewer: Oh, OK, OK, go on, so all the other three girls ...
Girl 2:   All the other three girls are really girly and we're a bit more
                 tomboy-ey.
Interviewer: Ah, OK, so is it something that more tomboy-ey people like?
Girl 1:   Yeah.
                 (Year 3, state school, girls group)

It was surprising that there seemed to be no clear unisex brands. Even *The Simpsons*, which features strong male and female characters, was seen as the domain of boys. Indeed, instead of seeking unisex brands the children made a point of distinguishing between a number of different product-related gender positions – 'girly girls', 'girls', 'boys' and 'tomboys' – such that they could categorize their own and other children's identities according to the brand or product. 'Tomboys' were constituted as girls who are 'just like boys' in appearance and demeanour, such that 'girl-ness' is treated as an inherent quality that can be masculinized into the category of the 'tomboy', or (further) feminized into the 'girly girl'. The discussions about Action Man and *The Simpsons* above show how this works.

Our study also supports Renold's (2005) findings that the position of the tomboy ceases to be available to girls as they move towards puberty. The conversations of the Year 6 children were still highly gendered, but the position of 'tomboy' began to be disparaged as an indication of lesbianism (Griffin et al., 2006). In this way the children's talk about everyday consumer objects serves to reinforce the traditional distinction between masculinity and femininity, and polices the path to heterosexual 'normality'.

To sum up, the period between 7 and 11 does seem to be a time when brand symbols play an important part in the daily lives of children, concurring with Belk et al. (1982, 1984), Achereiner and John (2003) and Chaplin and Lowrey (2010). But beyond showing that older children have a more conceptual (and perhaps more rigid) understanding than younger children, a consumer culture approach also allows us to see how children use brands to carve out their own spaces within their peer group in terms of being 'in' or 'out', 'tomboy' or 'girly girl', babyish or mature or savvy enough to know when to get that old Lego out of the loft and sell it on eBay.

The darker side of brand activity

Whilst brands can play a constructive part in children's everyday lives in terms of acting as tools for forging identities and social roles, there are also downsides to the ubiquitous presence of brands in children's culture. The ownership of particular brands can mean the difference between popularity and acceptance or rejection and stigmatism by the peer group and can put a financial and social pressure on parents to pay for their children to keep up with the latest trends. This can be particularly damaging for families with restricted financial means. Whilst we found few differences by social class in our study, Elliot and Leonard's (2004) research with children from seriously deprived backgrounds in the UK demonstrated how failing to wear the right brands can place a tremendous stress on children. The 8 to 12 year olds they talked to had developed incredibly strong brand stereotypes for trainers and all felt passionately attached to Nike, which were seen not only as cool but also as powerful enough to make you run faster. For them, owning Nike trainers was a passport to fitting in and being popular with others. Some of the children went so far as to say that they would be ashamed to even talk to another child who was not wearing branded trainers. This reflects the dynamics found in an earlier study of the influence of TV advertising on children's behaviour (Goldberg and Gorn, 1978) which showed that children would rather play with someone who had an advertised toy than one that did not appear on TV. Other studies have also shown how children from poorer backgrounds use brands as a means of disguising their poverty (Wicklund and Gollwitzer, 1982). More generally, another study in the UK (Nairn et al., 2007) showed that children from poorer backgrounds attached much greater importance to material possessions than their affluent counterparts. Whilst 47 per cent of deprived children said they'd 'rather spend my time buying things than doing almost anything else', only 23 per cent of children from affluent areas said the same and 69 per cent of deprived children versus 28 per cent of affluent children agreed that 'the only kind of job I want when I grow up is one that gets me lots of money'. The same study showed a strong and significant link between materialism and self-esteem in children from all backgrounds: the more materialistic children are, the lower their self-esteem. It also showed that materialistic children have poorer relationships with their parents and argue more with them. Involvement with brands clearly comes at a price.

In adulthood, it is evident that materialism has a high correlation with negative psychological outcomes such as low self-esteem and life dissatisfaction

(Burroughs and Rindfleisch, 2002). Tim Kasser explains these findings largely in terms of his Aspiration Index (Kasser, 2005) where an undue focus on extrinsic goals, such as making money and acquiring status possessions, inhibits the satisfying of intrinsic needs, such as friendship and community feeling. Ultimately, satisfying these intrinsic needs leads to greater wellbeing. This point is elaborated and backed up with substantial empirical evidence in Lord Layard's (2005) book *Happiness*.

Whilst the negative emotional and psychological effects of materialism on adults have been studied for some time, it is a relatively new area for study on children. However, studies to date have shown remarkable consistency in results. High levels of materialism have repeatedly been shown to correlate with life dissatisfaction, low self-esteem, depression and anxiety (Buizjen and Valkenburg, 2003; Goldberg et al., 2003; Schor, 2004; Chaplin and Roedder-John, 2007; Day et al., 2007; Nairn et al., 2007). It should be noted that all the studies so far have been conducted at one point in time so this relationship can only be treated as a correlation and not causation and we cannot yet say whether materialism causes low self-esteem or low self-esteem causes materialism. On the one hand, it is possible that a constant craving for more and more leads children to be less satisfied. On the other hand, it is also possible that when kids feel bad about themselves they think that the latest 'cool' object will improve their social status and make them feel better (as in Elliott and Leonard's (2004) study). Kasser's Aspiration Index would point to materialism resulting in less personal satisfaction, but other US researchers have claimed that variations in children's materialism levels are caused by age-related changes in self-esteem (Chaplin and Roedder-John, 2007). They argue that as tweenagers become more self-conscious with the onset of puberty they seek to redress uncertainties about themselves with money and possessions. So materialism doesn't make you unhappy but being unhappy makes you materialistic. Currently we just don't know which way round this works: both explanations are plausible and we await longitudinal research. In the meantime, it seems highly likely that this dynamic works both ways with a reinforcing cyclical effect.

Brand engagement: families and friends

Within the family, both children and adults experience great pleasure from the giving and receiving of material goods and with brand engagement. Treats in the form of toys or sweets are used to thank, encourage or reward children. Gifts are purchased and exchanged as tokens of love, affection and appreciation, and the commercial world can supply experiences that create family bonds – from watching *The X Factor* together on the sofa to screaming together at Alton Towers.[2] The new Nintendo Wii is being hailed as a modern age replacement for the board game, with families rediscovering 'together time' in the living room playing virtual tennis, boxing and golf.

There is a balance to be struck, however, and we can see that, whilst there is still research to be done, a picture is emerging where a society whose children attach too high a value to material objects, whether as a means to happiness, as a way to gain status in the playground or simply as a way of life, is a society whose families function less well. There is evidence that parents increasingly feel that the commercial world is infringing family life. In a 2003 MORI poll for the National Family and Parenting Institute, 84 per cent of parents thought that companies targeted their children too much. In 2007 a survey for Care for the Family found that this percentage had risen to 97 per cent and that 88 per cent felt that pester power was a real problem for most parents. Policy makers seem to agree as 94 per cent of MPs in 2008 agreed with the statement 'Young people in the UK have too many commercial pressures put on them'. The US author Juliet Schor (2004) believes that many brand marketers deliberately try to drive a wedge between parents and their children. She puts it like this: 'It's important to recognise the nature of the corporate message: kids and products are aligned together in a really great fun place while parents, teachers and other adults inhabit an oppressive drab and joyless world. The lesson to kids is that it's the product not your parent who's really on your side' (2004: 55).

In response parents are finding ways to cope with brand pressure. As one parent put it in the Care for the Family survey: 'If my teenager wants new trainers I look around at what I think are reasonable trainers and find the average price, say £25. Then I give them that as a budget and if they want a £50 pair that is fine but they have to make up the shortfall out of their pocket money – it tends to make the cheaper trainers much more attractive!' And children are becoming increasingly cynical about marketing and advertising. So businesses now have to find more and more creative ways of having their brand message heard and taken seriously. One of the best ways of doing this is to get children to market to each other. As one teenager told me in research for a recent book (Mayo and Nairn, 2009), 'The best way to market to kids is using other kids'. Companies now recruit children as 'brand ambassadors' to do research and sell to each other. The Girls Intelligence Agency is a peer-to-peer marketing company in the USA. Girls between 8 and 18 are invited to become 'secret agents' with the offer of cool free products in return. What they have to do to gain these is show off these free products to their schoolmates. This often involves a sponsored sleepover where products are tried out and discussed. The secret agent has to video the proceedings and report back to HQ. Whilst this is a highly effective, very cheap and, most importantly, new method of marketing, it does raise serious ethical issues about whether children's friendships should be effectively 'commercialized'. In particular, we have to question the instructions to the girls to be 'sneaky' with their friends (see Schor, 2004: 76–77). UK companies also run brand ambassador programmes: Mattel, for example, ran a campaign in 2007 to recruit 7 year old girls to promote the Barbie Girls MP3 player to their friends (Mayo and Nairn, 2009). These little ambassadors had to belong to extra-curricular clubs and have a presence on at least one social networking site. They were also required to take the MP3 player to all of their activities and take pictures of themselves promoting the product. These pictures were then emailed back to Mattel and if they showed that the ambassador was selling hard she could then be eligible for a bonus.

Vignette 2: Secret Agents!

The GIA (or Girls Intelligence Agency) describes itself as a unique organization with around 40,000, 8–29 year old female 'secret agents' based in the United States. Selectively recruited, these 'influencers' or 'alpha girls' offer insights into the female youth market. As GIA state on their website:

> Girls Intelligence Agency stays totally up-to-the-minute by running on-going shopping trips, hosting slumber parties and off-sites and doing in-room hang-outs. GIA provides the girls a place to voice their opinions, make a statement or simply text and IM with other like minded agents. During these sessions, analysts listen to their music, watch their body language, and hear how they relate and communicate with friends.

One of their key services is the 'Slumber Party in a Box'. A young host invites 10 to 12 of her closest friends for a sleepover where there is a secret box of new 'cool' products that they are invited to sample and provide feedback on. Moreover they have an impressive list of clients in the food, toy and entertainment industries.

Source: http://www.girlsintelligenceagency.com/ and http://girlsintelligenceagency.com/60min/choice.htm

---

Of course the sort of activity depicted in Vignette 2 which involves children very directly with brands can be seen as empowering for them. They have their voices heard and an input into the brands which are important to them. This sort of peer-to-peer marketing is also used by government agencies and charities who realize that a message is more believable to a child when it comes from another child than when it comes from a company or even any grown-up. However, currently it is an ethically grey area which has yet to be seriously debated by policy makers.

Conclusion

We have seen that children start to develop brand awareness when they can barely walk and will spontaneously articulate a brand preference for the most heavily advertised products (sweets and snacks) just as they start school. Much research has concentrated on identifying the age-stages or developmental milestones in children's emerging competence to use brand symbolism. This has taught us a lot about how children move from a perceptual to a conceptual understanding of products and brands and when stereotyping begins. More recently, consumer culture theory has allowed us to frame children's engagement with brands as part of their ongoing engagement with identity projects and negotiated peer relationships. However, as brands become a more immersive part of children's lives we now need to understand how brand relationships affect children socially and emotionally. Children are, at the same time, savvy and vulnerable and increasing demands on their competencies are made as marketing moves from easily recognizable TV advertising to new forms of communication such as mobiles, the internet, viral and peer-to-peer. Brands offer children tools for self-expression and identity play but they can also create family and peer tensions. There remains much research to be done on the social implications for an increasingly branded childhood.

Future research directions

In particular we need to research the relationships between relatively benign brand stereotyping and the much darker issue of prejudice created or reinforced through brands. When and how does stereotype become prejudice and what can companies do to mitigate prejudice? How can brands be harnessed as positive and inclusive symbols rather than as signs of inclusion and exclusion? More work is also needed in disadvantaged communities where brands seem to wield enormous power whilst simultaneously putting a huge financial and social pressure on families who are already hard pressed. We know that there are strong correlations between materialism and negative wellbeing but we need more longitudinal work to understand the direction of causality in this dynamic. And as brands become part of children's everyday lives we also need more ethnographic research which explores how brands are used in family power plays and within the complex dynamics of the playground.

Discussion questions

1 Why are brands such an important part of children's lives today?
2 How can the two approaches of developmental cognitive psychology and consumer culture theory help us understand children's relationships with brands?
3 How do brands impact on family life?
4 Should 'peer-to-peer endorsement' be allowed, regulated or banned?

Further reading

Goldberg, M.E., Gorn, G.J., Peracchio, L.A. and Bamossy, G. (2003) 'Understanding materialism among youth', *Journal of Consumer Psychology*, 13(3): 278–288.

Kasser, T., Ryan, R.M., Couchman, C.E. and Sheldon, K.M. (2004) 'Materialistic values: their causes and consequences', in T. Kasser and A.D. Kanner (eds), *Psychology and Consumer Culture: The Struggle for a Good Life in a Materialistic World*. Washington, DC: American Psychological Association. pp. 11–28.

Richins, M.L. (1987) 'Media, materialism and human happiness', in M. Wallendorf and P. Anderson (eds), *Advances in Consumer Research*, 14: 352–356. Provo, UT: Association for Consumer Research.

Richins, M.L. (2004) 'The material values scale: measurement properties and development of a short form', *Journal of Consumer Research*, 31(1): 209–219.

Roberts, J.A., Tanner Jr., J.F. and Manolis, C. (2005) 'Materialism and the family structure-stress relation', *Journal of Consumer Psychology*, 15(2): 183–190.

References

Achereiner, G.B. and John, D.R. (2003) 'The meaning of brand names to children: a developmental investigation', *Journal of Consumer Psychology*, 13 (3): 205–219.

Arnould, E.J. and Thompson, C.J. (2005) 'Consumer culture theory (CCT): Twenty years of research', *Journal of Consumer Research*, 31 (March): 868–882.

Belk, R.W., Bahn, R.N. and Mayer, R.N. (1982) 'Developmental recognition of consumption symbolism', *Journal of Consumer Research*, 7 (June): 4–17.

Belk, R.W., Mayer, R.N. and Driscoll, A. (1984) 'Children's recognition of consumption symbolism in children's products', *Journal of Consumer Research*, 10 (March): 386–397.

Bourdieu, P. (1984) *Distinction: A Social Critique of the Judgement of Taste*. London: Routledge and Kegan Paul.

Buijzen, M. and Valkenburg, P.M. (2003) 'The unintended effects of television advertising: a parent–child survey'. *Communication Research*, 30: 483–503.

Burroughs, J. and Rindfleisch, A. (2002) 'Materialism and well-being: a conflicting values perspective', *Journal of Consumer Research*, 29 (December): 348–370.

Chaplin, L. and Lowrey, T. (2010) 'The development of consumer-based consumption constellations in children', *Journal of Consumer Research*, February (published online 24 June 2009).

Chaplin, L. and Roedder-John, D. (2007) 'Growing up in a material world: age differences in materialism in children and adolescents', *Journal of Consumer Research*, 34 (December): 480–493.

ChildWise (2008) *The Monitor Report*. Norwich: ChildWise. Available at http://www.childwise.co.uk/ChildWise-monitor-survey.asp

Day, J., Dunn, V. and Goodyer, I. (2007) 'Results from the ROOTS Consumer Involvement Scale'. Working Paper, Department of Developmental Psychiatry, Cambridge University, UK.

Elliott, R. and Leonard, C. (2004) 'Peer pressure and poverty: exploring fashion brands and consumption symbolism among children of the "British poor"', *Journal of Consumer Behaviour*, 3 (4): 347–359.

Foucault, M. (1974) *The Archaeology of Knowledge*. London: Tavistock.

Foucault, M. (1978) *The History of Sexuality: Volume 1: An Introduction*. Harmondsworth: Penguin.

Goldberg, M.E. and Gorn, G.J. (1978) 'Some unintended consequences of TV advertising to children', *Journal of Consumer Research*, 5 (1): 22–29.

Goldberg, M.E., Gorn, G.J., Peracchio, L.A. and Bamossy, G. (2003) 'Understanding materialism among youth', *Journal of Consumer Psychology*, 13: 278–288.

Greenfield, S. (2006) 'Education: Science and Technology', *Proceedings of the House of Lords*, 20 April, Column 1219–1223.

Griffin, C. (2007) 'Being dead and being there: research interviews, sharing hand cream and the preference for analysing "naturally occurring" data', *Discourse Studies*, 9 (2): 246–269.

Griffin, C., Nairn, A., Gaya Wicks, P., Phoenix, A. and Hunter, J. (2006) 'Girly girls, tomboys and micro-waving Barbie: Child and youth consumption and the disavowal of femininity', 8th ACR Conference on Gender, Marketing and Consumer Behaviour, 29 June–1 July, Edinburgh.

Kasser, T. (2005) 'Frugality, generosity and materialism in children and adolescents', in K.A. Moore and L. Lippman (eds), *What Do Children Need to Flourish? Conceptualizing and Measuring Indicators of Positive Development*. New York: Springer Science. pp. 357–374.

Klein, M. (2000) *No Logo*. London: Flamingo.

Layard, R. (2005) *Happiness: Lessons from a New Science*. London: Penguin.

Marshall, D. and Aitken, R. (2006) 'Putting brands in the picture: children's drawings of their favourite things', in *Asia-Pacific Advances in Consumer Research Volume 7* (eds Margaret Craig Lees, Teresa Davis and Gary Gregory). Sydney, Australia: Association for Consumer Research. pp. 268–276.

Mayo, E. (2005) *Shopping Generation*. London: National Consumer Council.

Mayo, E. and Nairn, A. (2009) *Consumer Kids*. London: Constable and Robinson.

Moore, E. (2005) 'Alternative to what? Subcultural capital and the commercialisation of a music scene', *Deviant Behaviour*, 26: 229–252.

Nairn, A., Griffin, C. and Gaya Wicks, P. (2006) 'The Simpson's are cool but Barbie's a minger: the role of brands in the everyday lives of junior school children'. Report published by University of Bath, Bath.

Nairn, A., Griffin, C. and Gaya Wicks, P. (2008) 'Children's use of brand symbolism: a consumer culture theory approach', *European Journal of Marketing*, 42 (5/6): pp. 627–640.

Nairn, A., Ormrod, J. and Bottomley, P. (2007) *Watching, Wanting and Wellbeing*. London: National Consumer Council. Available at http://www.agnesnairn.co.uk/policy_reports/watching_wanting_and_wellbeing_july_2007.pdf

Nancarrow, C., Nancarrow, P. and Page, J. (2002) 'An analysis of the concept of cool and its marketing implications', *Journal of Consumer Behavior*, 1 (4): 311–325.

Piaget, J. (1960) 'General problems of the psychological development of the child', in *Discussions on Child Development: Proceedings of the World Health Organisation Study Group on Psychological Development of the Child IV* (J.M. Tanner and B. Elders (eds)). New York: International Universities Press.

Pole, C. (2007) 'Researching children and fashion: an embodied ethnography', *Childhood*, 14 (1): 67–84.

Renold, E. (2005) 'Queering "girlie" culture, negotiating heterogendered childhoods: tomboys, topgirls and moshers', Paper presented at the British Educational Research Association Conference, University of Glamorgan, September.

Russell, R. and Tyler, M. (2002) 'Thank heaven for little girls: "Girl heaven" and the commercial context of feminine childhood', *Sociology*, 36 (3): 619–637.

Schor, J. (2004) *Born to Buy*. New York: Scribner.

Swain, J. (2002) 'The right stuff: fashioning identity through clothing in a junior school', *Gender and Education*, 14 (1): 53–69.

Thompson, C.J. and Haytko, D.L. (1997) 'Speaking of fashion: consumers' uses of fashion discourses and the appropriation of counterveiling cultural meanings', *Journal of Consumer Research*, 24 (June): 15–42.

Wicklund, R. and Gollwitzer, P. (1982) *Symbolic Self-Completion*. Hillsdale, NJ: Lawrence Erlbaum.

Notes

1 Between 2005 and 2008 Britney Spears experienced a turbulent personal life including highly publicized custody battles for her two children and periods of time in various drug and alcohol rehabilitation centres.
2 Alton Towers is a UK theme park located in the Staffordshire peak district in England (see http://www.altontowers.com/). *X-Factor* is a television music talent show (see http://xfactor.itv.com/2009).

7 Children and Advertising

Brian Young

Chapter aims

- To describe how children develop an understanding of advertising and promotional activity from birth to adolescence.
- To deliver this understanding within a framework of what is now known about child psychology.
- To explore the influence of advertising in children's lives in two areas materialism and obesity.
- To identify areas where we need future research.

Introduction

Advertising is pervasive in the culture of the twenty-first century and indeed it would be hard to identify a country on earth that doesn't have some form of advertising.[1] This would suggest that many of us have what is sometimes called a folk understanding or lay theory of what advertising is, although we're less than sure of the distinctions and differences between advertising, marketing, and promotional activity. As a communicative genre, advertising tries to get us to do something like purchase brands of goods and services or (much less frequently) whole categories of goods. So it persuades. It also informs and indeed the small ads found in newspapers constitute a very common and frequently neglected type of advertising that provides valuable information. Advertising can be entertaining and imaginative and many of our internationally known film directors cut their creative teeth producing TV ads. So advertising can be sexy and exciting as well as dull and routine. Although much of the research in the last thirty years or so has focused on children and television advertising, it should not be forgotten that advertising is common in many of the newer forms of media such as SMS texting, social networking sites, and web pages (see Tufte and Rasmussen, Chapter 11 in this book). In addition we should not forget the branded presence in all our stores and retail outlets, in and on public transport, on shopping bags, and carefully located in school educational material. And it's there as an essential part of a mixed economy encouraging people to consume, discovering and sometimes creating real or even imaginary problems which brands can magically solve. Feeling bloated? Are your shirts not whiter than white? Our brand will provide the solution.

But the purpose of this chapter is not to explore all the different varieties of the advertising experience nor is it to draw subtle distinctions between advertising and marketing and promotional activity. Instead it will look at what happens when children become part of the picture. Why does putting children and advertising together create anxieties so that people feel the need to protect them from these seductive communications? Do children understand advertising in the same way as adults? This chapter will examine some of the most recent theories and findings in child psychology that inform our understanding about how children respond to advertising from birth to adolescence, looking specifically at its effect on materialism and obesity. Finally we'll look at what we don't know and what research still needs to be done.

Vignette 1: Interacting with the commercial environment from an early age

Rosie, at 12 months old, is a regular visitor to the supermarket where she is wheeled around in the supermarket trolley, sitting facing her mum who is doing the shopping. She can see all the brightly coloured packages and gurgles with pleasure when she recognizes brands and characters like the Teletubbies[2] on the packs. This recognition and linking the different experiences with brands – in the supermarket, in the fridge at home, on TV when the commercials come on – will develop into the second and third years of life as the growing child develops and learns more about the commercial world. Although Rosie might not be talking and using language until the second year of life, she might already have what is known as proto-language where she can draw Mum's attention to a favourite brand (e.g., with 'dere, dere') and make basic demands (e.g., 'gimme, gimme'). These two basic functions of social interaction with others mean that Rosie is interacting with the commercial world even from an early age.

What do child psychologists tell us?

During the first two years of life the child is in (what Jean Piaget, the famous Swiss developmental psychologist called) the sensori-motor period of development (Ginsburg and Opper, 1988). Most of the child's behaviour is driven by information that is available through the senses which then affects the way the child behaves on the world i.e., motor behaviour. According to Piaget the world is not yet mentally represented by the child with thoughts and ideas. Children's minds at this stage don't yet have symbolic representations. They have what he called schemata or mental structures, but these are only based on their actions. Although much of what Piaget claimed the child could or could not do has been revised in the light of new evidence from experimental child psychology, his theories are still very useful to gain a broad picture of what children are like.

During the sensori-motor period from birth to 2 years the child begins by acting on her surroundings with little regard for the nature of that environment (Vignette 1). Grasping and looking – both of these behaviours will be fired off in an attempt to act *on* the environment. Gradually the child learns to act on the objects in her environment and take their characteristics into account when exploring them. She looks and grasps, inspects, and turns toys over. So at the level of action children develop from being egocentric (or self-centred) at the beginning of the sensori-motor period to being allocentric (or other-centred) later in that period.

The next big stage of development according to Piaget is the pre-operational period (2–7 years). During this period the child thinks that the world that he sees is what the world is actually like. Appearance dominates. Early on in this period the child is egocentric – at the level of perception – and thinks that his or her view is the same as everyone else's.

This is followed by the concrete operational period (7–11 years) and the formal operational period (11 years and older). It is not until the concrete operational period that the child can think and reason systematically about the world of objects or concrete[3] reality and realize that the amount of stuff only changes when you add or take away, and it doesn't depend on the shape or size of the container for example. When children become older and enter the formal operational period they begin to reason abstractly and systematically. But they are still egocentric at this new level of abstract reasoning and can't take into account other people's views. So the young teenager is idealistic. Why can't we have a world without war with peace and love across the globe? We must save the planet. (I'll come back to this when we talk about materialism and advertising.) During each of these periods there is a gradual development from being egocentric to being allocentric.

Not surprisingly there has been little written about children's consumer behaviour in infancy, although McNeal (2007) is valuable both for his reputation as one of the most respected and important writers in the field as well as the uniqueness of his contribution. To summarize what we know – from birth to 6 months the young child will probably have made her first trip to the marketplace (often the local supermarket) with her parent(s) and will have established an association between the sights, smells and sounds of that place and the experience of being there which often will be pleasurable. During the latter part of the second year of life the child becomes able to walk and talk and can start making requests.

Advertising, however, is not seen as anything more than fun and entertainment and there is a general consensus that children under the age of 5 years do not understand the intent of advertising – what it's there for and what it's trying to communicate. Certainly many children by 3 or 4 years old can distinguish television spot advertising from programming on the basis that ads are little breaks in the programmes, but they are unable as yet to make inferences about the nature of the genre called advertising or promotional activity (Young, 2008). Both of these observations are predictable from Piaget's theory of child development where the preoperational child makes judgements based on the perceptual qualities of their environment (ads are short, programmes are longer), but concrete operational children are more able to 'dig deeper' mentally and make inferences about the essential nature of their concrete – as opposed to abstract – worlds and draw conclusions that go beyond the mere appearance of things.

Recent research in child development has established that, between 3 and 4 years of age, children become aware of the intentions and beliefs of other people and more importantly that these psychological states might be different from their own. Although this research was originally called theory of mind, a better term might be the child's emerging folk psychology – a growing understanding of the nature of one's own psychology and the psychology of others. It is not difficult to see that knowing what other people are up to and being able to work this out from a person's behaviour is an essential set of tools and skills for the survival of the child who is beginning to form social relationships with his or her peers and other adults in a world where scheming and other Machiavellian manoeuvrings are commonplace. Surely this ability then will help the child understand the point of advertising? After all it is a form of communication where the sender often has different interests from the audience at the receiving end and is able to use rhetoric and present the virtues of the brand in a way that optimizes the chances of a member of the audience being persuaded to buy. And yet it will be another four or five years before the average child will grasp the idea that advertising is there to 'persuade you to buy stuff'. As yet, there is no consensus on when most children understand the persuasive nature of advertising as it seems to depend on the methods used to establish it (Moses and Baldwin, 2005). This gap in development between having a theory of mind and understanding advertising is a real problem for the developmental psychologist. Some children, from about 7 years of age, are quite capable of asking critical questions about different kinds of processes like 'where does that come from?' or 'why is that there?' as the following Vignette shows.

Vignette 2: But not all children are the same

Jenny is an attentive 7 year old who can be relied on in class to ask questions about everyday parts of her environment and her teachers know this. Her parents are older and this is their only child so much has been invested in her. They go over her homework and sit down together at dinner each evening where Jenny is encouraged to talk about her day. Her favourite word is 'why?' and often her parents don't feel like answering but believe that they need to satisfy her constant curiosity about this new world she is discovering every day. She has many friends and good social skills, helping the younger ones. This rather 'Pollyanna' portrait is an idealization but it shows that such a critical stance is encouraged by involved parents and present in good schools as part of a history and geography lesson or everyday life, for example when the teacher tries to get children to question where the humble bottle of milk comes from – from cows on farms and through supermarkets to our homes.

Contrast Jenny with Fred who is two years older than Jenny. Fred is a solitary child and his parents who both work are too busy to pay much attention to him, explaining that he 'prefers his own company'. Fred doesn't talk much in class and most of the teachers say he's a quiet child. He thinks it's cool to be uninvolved and unemotional and if you ask him why ads are on TV he shrugs and uses his favourite word 'dunno'. He is often ignored by teachers and is accepting of his environment. Curiosity seems to have passed him by.

Many children do acquire a questioning style but other children are accepting of their environment and rarely question why things are as they are.[4] So for them TV is like moving wallpaper and ads are 'just there'. On this basis we would expect children in the former group, with the questioning style, to grasp that there is a source behind advertising at an earlier age than the latter ones who are uninterested and accept things as they are. Knowing that there is a source[5] that generates promotional communication is one of the skills of literacy with advertising. We would also expect children who understand the source to acquire an understanding of the intent behind advertising at an earlier age than those who see advertising as just moving wallpaper.

Unfortunately there is not much research on differences in understanding how children relate to advertising across other variables apart from age. Using age as a variable usually produces significant results in developmental psychology[6] and tends to be the dominant independent variable used in the literature. However, Martin (1997) in a meta-analysis of the research on the child's understanding of advertising did find socio-economic differences between children – evidence that supports the argument outlined here.

Children under five years of age do not see advertising as anything more than entertainment and there is a consensus on this conclusion in the vast majority of the literature. At about 6 to 7 years old, on average, children begin to separate television advertising from other forms of communication such as programmes not on the basis of their perceptual features but on the basis of a deeper, more inferred property of the communication. We would predict this from Piaget's theory. In a classic paper, Robertson and Rossiter (1974) interviewed over 250 boys in the USA about the intent behind ads in TV commercials. They established that there were two types of attribution of intent. One, called assistive, is where the child sees commercials as informative as in 'commercials tell you about things' and the other, called persuasive, is where the child sees commercials as 'trying to make you buy things'. Although both types of attribution of intent can co-exist in the individual child, there is a trend towards persuasive intent attribution, as compared with assistive intent attribution, becoming more frequent as the child gets older.

By 10 to 11 years of age, practically all children are able to attribute persuasive intent. Also, children of parents with higher educational levels will tend to attribute persuasive intent at an earlier age than children of parents with lower educational levels. Older children will tend to see ads functioning more as persuaders than providing helpful information. In addition those children who were categorized as attributing persuasive intent to television commercials also tended to possess all of the antecedent skills that Robertson and Rossiter had argued were necessary for the comprehension of persuasive intent. These were: they could distinguish programme from commercial; they understood about an external source or sponsor; they saw that an audience was intended for the commercial; they were aware of the symbolic nature of commercials; and they cited instances of negative discrepancies where the product did not come up to expectations as extolled by the advertisement. Those children who attributed assistive intent to commercials as in 'commercials tell you about things' tended to be capable of perceiving the idea of an intended audience and also capable of seeing a source for the message.

Understanding that ads persuade has a special privilege as a significant milestone in the child's literacy with advertising. Robertson and Rossiter's paper is important as it blends together empirical work with a tight argument about the psychological processes involved. Being able to detect assistive intent without persuasive intent would imply a great susceptibility to advertising as ads are seen as transmitting information about brands but without the child being aware that this information is there to get you to buy something i.e. that it is deliberately designed for this purpose. It should be noted however that the results from this paper were published some time ago when the dominant mode of advertising to children was spot advertising on TV. The media landscape has in the interim changed beyond all recognition, with advertisements on the web and in computer games. Consequently we need to explore (and there has been very little research in this area) how children cope with and comprehend these various different forms. Advertising and marketing are much more pervasive now in children's lives and we just don't know whether they understand, for example, the purpose of banner advertising on websites. What we can say is that the essential cognitive ingredients for understanding that there is a genre which persuades and tries to sell stuff should be there at some time in middle childhood. Another function of advertising is its promotional aspect. Some years ago I did some research (Young, 2000) that looked at young children's (aged 4 to 9 years old) understanding of promotional intent which is that advertising only provides positive information[7] about brands. Children of different ages were shown videos of TV ads with the end part missing and various optional endings on cards. One ending was funny but broke the golden rule in that it wasn't flattering about the brand and effectively mocked it. Another ending was promotional and there was also a control option which was neither funny nor promotional. As we had anticipated, the youngest children under about 6 years of age tended to choose the 'funny but negative-about-the-brand' option and the older ones picked the promotional one and firmly rejected the amusing but negative ending. So what can we conclude? Children between the ages of about 6 to 9 years are beginning to learn why TV ads are there as they are able to reason beyond the surface qualities of advertising that it is funny and entertaining. But why does that matter? The reason is partly psychological, but mostly legal, as the next section shows.

Do we need to regulate advertising to children?

Being able to understand advertising does not mean advertising has no effect on you. In the case of children then there is a good case that advertising has a greater effect than with adults. Roedder-John (1999) assumed that there were three stages in the processing of information. Children under 7 years of age are seen as limited processors. In the language of information processing they have mediational deficiencies where storage and retrieval are difficult even when they are prompted and cued to do so. Children over 12 years of age on the other hand are able to use various strategies for storing, retrieving and utilizing information and that can be done in the absence of prompting and cueing. Between the ages of 7 and 11, however, although children might be able to deploy strategies to enhance information storage and retrieval that are similar to those used by older children, they also need to be aided by explicit prompts and cues. Consequently, although children might be able to understand a lot about the intention behind advertising by 8 years of age, they still have a problem with advertising until 12 years of age. This problem is to do with access to and utilizing that knowledge. In a sense although the understanding is there and can be used to cope critically with advertising, it may not necessarily be accessed and used in evaluating advertising messages.

In the same paper Roedder-John, drawing on the work of Selman (1980), argues that there is a skill concerning the child's ability to take the perspective of other people that develops from early childhood to adolescence and that these developmental stages should be taken into account when considering children's understanding of advertising. Children before the age of 6 years old are unable to take the perspective of other people and view the world from their own point of view. Between 6 and 8 years of age children will realize that others have different opinions or motives, but will believe that this comes from the other person having different information rather than adopting a different perspective on a situation. Between 8 and 10 years old children acquire an understanding that people with the same information can have different opinions or motives and can take this into account and consider another person's point of view. Development does not stop at 10 years of age however and being able to consider simultaneously the other person's point of view emerges from 10 to 12 years old. This skill is vital in interpersonal negotiation and persuasion when people interact socially. Finally, the young adolescent can take the mature detached position of seeing another person's perspective as relating to social group membership or the social system within which they operate.

Both of these developmental sequences – information processing and perspective taking – are important when considering how literate children are when coping with advertising in all its multifunctional aspects. Being able to acquire and, importantly, utilize understandings about advertising and being able to understand the advertiser's point of view seem to be important elements of advertising literacy.

There is a well-defined trajectory of development that describes the child's understanding of advertising and the various skills in the psychology of child development that constitute advertising literacy have been outlined. Yet it is important to recognize that the theory and evidence in this area are limited to television advertising as most advertising that children watched at the end of the twentieth century when much of the research was published was in that medium. Furthermore, most of the regulation centred on television advertising.

The history of regulating advertising to children can be traced back to the US federal government proceedings of the 1970s and in particular the Federal Trade Commission (FTC) and Federal Communication Commission (FCC) submissions (for references and history, see Young, 1990; Chapter 2). At one point in the late 1970s it looked possible that the FTC would be able to ban television advertising to children on the grounds that such advertising was unfair to children. 'Unfair' in this context suggests that there is a generic category of communications, called advertisements, and that there is a case that certain individuals are not in a position to understand the point or intention behind these communications. Young children below a certain age could fall into this category. Psychologists would have a role here if they were in a position to provide expert evidence on the age when children can understand advertising intent. In fact, after much pressure from commercial lobbies the FTC was effectively emasculated in that they were only permitted to consider deceptive advertising which consisted of communications from sellers to buyers which were false or misleading and which induced purchases. In a European context various different legislative positions have been adopted. For example, Sweden has banned advertising to children for many years and is often held up as a model of protecting children from the onslaught of TV advertising. In the UK, advertising to children was regulated but permitted if it adhered to certain principles although certain categories of products (such as alcohol) were off limits. However, in the wake of the so-called 'obesity epidemic' which applies to children as well as adults Ofcom (the main UK regulator of media) has banned any advertising to children on TV of high fat, sugar, and salt (HFSS) foods. By January 2009 there was no advertising of HFSS foods and drinks to children aged 4 to 15 years in programmes made for or of a particular appeal to children.[8] Presumably in both these cases if there is a political will and a cultural ethos that supports this sort of legislation then it will be enacted.[9]

Materialism: does advertising have a role to play?

In the second part of this chapter we shall explore the two issues of obesity and materialism. In both of these areas it has been claimed that advertising has an effect in the sense that being exposed to ads encourages or promotes these dispositions in children. I shall develop a case, again relying on arguments taken from psychological theory and evidence, that issues in both these areas are quite problematic.

The academic literature defines materialism either as 'the importance a consumer attaches to worldly possessions' (Belk, 1984: 291) or 'the importance a person places on possessions and their acquisition as a necessary or desirable form of conduct to reach desired end states, including happiness' (Richins and Dawson, 1992: 307). The literature on how materialism develops in children is sparse, but a seminal paper by Chaplin and Roedder-John (2007) claims that materialism changes over childhood and adolescence, rising through middle childhood and declining from early to late adolescence. They attribute these changes largely to changes in self-esteem that occur during this period of the lifespan. While not wishing to criticize this plausible explanation of an interesting developmental trajectory, I would argue that there are also good theoretical reasons in development in general to assume that a change will occur and that these reasons can be explained by

Piaget's general principles as outlined earlier in the chapter. If we look at survey research we will find a general tendency for children to value non-materialistic goals such as friendship, love, and helping others and as Nairn et al. (2006) also found almost 40 per cent of children disagreed with the statement 'I really like to go shopping'.[10] Much of the concern that some adults feel about an increasingly materialistic world is often not validated by the research evidence.

As we have seen, during the pre-operational period of development the child is driven by the appearance of things and the world of the supermarket and shops is very appealing, with bright primary colours, interesting sounds and fascinating smells. Children at this age will focus on the dominant features of packages and displays and respond by demanding and pointing to one feature, such as the presence of a character or cartoon on a package. By the time the child is at school and beginning to understand the rudiments of advertising she is also making deeper inferences and using systematic (i.e., operational) thinking on the material world. In a classic paper, Belk et al. (1984) established that children in middle childhood acquire what is known as consumption symbolism. This means that certain goods are not just valued in terms of their functionality and aesthetic properties ('this is a pretty dress'; 'this coat has so many pockets'), but also in terms of the social status they confer ('this car is owned by really wealthy people'; 'these trainers are cool'). So in other words, the perceived value of goods and services increases in middle childhood just because the symbolic value is recognized and added to desirable goods (and presumably reduced for 'uncool' stuff). These are not just trainers, they are Nike trainers. This is not just food, it's M&S food.[11] It's not surprising then that as the value of goods and services becomes inflated for desirable brands that the interests of the tweenie[12] child in material aspects of his culture are raised and an involvement in browsing, choosing, shopping and so on becomes higher. It's against this backdrop of cognitive developmental changes that we should assess the relative influence of other factors such as self-esteem (Chaplin and Roedder-John, 2007) and peer group pressure (Banerjee and Dittmar, 2008).

So what explains the apparent drop in materialism as the child moves through adolescence toward adulthood? When the child moves into the formal operational period of thought then an abstract vision of the ideal and a perfect solution to problems are now available as a brave new world that the adolescent can explore and evaluate. But as this is a new period of development it is highly egocentric and it will take some years and plenty of experience before the non-ideal practical solutions to social problems are acceptable (Elkind, 1994). And as the opposite of materialism is idealism, then idealism – a rejection of the trappings of consumption as having no place in the perfect solution – emerges. 'Imagine no possessions …' is easy for the egocentric and idealistic young person. But materialism is still there in the world and the conflict between the two poles of the spectrum could act as a forceful dynamic for change in the individual child.

Obesity: does food advertising make children fat?

Finally let's look at the question of advertising and childhood obesity. There are several areas where advertising to children has a particularly negative resonance with the public and these have included the advertising and promotion of alcohol and tobacco which, although they are legal products for adults, are generally off limits to minors and most societies try to keep it that way. Restrictions on the advertising of foods high in fat, sugar, and salt (HFSS) to children have been discussed above. Why have these regulations been introduced? Evidence has been presented in several authoritative reviews worldwide that advertising has a role to play in the multi-factorial problem that is obesity. However, a closer examination suggests the picture is not as clear as perhaps the press have claimed. For example, the Institute of Medicine of the National Academies (IMNA) published a report on food marketing to children and youth in 2006 which claimed that there was strong evidence that television advertising influences the food and beverage preferences, purchase requests, and *short-term* consumption of children aged 2 to 11 years but that 'the causal evidence is not sufficient to arrive at any finding about a causal relationship from television advertising to adiposity' (IMNA, 2006: ES-7). So what's the truth here?

The research base that has been built up over twenty years is concerned with the role of television advertising on children's food preferences and choice. The first UK review in this area was commissioned by what was then known as MAFF (a government department covering agriculture, fisheries, and food) and published by Young et al. (1996). The second UK review was by Hastings et al. (2003), and most of the small number of studies that show some sort of effect of advertising on food consumption (usually quite small with less than 5 per cent of the variance accounted for) are common to both reviews. However, the conclusions that the two reviews came to differed in one important respect. There are a set of experiments that use a particular research technique which Hastings et al. found acceptable and valid as they cite them in support of their conclusions, but which Young et al. saw as not really simulating how children are influenced by advertising. One of the paradigms involves watching a video presentation (which might include TV commercials for a particular brand) and then afterwards being offered an array of foods. The children chose from this mixed set of alternative brands and products. In general young children's short-term snack and breakfast food preferences tended to reflect their exposure experience. Children were more likely to select highly sugared foods if they had previously viewed television commercials for them and they were more likely to choose nutritious snack and breakfast foods if they had just seen pro-nutrition public service announcements. The difference between the two reviews lay in what to make of these results.

Young et al. claimed they were so far removed from the everyday process of consuming advertising and making choices that the studies weren't just irrelevant to how children were influenced by advertising but also provided dangerously distorted evidence of its influence. In other words they lack external validity. Hastings et al. cited them extensively on the other hand as providing sound empirical findings that could inform the debate. On this basis the Hastings review claimed that advertising to children had an effect not just at the level of the brand but at the product level too. The implication here is that exposure to a brand of HFSS food would not just increase the salience of that brand when food is chosen but the influence of that exposure would extend to other HFSS foods as well.

The importance of establishing that brand advertising has a generic effect cannot be underestimated in the debate about whether food advertising increases the child's consumption of HFSS foods. There is no consensus that brand advertising has a generic effect, although the possibility of a cumulative effect of individual food advertising on young children is a distinct possibility. But the effect size of advertising is small relative to the effects of family, friends and culture in determining food choice.

But where is obesity in the debate? The dominant model in most of the research about determinants of obesity is based on a simple 'balance sheet' where food intake implies 'energy in' and exercise is 'energy out'. Too much of the former, especially if it's calorifically dense, and too little of the latter means running the risk of becoming fat. This balance metaphor also has a moral resonance of gluttony and laziness (Gard and Wright, 2005) which would suggest it is easy enough for the average person to adopt as a common-sense explanation of obesity. In addition there are cultural, physiological, environmental (the so-called obesogenic environment), genetic, and social factors that promote or attenuate obesity prevalence. Note that food choice is but one input variable in a multifactorial mix here and we have seen that food choice itself is an output variable in another multifactorial system of which food advertising is but a small part. It seems highly likely then that the already small contribution that advertising makes to individual differences in diet will be even less when we consider the differences between people on obesity.

So does advertising have a small and insignificant effect on obesity and is the new regulatory framework based on bad science? The role of food advertising in obesity in children is one of many factors and there is no consensus yet on how powerful a role advertising plays, although there is an emerging consensus on issues of diet and the role that advertising plays in children's dietary habits. Moreover, this is not devoid of a political dimension. It's difficult and expensive to change diets or promote exercise but cheap and efficient to introduce regulations on advertising to children. Also it should be remembered there is no direct evidence of the cumulative effect on children of watching many different food advertisements over a long period of time. However, there is a way forward which we shall look at in the section on future research (see Kline, Chapter 14 in this book). But first here is a summary of our conclusions so far.

Conclusion

Four aims were listed at the beginning of this chapter. The first was to provide a description of how the child's understanding of advertising and promotional activity develops from birth to adolescence using different streams of development that have been described and theorized by psychologists. So, for example, the very young infant taking her first tour of the supermarket in a trolley pushed by mum or dad has to make sense of a new brightly coloured world of goods and lots of other people also doing this strange new activity. It's the young child's job to make sense of this place. She will draw associations between the brands found there and those at home and in ads on TV. She will see these people line up and pack stuff and hand over money (or more commonly hand over a card) and later on will begin to understand what that means. This site – the marketplace – has been a core activity for adults and their families since trading began in society. Children have played and will always play an important role there as their growing up starts in the supermarket and ends up by hanging out at the mall.

Two of the most common aspects of what have been called the 'unintended' consequences of advertising are obesity and materialism. The ebb and flow of materialism across the lifespan from childhood through adolescence is described and the possibility of more than one explanation is explored. There are also definitional issues surrounding a slippery concept like materialism and we should be sceptical of easy solutions to this complex problem. The unique cocktail of social influences involving parents, friends, media, and most importantly how each child resolves these different pressures, must be considered when answering the question – what makes children more or less materialistic?

Obesity is part of a multifactorial problem, variously attributed to a balance sheet where there's too much coming in (diet) and too little being expended (exercise); to an environment where the cards are stacked in the direction of too much sedentary sitting around and too much high energy food being eaten; to cultural influences, and genetic factors, and individual differences in the physiology of metabolism – and the list grows longer every day. So where is advertising in all this? Most commentators believe that advertising and marketing have an influence on diet and that this influence, as measured by effect size, is not very strong. Diet itself has a major influence on obesity. And how do we put all these together? Well let's see where research should be going in these areas.

Future research directions

If advertising had a role to play in shaping and moulding children's food preferences then it would play out against an already established backdrop of dietary habits. It is well-known that children's dietary habits emerge early in childhood using the basic psychological mechanisms of associative conditioning. Therefore family influences on children's diets are important in the early development of each child when tastes and preferences are formed (Birch, 1990). Other dietary influences on the family would include not just the advertising of HFSS foods but also the whole culture associated with media representations of food and the commercial presence of food products in stores, as well as the contrasting culture offered by celebrity chefs and health professionals. This conflict between different food cultures and how it impacts on families is largely unexplored and it is important to discover the ways families negotiate their own identities in the face of these differing images and representations. For example, the culture of 'fun foods' is promoted by food manufacturers as it is received positively by children and by some parents whose main concern is to get their children to eat (see Marshall and O'Donohoe, Chapter 10 in this book). Jamie Oliver, a popular UK celebrity chef, promotes healthy eating in schools and a different culture of fun and pleasure in cooking using basic ingredients such as pasta, fish and vegetables, thus setting himself against the interests of 'big food' with their high value-added products. Food and diet are resources with a political resonance and in a country like the UK politics and class lines of demarcation can still coincide. Recently Oliver's attempts to change the school meal culture were opposed by some determined mothers who handed burgers and chips to children in their school playground through a fence. Such conflict feeds back into the media and only exacerbates the problem. It would be helpful if future scholarship and research explored issues of social identity, food-related class groups, and whether what could be called an HFSS family-based culture does exist.

Discussion questions

1 You might have been brought up in a world very different from Rosie and her mum, described at the beginning of the chapter. Discuss in a group your own upbringing and culture and when you first became aware of advertising and marketing.

2 I have described two 'unintended' consequences of advertising. Can you think of any more? If you have time, see if you can find out anything about them using internet-based resources.

3 Make a list of the things you really really wanted when you were a young adolescent. How many of these did you want just to look 'cool'?

4 If you were in charge of regulating marketing to children, what techniques used in advertising do you think you might want to control? Make a list and then see if you can find if there are regulations that ban them.

Further reading

Advertising Education Forum – http://www.aeforum.org/

Government Office for Science (2007) *Foresight. Tackling Obesities: Future Choices.* London: HMSO.

Gunter, B., Oates, C. and Blades, M. (2005) *Advertising to Children on TV: Content, Impact, and Regulation.* Mahwah, NJ: Lawrence Erlbaum Associates. (Chapter 5: 'Theoretical approaches to studying children's understanding of advertisements': pp. 62–80.)

Moses, L.J. and Baldwin, D.A. (2005) 'What can the study of cognitive development reveal about children's ability to appreciate and cope with advertising?', *American Marketing Association,* 24(2): 186–201.

Kaiser Family Foundation (2004) *The Role of Media in Childhood Obesity.* Available at http://www.kff.org/entmedia/7030.cfm

Kunkel, D., Wilcox, B.L., Cantor, J., Palmer, E., Linn, S. and Dowrick, P. (2004) *Report of the APA Task Force on Advertising to Children.* Available at http://www.apa.org/releases/childrenads.pdf)

References

Banerjee, R. and Dittmar, H. (2008) 'Individual differences in children's materialism: the role of peer relationships', *Personality and Social Psychology Bulletin,* 34: 17–31.

Belk, R.W. (1984) 'Three scales to measure constructs related to materialism: reliability, validity and relationships to measures of happiness', in T. Kinnear (ed.), *Advances in Consumer Research.* Provo, UT: Association for Consumer Research. pp. 291–297.

Belk, R., Mayer, R. and Driscoll, A. (1984) 'Children's recognition of consumption symbolism in children's products', *Journal of Consumer Research,* 10: 386–397.

Birch, L.L. (1990) 'Development of food acceptance patterns', *Developmental Psychology,* 26 (4): 515–519.

Chaplin, L.N. and Roedder-John, D. (2007) 'Growing up in a material world: Age differences in materialism in children and adolescents', *Journal of Consumer Research,* 34: 480–493.

Elkind, D. (1994) *A Sympathetic Understanding of the Child: Birth to Sixteen* (3rd edition). Boston, MA: Allyn and Bacon.

Gard, M. and Wright, J. (2005) *The Obesity Epidemic: Science, Morality and Ideology*. London: Routledge.

Ginsburg, H. and Opper, S. (1988) *Piaget's Theory of Intellectual Development: An Introduction* (3rd edition). London: Prentice-Hall.

Hastings, G., Stead, M., McDermott, L., Forsyth, A., MacKintosh, A.M. et al. (2003) *Review of Research on the Effects of Food Promotion to Children: Final Report* (2 vols.). The University of Strathclyde, UK: Centre for Social Marketing.

Institute of Medicine of the National Academies (2006) *Food Marketing to Children and Youth*. Washington, DC: The National Academies Press.

Martin, M.C. (1997) 'Children's understanding of the intent of advertising: a meta-analysis', *Journal of Public Policy & Marketing*, 16 (2): 205–216.

McNeal, J.U. (2007) *On Becoming a Consumer: The Development of Consumer Behavior Patterns in Childhood*. New York: Elsevier.

Moses, L.J. and Baldwin, D.A. (2005) 'What can the study of cognitive development reveal about children's ability to appreciate and cope with advertising?', *Journal of Public Policy and Marketing*, 24 (2): 186–201.

Nairn, A., Ormrod, J. and Bottomley, P. (2006) *Watching, Wanting and Wellbeing: Exploring the Links*. London: National Consumer Council.

Richins, M.L. and Dawson, S. (1992) 'A consumer values orientation for materialism and its measurement: scale development and validation', *Journal of Consumer Research*, 19: 303–316.

Robertson, T.S. and Rossiter, J.R. (1974) 'Children and commercial persuasion: An attribution theory analysis', *Journal of Consumer Research*, 1 (1): 13–20.

Roedder-John, D. (1999) 'Consumer socialization of children: a retrospective look at twenty-five years of research', *Journal of Consumer Research*, 26 (3): 183–213.

Selman, R.L. (1980) *The Growth of Interpersonal Understanding*. New York: Academic.

Young, B.M. (1990) *Television Advertising and Children*. Oxford: Oxford University Press.

Young, B.M. (2000) 'The child's understanding of promotional communication', *International Journal of Advertising and Marketing to Children*, 2 (3): 191–203.

Young, B.M. (2008) 'Media and advertising effects', in S.L. Calvert and B.J. Wilson (eds), *The Handbook of Children, Media and Development*. Oxford: Blackwell. Chapter 18: pp. 407–431.

Young, B.M., Webley, P., Hetherington, M. and Zeedyk, S. (1996) *The Role of Television Advertising in Children's Food Choice*. Report to the Ministry of Agriculture, Fisheries and Food (MAFF).

Notes

1 After some head-scratching a colleague suggested North Korea as an advertising free zone. A few minutes on the Web uncovered a sole billboard in Pyongyang advertising automobiles! (http://www.gadling.com/2007/12/16/infiltrating-north-korea-part-11-north-korean-style-advertising/Retrieved 5 March 2009).

2 *Teletubbies* is a children's programme on the BBC featuring four main characters – Tinky Winky, Dipsy, Laa-Laa and Po. See http://www.bbc.co.uk/cbeebies/teletubbies/

3 'Concrete' is used here to refer to things (and representations of them) that you can touch and see in contrast to 'abstract' ideas.

4 Children who do not question like this may be cognitively incapable or unwilling to do this for developmental reasons. But they can also be socialized this way – to be 'seen and not heard' is unfortunately often a strategy that ensures a quieter, safer life for many children. In addition some cultures encourage an independent, assertive style in children from an early age whereas others require children to be more compliant and obedient for many years of that period in the lifespan.

5 Knowing that there is a 'source of a communication' in an interpersonal encounter means that the receiver (e.g., the child who is listening to the parent) understands that that person has beliefs and intentions. Knowing that there is a 'source' behind an advertisement is similar – there is some agent out there whose intentions are getting you to buy the brand advertised. The child need not be aware of the detailed arrangements whereby ads appear in different places.

6 It is a truism to say that children perform differently at different ages: they usually get better at doing things as they grow up. Consequently, experimental psychology using children will sample different age groups as a matter of course in order to obtain significant differences and if a multivariate design is used with for example socio-economic status (SES) as another variable the dominant effect of age tends to 'drown out' the possible influence of SES.

7 In this sense advertising is advocatory. Adults know this and expect to hear only positive information about the brand.

8 Programmes 'of particular interest to children' were defined as those where the proportion of children in the audience was 20 per cent higher than their proportion in the available TV audience. Retrieved from http://www.ofcom.org.uk/research/tv/reports/update/briefing.pdf on 23 August 2009.

9 Although it is beyond the purpose of this chapter to review legislation on advertising to children in different countries, a useful source is the Advertising Education Forum (http://www.aeforum.org/) where different regulatory environments in different countries are described. The journal *Young Consumers* has a regular feature of advertising regulation concerning children in different countries.

10 'Shopping' is a notoriously slippery concept with various meanings. Obviously some children won't like going round the supermarket with mum or dad but will like the social side of going round the clothes shops with their friends on Saturday mornings.

11 This strap line was used by Marks and Spencer to promote their 'simply food' range of stores and proved to be a great success in 2008/09. A clever use of visual and spoken hyperbole hints at a slightly self-mocking irony which effectively seduces the more upmarket customers who would not always be influenced by the hard sell.

12 The 'tweenie' or 'tweenager' is a marketing creation and doesn't correspond with any of the main periods of development that Piaget identified. Ages are approximately 8 to 13 years and these children are pre-adolescent in the early stages of tween. This time of life has been identified as one when children face an onslaught of marketing specifically directed at them.

8 Children and Shopping

Julie Tinson and Clive Nancarrow

Chapter aims

- To consider the developments in studies on the shopping behaviour of children, in particular tweenagers (8 to 12 years old).
- To establish the perceptions by children (in particular tweenagers) and by the mother of the child's role and the influence on purchases for themselves and family purchases.
- To determine the strategies employed by parents to cope with their children's involvement in consumer purchase decisions.
- To explore children's shopping 'savvy', how this can be measured and different types of shopping 'know-how'.
- To develop avenues for future research in the area of children and shopping behaviour.

Vignette 1: The new pink pound

The tweenage magazine market is growing ever stronger on a diet of princesses, ponies, pals and puzzles. It's an unusual publishing story in the current climate – an expanding market and some outstanding successful new launches. Although the teen market is down and the pre-school market is static, pre-teen is very buoyant. 'Girl Talk' has been established for ten years and despite now competing with seven or eight other titles the market has simply expanded. Growth in this market has been fuelled as the tweenage market does not suffer from competing websites, mobiles and MSN. These online options are very much on the periphery for the 'Girl Talk' reader, as tweenagers are still governed by parents who do not want their children exposed to this medium.

Source: adapted from *Wignall* (2008)

Introduction

There is widespread interest in the child shopper as childhood habits will more than likely shape adult shopper behaviour. What is known about the child consumer is that children shop for much the same reasons adults do: convenience (economic) motives and recreational motives (Bellenger et al., 1977). Although the majority of studies on children and shopping focus on grocery trips (see, for example, Rust, 1993; Pettersson et al., 2004) or the role of *teenage* children (see, for example, Lee and Beatty, 2002), this chapter includes the findings of a number of studies that go beyond pester power and consider the negotiating and shopping skills that *tweenagers* display.

Tweenagers enjoy shopping and it is said that children in the UK have greater brand awareness but are less satisfied than US children with what they have to spend (Mayo, 2004). It is clear from Vignette 1 that tweenagers as a target audience display specific characteristics e.g., spend less time online than teenagers yet also seek entertainment and have a disposable income. Whilst tweenagers' 'income' may principally be sourced from other family members such as parents, older siblings and grandparents, their spending power and influence on spend are of considerable importance for marketers, policy makers and academics alike. 'Becoming' a consumer has already been explored in this text and as such the initial section of this chapter will focus on the role children play in individual and family decision-making purchases and in the latter section of the chapter the shopping 'savvy' skills needed and displayed for shopping will be addressed. The role of the child will be considered in relation to their age, family type and their shopping 'know-how' or savvy.

The role of children in shopping decision making

When examining purchase decision making in a household it is important to take into account who will become involved in the process. This will vary depending on the type of product being bought, the expectations of whom should be involved in the household for this type of purchase and what role or roles each should fulfil in different types of family structures (see, for example, Holdert and Antonides, 1997; Ahuja et al., 1998).

It is widely recognized that children are often involved in some aspect of family purchase decision making and it is thought that this involvement occurs at a younger age than in the past (Roedder-John, 1999). It has been reported that children are involved in both simple impulse purchasing as well as in more planned purchases (Kuhn and Eischen, 1997). Indeed, these two researchers argue that the child may in many cases be the primary instigator, decision maker, and shopper within the family. Whilst socio-economic changes may in part explain this decision-making role, it is likely that the consumption of brands is becoming more important for children as a way of expressing their personality to others as well as to themselves – a sort of self concept or ego-reinforcement. This was reported to be the case for tweenagers (8 to 11 year olds) regarding what they included in their school lunchboxes (Piacentini and Tinson, 2003).

A frequent basis for analysis for those in a family involved in decision making (taking account of the role and the degree of influence) is to examine these questions using three stages of decision making. These three stages comprise the initial stage of searching for information about the product category and/or brands, secondly the stage of discussion with regard to the options, and lastly the final decision or outcome stage. Of course, this presumes a new, non-routine and non-impulse purchase and when this is not the case the stages may collapse and post purchase dissonance management may also become relevant.

Previously, findings have consistently indicated that children are involved in and exert influence on the information search stage of decision making but not necessarily on the final outcome stage. Yet recent studies in New Zealand suggest that adolescents do become significantly more involved in the final stages of decision making and given the extent to which tweens are known to wield influence over family purchase decisions (Field, 2007) it is likely also that their level of involvement may have changed over time. This being so, future research needs to examine the role of adolescents and children given their growing involvement in family purchases at all stages of decision making (Lee and Beatty, 2002).

Shoham and Dalakas (2005) summarize a number of variables to explain children's influence on decision making. The degree of influence the child consumer has is likely to be related to the age of the child, parental attitudes towards advertising, the stage of decision making (search, discussion, etc.), the type of product or brand (whether it is only for the child's personal consumption or part of a wider family activity), and its importance in relation to peer group affiliation in particular. It is known that parental acquiescence in a shopping context escalates as the child's age increases and more recently mid/late teenagers have been identified as engaging in a 'consultancy' role for family holidays (Dunne, 1999). It has also been noted that children have greater influence, in some cases, in all stages of decision making, if the product is 'child-centred' rather than a family purchase (Shoham and Dalakas, 2003).

Kids growing older younger

There is a prevailing belief in youth marketing that young people are getting older younger (Geraci, 2005). This notion has been the thrust for much of the debate surrounding the children's marketplace in the last decade (Kurnit, 2004). In effect the youth market has changed, with the implication that tweenagers are the new teenagers in terms of mindset (e.g., desires, ideals and knowledge). However, what is not necessarily taken into account in the 'older younger' debate is that children develop along a number of dimensions. Evidence suggests that whilst tweens are developing more quickly cognitively and physically they are not inevitably progressing at the same rate emotionally or socially (Geraci, 2005). To that end, although the target audience for toy brands, for example, is very narrow and becoming narrower (Tutt, 2001), Kurnit's (2004) suggestion that children just want to be 'kids' can be very relevant for some tweens.

Children may be under the illusion that they are more involved in decision making than is actually case. Although the child may think that they have had a say in the final outcome it may be that the parents have already narrowed their choice and have allowed the child to choose the detail. That is, the parent/s could decide on the model of car and the child could be given the opportunity to choose the colour (see Ekström, Chapter 3 in this book). Erduran (1999) supports this theory by suggesting that there is a difference between making a decision to purchase a product and deciding on a brand. This was researched and supported by the work of Tinson and Nancarrow (2007) in the context of younger children. They established that tweenagers (10 to 12 year olds in their study) were less influential in the final stage of decision making than they considered themselves to be. It may be that the acronym KGOY (Kids Growing Older Younger) is not necessarily always true as suggested by Kurnit (2004) and that whilst the aspirations of tweenagers' involvement may increase their influence does not always match this.

Children's products versus family purchases

Tinson and Nancarrow (2007) also illustrated that both tweenagers and mothers report that there is a higher degree of involvement by children when *looking around* at choices and *having the most say* when buying casual clothes than is the case for a family holiday. This contrasts with the findings of Lee and Beatty (2002) who suggest that adolescents in New Zealand are as involved in the final stage of decision making for family purchases as they are in earlier stages. This may be as a consequence of the age, cognitive development, experience and 'savvy' (see later) of the adolescents in their sample.

Tinson et al. (2008) noted a growing significance of different family types in the West and explored the relationship between the complexity of family relationships typified in single parent, blended and intact families and the involvement of children in purchase decisions. This quantitative study considered children's products versus family products and indicated that there were a number of influences on the role children play in decision making.[1] In addition, whilst there are a number of ways to determine family 'type', including considering communication patterns within the family and parenting style, the Tinson et al. study categorized families by their family structure, namely single parent families, blended families (living with a step-parent and a natural parent) and intact families (children living with both their natural parents). It was found that family structure impacted on the say children have on purchases. For example, in the context of going on holiday children raised in blended families were more involved in *looking around* at options than children raised in intact households according to their mothers. Perhaps this was a token involvement that was more manageable than an actual involvement in the final decision. Interestingly, children raised in blended families were less often involved in *having a say* than children with single mothers, probably because of the number of family members which complicated the management of decision making.

Children and mothers from single households in the Tinson et al. study also agreed that their children *talked* a lot more about the best place to go for a holiday than children in other families. This could be because there are less people involved in the decision-making process, the single mum is dependent on the child and their opinion to a greater extent (as it may be no one else is available), because it is perhaps more important to 'get it right' (with possibly fewer resources/opportunities to recover the situation) or that there is the possibility of a holiday with an absent father that needs to be taken into consideration. This is true also of having the final say.

In terms of family purchases (computers for family use, a family car and various family outings for instance) Tinson et al. (2008) reported that children had a lower frequency of having the final say in a decision according to both mothers and children and that this was the case for all three family settings. However, the children reported their involvement was higher than those of their mothers. This supports the findings of Foxman et al. (1989) and Erduran (1999). As the Foxman et al. study considered adolescents as opposed to tweens it is interesting to note the similarity in perceived influence between adolescents in the late 1980s and tweenagers in the year 2008. There were no differences between family types in relation to these family purchases.

However, in terms of purchases for the child Tinson et al. (2008) reported that mothers from blended households claimed to allow their children to have the final say on sweets, drinks and comics/books to a greater extent than was the case for single mothers. This could be the mother in a blended family making an easy concession either out of feelings of guilt and/or because of the greater complexity of a blended household. This may have meant that it was easier to devolve some decision making – particularly where personal tastes were involved. Children's reports did not mirror the above differences, however. It is important to bear in mind that when considering the differing perceptions of two family members there are a number of possible explanations. This has been described as a Distortion of Interpersonal Perception (DIP) in Tinson and Nancarrow (2007). The DIP phenomenon includes posturing (inflating one's own importance), subtle persuasion (influencing the child without the child being aware of this – akin to 'hidden influence'), being out of the loop (not being aware of all the interactions of family members), and taking into account believed preferences (using experience to take other's believed views into consideration without discussion), and indeed all of these may partly explain the different perceptions of each others' involvement in family decision making. Managing expectations as well as interpersonal perceptions may require the parent(s) to employ strategies to minimize conflict and disruption in households. Given DIP may be relevant for some product categories as opposed to others, further research in this area would be useful.

Strategies to manage purchase decisions

While pester power has been explored in the literature (see, for example, Tylee, 1997; Spungin, 2004 and Ambler, 2007), few studies have examined the strategies employed by mothers and children when deciding on what to purchase and when. Tinson et al. (2008) illustrated a variety of different decision-making strategies (which could be considered as accommodating or consensual) employed within families to manage decision making and the family shopping culture. Of course some of these strategies can be used in parallel in the same family decision-making scenario. These strategies include: as a family discussing all the options until they all can agree on one; parents narrowing the options then allowing the child to choose from these; parents listening to the views of the child but making the final decision; and Mum simply tending to side with or cave in to the child. These can be seen in Vignette 2.

Vignette 2: Decision-making strategies to manage the shopping culture

- As a family all the options are discussed until one can be agreed on.
- Parents either overtly or covertly narrow down the options and allow the children to choose.
- Parents listen to the child's point of view but make the final decision.
- Mum tends to side with the child.
- Dad/Mum's partner tends to side with the child.
- Parent gives in if the child is very upset.
- Parent gives in if the child offers to do something in exchange.
- Parents would give in if the child begged or pleaded.
- Parents would give in if the child provided a logical reason.
- Parents listen to all points of view and jointly make the final decision.

Source: Tinson et al. (2008)

Tinson et al.'s findings illustrated when purchasing casual clothes there was a similar level of reporting from the mothers and children that the mothers sided with the child. However, the children did not seem to acknowledge the narrowing down of options by the parent(s) to the same extent as reported by their mothers. This is perhaps unsurprising as this may well be executed in such a subtle way that the child is simply unaware of the tactic or it may be that the choice is narrowed down to such an extent that the child feels all choice has been taken away – the choice they really wanted having been excluded – and therefore they would consider there to be no 'choice'.

Likewise mothers reported a very democratic process of consensus-seeking to a much greater extent than their children. Qualitatively they also recognized that involvement in family decision making has changed: 'When I was young, my parents made all the decisions but the kids are getting more of a say now'. Mothers were also more likely than children to report that they listened to their child's point of view but then made the final decision: 'They know when not to push that button ... when I have put my foot down ... then that's it ... but if they sense the slightest indecision ...'. Children and mothers broadly agreed on the degree of bartering with emotions or something in exchange which was relatively infrequent: 'The children will say "Muuuuum, ... you know we really love you" ... Sometimes it works sometimes it doesn't it ... Depends on what it is'. However, mothers reported the logical reasoning argument to be more successful to a greater extent than the children: 'I talk it through ... ultimately if we are still arguing over which to buy, I say alright we won't buy anything ... then they come to their senses ...'. On the other hand, children reported tantrums 'mostly' working to a greater degree than mothers.

Children were typically more inclined to think that all options were discussed until one was agreed upon but interestingly these strategies also differed by family type. In terms of children's perceptions, those raised in single households thought themselves to be more involved discussing all the options for casual clothes until everyone could agree. In terms of single parent mothers, however, this finding was not reflected in such an obvious way. The child possibly believed s/he was more involved in this way (and may have generalized from other situations in the household – a 'halo' effect). The mother of a blended family reported taking the democratic route slightly less often than occured in other families.

Given the leaning to the apparently more democratic route it may have been expected that single mothers were less likely than other mothers to report narrowing down the options and this was mirrored to some extent by their children. Single mothers also admitted more often that they were likely to succumb to pleading whilst mothers in blended families were least likely to give in. Perhaps single mothers were managing fewer emotional situations whilst blended mothers had to manage a more complicated family life and so could not afford to set a precedent.

Children raised in intact or traditional households claim if they did something in exchange the parents were more likely to give in (e.g., walk the dog, wash the car or tidy their bedroom). However, this difference was not supported by the reports from mothers. The mothers from intact/traditional family households may not have wanted others to think that their children had to 'work' for what they 'needed' or perhaps to know that the exchange often did not come to fruition. It may be that this offer of 'exchange' suggests that the child is more 'savvy' as s/he still manages to secure what it is s/he wanted without having to give anything in return.

Children's shopping savvy

In many societies consumption has become increasingly important, fulfilling functional as well as symbolic needs. As a consequence the media, schools, the family, peers and reference groups act more and more as socializing agents, helping children to deal with the consumer world and shopping. Children consequently are assumed, compared to earlier generations, to be more knowledgeable and strategically sophisticated in terms of shopping (having more 'shopping savvy') and so are also more likely to be invited to participate in purchase decisions (as suggested by Kuhn and Eischen, 1997) or, failing this, to express their unsolicited views more vociferously.

'Savvy' is an increasingly popular term applied to consumers by marketers and journalists. *Longman's Dictionary* defines savvy as 'practical know how' or in certain contexts being a 'shrewd judge'. This latter definition reflects the colloquial meaning of *consumer* savvy in a shopping context (Tinson and Nancarrow 2005; Brace et al., 2006) as opposed to *marketing* savvy[2] (Nancarrow et al., 2008).

The notion of consumer savvy runs counter to the traditional model of the passive consumer as a savvy consumer will bring past experience and knowledge from other sources to the marketers' 'touchpoints' such as communications, service, and so on, and in many situations will analyse, evaluate and form a decision on what is on offer based on what is perceived within this context. To gain more *consumer savvy* involves consumers moving from a basic awareness of and simplistic reactions to marketing per se towards a greater understanding and evaluation of marketing communications, products and services. This may lead consumers to become shrewder in their consumer behaviour though of course there may be barriers, for instance, a lack of money and no access or limited access to sources of information or distribution channels. In some cases there may even be a lack of interest and motivation to execute such savvy shopping and consumption. Consumer savvy can apply to both adults and children.

In recent years interest has been shown in the characteristics of the 'savvy' or the marketing literate consumer (see, for instance, Goodyear, 1991; Ritson and Elliot, 1999; Barker et al., 2002; Tinson and Nancarrow, 2005; Brace et al., 2006; Eagle, 2007). This includes interest in the degree of marketing sophistication in different cultures (Goodyear, 1991), the nature of media literacy (Ritson and Elliot, 1999), and whether consumers are gaining more savvy (Barker et al., 2002).

The development of intellectual skills (numeracy, verbal, reasoning, etc.) coupled with consumer socialization underpins the ability to behave in a savvy fashion. Consumer socialization has been the subject of a review by Roedder-John (1999), although the definition of the concept of savvy and a discussion of ways of measuring it have, for the most part, not been so thoroughly explored. Problems associated with the definition of intelligence are echoed in the psychology literature (Kline, 1991) and at some point there will be a need to explicate the various psychometric properties of shopping savvy in greater detail. Nancarrow et al. (2008) adopted the earlier 'working' definition (Tinson and Nancarrow, 2005) of being a 'shrewd judge' within a shopping environment or group culture. That is, the extent to which a child's or an adult's input into a purchase decision would be welcomed and possibly influential seems likely in part to rest on their perceived product knowledge and ability to evaluate different propositions and see through any hype, 'puffery' or spin, amongst other things.

Barker et al. (2002) examine the concept of consumer 'savvy', namely the degree to which consumers are 'more knowledgeable, more demanding, more confident, more powerful, more cynical, more sceptical'. However, the closest the topic of savvy has come to a thorough discussion of its definition has been in the attention paid to advertising literacy (Eagle, 2007). It is clear consumer savvy is relevant in a wider context than just advertising and it is consumer savvy that is discussed here.

Measuring consumer savvy

The authors have identified that there are three ways of measuring consumer savvy. That is, there is an objective measure, a surrogate measure, and a measure of perceived savvy by key informants. The first way of assessing consumer savvy in an individual is an *'objective' measure* equivalent to an intelligence quotient (IQ) test, but focused on a knowledge and understanding of consumer issues and a critical evaluation of communications and product choices. In the field of psychology there are over one hundred years of development of 'intelligence tests' from which we can learn. Realistically the development of objective measures of consumer savvy seems likely to be a long and demanding one, with new challenges such as ensuring the measures reflect the changing consumer environments. As is the case for IQ tests, the successful administration and marking of a literacy or consumer IQ test for children requires both time constraints and 'invigilators', as speed of thought, knowledge, the ability to evaluate and the prevention of 'cheating' are key factors. This is clearly not feasible in many commercial marketing research projects, particularly those involving self-completion question-naires (e.g., such as online or mail surveys). Nonetheless, it is necessary to develop an 'objective' measure to examine the relationship with other possible indicators or surrogate measures of savvy as described below.

A *surrogate measure* will be needed in many situations when 'objective' testing is not feasible, say, when self-completion questionnaires are used (e.g., online) and no interviewer is present to 'invigilate'. One possible sur-rogate measure is simply to ask respondents how savvy they think they are relative to the people they know. This is an approach that has been used to identify opinion leaders (see Flynn et al., 1996). With this measure one prob-lem that may arise is that asking respondents how intelligent they are might lead to posturing to a greater degree than would be the case for questions on early adoption and opinion leadership. Alternatively, there may be the reverse (an inverted snobbery response) of being dismissive of having an interest in shopping. Another possible surrogate measure is a declared involvement in different types of consumer behaviour on the basis that a greater involvement is likely to develop consumer savvy.

To develop the surrogate measure of savvy Tinson and Nancarrow (2005) examined existing measures of consumer activity, including the propensity to be an early adopter or an opinion shaper, and discussed these and the con-cept of savvy with marketing and marketing research experts and education-alists. Research was also conducted on parents and children, including open-ended questionnaires at ten schools (with space for drawing). Figure 8.1 depicts an illustration from one child who is trying to convey what a person would know if they knew a lot about shopping. For children, someone who 'knows about shopping' is likely to compare prices at a variety of shops, is likely to be female, will choose 'cool' items for purchase, will buy branded products and will watch adverts on TV. These comments reflected the views of what the adults thought would make their children 'savvy' (although the language used by the adults perhaps expressed in greater depth the notion of, for example, buying brands for durability and quality as well as for their symbolic value). Parents recognized that there were different types of savvy – 'Offers? Yes they are good at sorting these. BOGOF [Buy-one-get-one-free] is the one ...' – but that this 'savvy' could be selectively used: '[The children are] not good judges of value ... especially if it's something they want ...'. Cognitive development was also relevant: 'He looks at buy-one-get-one-free [BOGOF] ... understands this one ... others don't really regis-ter', as well as interpreting the advertising content: 'They do understand it's over-exaggerated and made up ... '.

This led to the development of a measure that included references to a child's involvement in various consumer-related activities, which in turn

Figure 8.1   A 'person' who 'knows' about shopping

Source: a boy aged 10

could also be translated by others in a family as an indication or degree of consumer savvy (Tinson and Nancarrow, 2005; Brace et al., 2006). Of course, it is quite possible that this measure might not reflect consumer savvy perfectly as it does not necessarily capture whether the accumulation of experience truly leads to learning.

Finally, from a social perspective, a relevant measure might be the *perception of how much consumer savvy a person has by key informants* (friends, colleagues, parents, etc.). As with the other measures, there are likely to be issues surrounding the accuracy of perceptions. With a child being judged by his/her mother there may also be a perceptual and response bias where other factors influence perceptions, such as pride in the child and perceptions of ability in other areas (e.g., schoolwork) being generalized to consumer savvy. Nonetheless, in terms of explaining purchase influence within a family for family products or products for others in the family it may be a very relevant measure.

Perceived savvy and shopping involvement

In a recent study by the authors (Tinson et al., 2009) perceived savvy was used to examine the shopping behaviour profiles of those children seen to be more savvy and those less savvy. To that end, 524 matched pairs of mothers and their children were asked how frequently they participated in various types of shopping activities and each was also asked independently about their involvement and influence in three phases of purchase decision making. This included considering a product for the child (casual clothes) and a shared product (a summer family holiday). Mothers were additionally asked how savvy their child was when it came to shopping in general and more specifically in the purchase of casual clothes or the choice of a family summer holiday. Over 50 per cent of mothers rated their child as extremely or very savvy when it came to shopping in general or for casual clothes for that child. However, when it came to a family purchase (e.g., a summer holiday) the number dropped significantly to just 22 per cent. Of course, a family summer holiday might in some cases have been hypothetical.

The children perceived to be more savvy claimed more often than their less savvy counterparts to be on the look out for bargains and were generally more involved in perusing catalogues, information online and new things or things no one else had. They were also more likely to go on shopping trips for their clothes. Interestingly, using the same frequency scale we asked how often the child's advice on a purchase was sought by the mother. It is evident from the findings that mothers were more inclined to seek advice from the more savvy children. Of course, the child's perception of involvement and influence might be misplaced or inaccurate so we analysed the same question with the mother's perception. This illustrated a remarkable consistency with the perceptions of children and indeed the more savvy child was clearly more involved and influential than his or her less savvy counterpart.

To this end, it is recognized that 'savvy' is not a one-dimensional concept. Children may have such 'savvy' in an economic sense (e.g., able to identify bargains or value items) or could be 'savvy' in relation to the symbolism attached to specific purchases (e.g., knowledgeable about fashion). Children may be 'savvy' in different contexts (e.g., girls may be more aware of fashion and boys may be more aware of technology). Understanding not only the degree of 'savvy' but also the way in which it is used will be an interesting avenue for future research.

Conclusion

This chapter sought to note developments in terms of children and tweenagers in particular as shoppers in the context of their role in purchase decision making comparing and contrasting family purchases and individual purchases. We also considered the development of the child consumer with specific regard to kids growing older younger (KGOY). Strategies employed by parents (and children) to manage purchase decisions were determined and the relevance of consumer 'savvy' and possible measures in relation to children were addressed.

The intention of this chapter was to move beyond studies on the retail (grocery) environment and pester power and to consider in greater depth the negotiating behaviour and shopping 'savvy' that tweenagers display. It has been established that an influence on individual and family purchase decision making is not simply age-related but that a number of factors, including family type, may determine the 'voice' of children in shopping decisions. Whilst tweenagers may consider themselves to have a significant influence on purchase decisions in the family, their perceptions often appear to be aspirational as opposed to the actual with specific relation to larger family purchases. Parent(s) and children do employ strategies to manage and/or influence shopping decisions, although not all of these strategies are successful for the child and parents and children will differ in their perceptions as to which ones work best.

Shopping skills have also been considered in the context of consumer 'savvy' or shopping 'know-how'. The different ways in which 'savvy' can be measured have also been summarized. Findings from a study using the surrogate savvy measure have been discussed and different types of savvy illustrated. The research detailed above generates an insight into the shopping skills and roles adopted by and ascribed to tweenagers. There are, however, ways in which these studies could be further developed.

Future research directions

Given the discussion above there appear to be four ways in which this research on children and their role and skills in shopping could be further explored.

Firstly, the Distortion of Interpersonal Perception (DIP) reported in Tinson and Nancarrow (2007) suggests that there are a number of reasons as to why children and their parents have different perceptions of purchase decision-making situations. Considering the DIP phenomenon in a variety of contexts may further explain the different perceptions of family members' involvement in family decision making.

Secondly, the research illustrated in this chapter shows that there are different types of influence and skills related to shopping behaviour and that these appear to be dependent on family type (e.g., single parent, blended and intact or traditional). Further work on different family types, their approach to communication and decision making and perhaps the Gender Role Orientation (GRO) and preference (ibid.) of both parents and children, may enhance our understanding of shopping decisions and facilitate a greater awareness of the way in which strategies are employed in different households to manage decisions and the shopping culture. By GRO we mean the expectations of and preferences for what is carried out by males and females in a household.

Thirdly, there is considerable work still to be conducted on the concept and measurement of savvy. An 'objective' measure of savvy equivalent to an intelligence quotient (IQ) test, but focused on a knowledge and under-standing of consumer issues and a critical evaluation of communications and product choices, needs to be developed. As in the field of psychology where there are over one hundred years of development of 'intelligence tests', realistically the development of objective measures of consumer savvy seems likely to be long and demanding with new challenges such as ensuring the measures reflect the changing consumer environments and different cultures.

Finally, the role that advertising plays in influencing young consumers (in addition to their influence on decision making and shopping behaviour) may generate both greater insight and a more holistic view of the shopping behaviour of children and how this is influenced by the media as well as by peers, parents and school. All of this needs further exploration.

Discussion questions

- To what extent are kids growing older younger (KGOY) in the context of shopping decision making?
- How might the changing family structure (and our understanding of what is meant by 'family') affect shopping decision making and behaviour?
- What different types of shopping savvy are there?
- Can you think of different types of communication approaches that would appeal to different types of 'savvy' consumers?
- What other strategies might be employed by parents or children when trying to manage decision making in relation to family and individual purchases?

Further reading

Beatty, S.E. and Talpade, S. (1994) 'Adolescent influence in family decision making: a replication with extension', *Journal of Consumer Research*, 21: 332–341.

Corfman, K.P. and Lehmann, D.R. (1987) 'Models of co-operative decision making and relative influence: an experimental influence of family purchase decisions', *Journal of Consumer Research*, 14: 1–13.

Claus Ebster, C., Wagner, U. and Neumueller, D. (2008) 'Children's influences on in-store purchases', *Journal of Retailing and Consumer Services*, 16(2): 145–154.

Flurry, L.A. and Veeck, A. (2009) 'Children's relative influence in family decision making in urban China', *Journal of Macromarketing*, 25(2): 145–159.

Rindfleisch, A., Burroughs, J.E. and Denton, F. (1997) 'Family structure, materialism, and compulsive consumption', *Journal of Consumer Research*, 23: 312–325.

Wilson, G. and Wood, K. (2004) 'The influence of children on parental purchases during supermarket shopping', *International Journal of Consumer Studies*, 28(4): 329–336.

References

Ambler, T. (2007) Response to 'International Food Advertising, Pester Power and Its Effects', *International Journal of Advertising*, 26 (2): 283–286.

Ahuja, R.D., Capella, L.M. and Taylor, R.D. (1998) 'Child influences, attitudinal and behavioural comparisons between single parent and dual parent households in grocery shopping decisions', *Journal of Marketing Theory and Practice*, Winter: 48–62.

Barker, A., Haynes, S. and Nancarrow, C. (2002) 'You are what you know: the savvy consumer, myth or fact?', *Market Research Society Conference Proceedings* (Brighton).

Bellenger, D.N., Robertson, D.H. and Greenberg, B.A. (1977) 'Shopping center patronage motives', *Journal of Retailing*, 53: 29–38.

Brace, I., Tinson, J. and Nancarrow, C. (2006) 'The family inheritance: are attitudes to advertising kept in the family?', *Market Research Society Annual Conference*, March, London.

Dunne, M. (1999) 'The role and influence of children in family holiday decision making', *International Journal of Advertising and Marketing to Children*, 1 (3): 181–191.

Eagle, L. (2007) 'Commercial media literacy', *Journal of Advertising*, 36 (2): 101–110.

Erduran, Y. (1999) 'Children are important consumers: a case study from a developing country: Turkey', *European Society for Opinion and Marketing Research Conference Proceedings*.

Field, K. (2007) 'Targeting tweens', *Chain Store Age*, 86.

Flynn, L.R., Goldsmith, R.E. and Eastman, J.K. (1996) 'Opinion leaders and opinion seekers: two new measurement scales', *Journal of the Academy of Marketing Science*, 24 (2): 137–147.

Foxman, E.R., Tansuhaj, P.S. and Ekstrom, K.M. (1989) 'Family members' perception of adolescents' influence in family decision making', *Journal of Consumer Research*, 15 (4): 482–492.

Geraci, J.C. (2005) 'Learning from youth marketers', *The School Administrator*, September: 22–26.

Goodyear, M. (1991) 'The five stages of advertising literacy: why different countries respond to different levels of ad sophistication', *Admap*, 26 (3): 19–21.

Holdert, F. and Antonides, G. (1997) 'Family type effects on household members' decision making', *Advances in Consumer Research*, 24. (Association for Consumer Research, Ann Arbor, MI, pp. 48–54.)

Kline, P. (1991) *Intelligence: The Psychometric View*. London: Routledge.

Kuhn, M. and Eischen, W. (1997) 'Leveraging the aptitude and ability of eight year-old adults: and other wonders of technology', *European Society for Opinion and Marketing Research Conference Proceedings*.

Kurnit, P. (2004) 'KGOY reconsidered: kids just want to be kids', *International Journal of Advertising & Marketing to Children*, 5: 19–24.

Lee, K.C.C. and Beatty, S.E. (2002) 'Family structure and influence in family decision making', *Journal of Consumer Marketing*, 19 (1): 24–41.

Mayo, E. (2004) 'Shopping generation', *Young Consumers*, 6 (4): 43–49.

Pettersson, A., Olsson, U. and Fjellstrom, C. (2004) 'Family life in grocery stores – a study of interaction between adults and children', *International Journal of Consumer Studies*, 28 (4): 317–328.

Piacentini, M. and Tinson, J. (2003) 'Understanding social influences on children's food choices', *European Association of Consumer Research* (EACR), Special Session on 'Children as Consumers', Dublin, June.

Ritson, M. and Elliot, R. (1999) 'The social uses of advertising: an ethnographic study of adolescent advertising audiences', *Journal of Consumer Research*, 26 (3): 260–277.

Roedder-John, D. (1999) 'Consumer socialization of children: a retrospective look at twenty-five years of research', *Journal of Consumer Research*, 26: 183–213.

Rust, L. (1993) 'How to reach children in stores: marketing tactics grounded in observational research', *Journal of Advertising Research*, (November/December): 67–72.

Shoham, A. and Dalakas, V. (2003) 'Family consumer decision making in Israel: the role of teens and parents', *Journal of Consumer Marketing*, 20 (3): 238–251.

Shoham, A. and Dalakas, V. (2005) 'He said, she said … they said: parents' and children's assessment of children's influence on family consumption decisions', *Journal of Consumer Marketing*, 22 (3): 152–160.

Spungin, P. (2004) 'Parent power, not pester power', *Young Consumers*, 5 (3): 37–40.

Tinson, J. and Nancarrow, C. (2005) 'The influence of children on purchases: the development of measures for gender role orientation and shopping savvy', *International Journal of Market Research*, 47 (1): 5–27.

Tinson, J. and Nancarrow, C. (2007) 'Growing up: tweenagers' involvement in family decision making', *Journal of Consumer Marketing*, 24 (3): 160–170.

Tinson, J., Nancarrow, C. and Brace, I. (2008) 'Purchase decision making and the increasing significance of family types', *Journal of Consumer Marketing*, 25 (1): 45–56.

Tinson, J., Nancarrow, C. and Brace, I. (2009) 'Profiling key purchase influencers: the consumer savvy', *Journal of Consumer Behaviour*, August.

Tutt, F. (2001) 'KGOY but can brand owners keep up?', *Brand Strategy*, November.

Tylee, J. (1997) 'Should advertising take 'pester power' seriously?', *Campaign*, 29 (11): 4.

UK Office of National Statistics (2007) *Social Trends*, 37. London: ONS.

Wignall, A. (2008) 'The new pink pound', *The Guardian*, 2 June.

Notes

1   Children's products versus family products were determined by qualitatively considering the relative level of involvement (high and low) with products and the number of people using the product, e.g., children's products included sweets,

soft drinks, fruit, and school shoes and family products included computers and holidays. The questionnaire specified 'for the child' or 'for the family' as opposed to assuming the respondents would hold the same view of child/family products.

2   *Marketing* versus *Consumer* savvy – there are two types of savvy. The first is a state of mind that questions the prevailing ideology i.e. a mind that questions capitalism and marketing per se and is sensitive to corporate and consumer social responsibility. We refer to this as being *marketing savvy*. The second type is a state of mind that accepts the way things are and simply tries to achieve the best outcome in a given shopping situation. This we term *consumer savvy*. Of course a consumer may switch from one to the other and *marketing savvy* may be part of the *consumer savvy* decision in some cases (choice of Green goods, Fair Trade, no animal cruelty involved etc.).

9 Children and Money

Christine Roland-Lévy

Chapter aims

- To compare the way in which children from different origins acquire their financial understanding.
- To trace the emergence of children as consumers and actors in the economic world.
- To identify both their impact on consumption and their role as independent consumers with a financial resource (pocket money).
- To identify how children learn about abstract economic concepts such as taxes, savings or credit.

Vignette 1: Pocket money given to children and teenagers in France

In France, 63 per cent of 11 year olds regularly receive pocket money. Up until this age money is normally provided on a weekly basis; after age 11 it is generally given monthly, which allows the child to learn how to budget the allowance. Parents who tend not to give pocket money represent 26 per cent of workers, 24 per cent of employees, 15 per cent of shopkeepers, and 13 per cent of white-collar parents. Pocket money is not provided in the same way according to the geographical area where one lives: in the most populated areas (100, 000 to 20,000 inhabitants) 31 per cent of the children receive pocket money on a regular basis, while in less populated towns (less than 20, 000 inhabitants) only 14 per cent receive pocket money; in most rural areas, as well as in the Paris area, 22 per cent and 23 per cent of the young people do not receive any pocket money. On average, an 11–14 year old in France receives about €20 per month, whereas a 15–17 year old gets on average around €50 per month.

Source: Boyer and Coridian, 2000; Le Bigot et al., 2004; Roland-Lévy, 2005

Introduction

What do children understand about their economic environment? How do they gain control over their economic conditions? Does understanding develop in the same order when the social, economic and political systems are radically different? These are some of the main questions that those interested in children's use of money and socialization might ask. The purpose of this chapter is to provide information about various studies related to these questions in terms of economic socialization. Economic socialization is a specific concept referring to the whole process by which a child will develop an understanding of the economic world. It is related to 'naive economics' – the economics of non-specialists. Even though children as well as many adults are 'naive' subjects, they are familiar with parts of the economic world and possess some knowledge and understanding of how it works. Economic socialization refers to the maturing child who is learning how to comprehend the world of adults.

This chapter looks at the development of economic socialization which is closely connected to receiving, or not having, pocket money on a regular basis (see the Vignette 1). In the chapter links between children and money are investigated, thus leading to the child as a consumer and actor in the economic world. It investigates both their impact on consumption and their role as independent consumers with financial resources. It also explores how children use and relate to money as a means to an end, and the way in which they acquire and manage their financial resources and learn about economic concepts through the practice of consumption (see de la Ville and Tartas, Chapter 2 in this book). As an opening, elements of the theoretical background of research in the field of economic socialization will be analysed. Some examples of specific themes in the economic world will be presented; among these, examples of studies on the understanding of issues around the topics of savings and taxation will be offered.

Why study economic socialization and pocket money?

If socialization is, as Zigler and Child wrote in 1968, 'a broad term for the whole process by which an individual develops, through transactions with other people, specific patterns of socially relevant behaviour and experience' (p. 455), then one might easily presume that in order to define economic socialization, it is necessary to include particular elements around the idea of exchange (see Chapter 2 this book). An economic way of defining potential transactions with other people would include specific ideas related to production, trading, or commerce. In this case, economic socialization covers the process by which individuals develop their competence in dealing with the economic world. This competence is gained through their experience of using money to purchase items, of negotiating exchanges (of any kind), as well as of persuading others to buy, exchange or sell a product. Such experience provides a better understanding of the need to budget; it develops the skills of negotiating and bargaining with others in connection to the economic world of production. This experience provides specific natural training which gradually develops skilful knowledge via an appropriate perception of economics, which in turn, little by little, constructs economic socialization. Economic socialization is concerned with the acquisition of the knowledge, skills, behaviour, opinions, attitudes and representations that are relevant to the economic world. An early understanding of the notions implicated in the economic world may, during adult life, help avoid some of the outcomes of credit use such as excessive levels of debt. In that sense, studying and understanding the mechanisms related to money and to the development of economic socialization are very useful.

Over the past fifty years there have been a number of studies concerned with the development of economic ideas and notions, along with their understanding, in children. Although the literature proposes various definitions of the main conceptual contents which are widely accepted, socialization refers to the problem of general education in any society, implying a process of interaction between children and their environment. Researchers tend to concentrate on children's understanding of specific topics (i.e., Berti and Bombi, 1988). More recently, there has also been a great deal of research concerning the influence, decision-making power and buying power of children, with this topic being related to the amount of pocket money they receive (cf. Roland-Lévy, 2005).

Different theoretical orientations

Two main theories dominate the field: the Piagetian developmental-cognitive approach and the environmental learning theory. Piaget proposes a transactional process which links children's cognitive stages to their experience of the world, emphasizing the primacy of children's actions in their development and maturation (Piaget, 1932, 1967/1947), while learning theory, based on behaviourism, stresses the effects of the environment on children's behaviour (Bandura, 1986). According to this second theory, a functional behaviour will be imitated because it previously appeared to be rewarding. As Youniss (1978) indicates, these two models are not really incompatible. The cognitive model is applied to the development of thinking processes while learning theory explains behaviour. Piaget's approach deals with the framework, while the behaviourists supply information concerning the content of socialization. The first model stresses intra-individual differences as the child grows up, while the second describes inter-individual variations among children of the same age. Both theories assume that contacts with social reality are necessary for the construction of a predictable pattern of behaviour.

For Piaget, the social evolution is very similar to the construction of intelligence. Each new step in the development of intelligence corresponds to a new phase in socialization. According to Piaget's theory, the basic units of intelligent behaviour are called 'schema'; schema are ways in which we try to organize and understand our experiences, they develop as a result of experience and are used as a basis for actions. New schema are formed and existing schema are developed by the processes of assimilation and accommodation. Assimilation is taking in pieces of information from the environment and reacting to them in the same way. In order to show how intelligence develops, Piaget (1932) proposed a transactional process called equilibration, which creates a balance between the cognitive level of a child at a specific moment of his/her evolution (stage) in relation with his/her experience of the environment: it allows their accommodation to a new situation.

In 1947, Piaget defined four main and distinct stages in the development of intelligence.

- The first stage, from birth to 2 years, is the sensory-motor stage. In this stage the child is egocentric, unable for a while to distinguish between him/herself and the rest of the world. By the end of this stage, they start to acquire what is called general symbolic function (e.g., they understand that a doll represents a person).
- The second stage, between 2 to 7 years old, he or she enters the phase of the pre-operational stage. During this phase, the symbolic thinking and language continue to develop. Piaget claimed that at this stage, the child couldn't yet see the point of view of another person. Until the child is able to de-centre, he or she is unable to classify objects in any logical way.
- At the age of 7 to11, the child should enter the stage of concrete operations. At this age, conservation is acquired (i.e., the child can now understand that the volume of something is the same, even if the shape changes). Operational thinking is now consolidated, but mainly if the object is concrete and physically present.
- When reaching the age of 11 to 12, and preadolescence, the child attains the fourth and final stage identified by Piaget which is the stage of formal operations. This stage implies that the logical thinking now allows solving problems related to various observations and situations. At this stage the child can use full adult reasoning and is capable of all forms of abstract thought. Deductive reasoning allows for a mastery of complex systems, such as science, mathematics or economics.

Piaget claimed that all children pass through these four stages in the same order but at different speeds. The notion of stages supposes that the child has reached a certain degree of maturation in order to allow these processes to occur and therefore to enter a new stage of cognitive development (see Young, Chapter 7 in this book, for a discussion of these ideas in relation to advertising).

The developmental-cognitive approach has been criticized when applied to economic socialization. Among the critiques, one can underline the fact that a child only encounters a few situations related to consumption and the economic world. On the other hand, Piaget's theory does not take into account individual variability, which is often related both to the individual's personality and to the cultural environment of the child. Therefore, the other interesting theory has also taken an interesting part in studying economic socialization, as it answers some of the critiques formed around Piaget's theory; it is known as the theory of social learning (Bandura, 1986). This theory focuses on the effect of the environment as a source of stimuli, implying that the specific behaviour of a child is going to be a response to the stimuli of his/her environment. In fact, the observed results of the behaviour of the child can be used, according to Bandura's theory, in order to produce new types of behaviour. If the outcome of the behaviour is rewarding the behaviour is reinforced, if the outcome results in a penalty the behaviour is weakened. In the case of economic socialization, money can be perceived as a powerful agent of reinforcement as it is often used as a reward. The act of saving, for example, will be reinforced if savings allow the child to acquire a specific object, which could not have been obtained without such saving. This specific type of conditioning supposes that the child has an active role in the world of consumption and economics.

How is the acquisition of notions and values approached?

By testing children of different ages corresponding to the stages defined by Piaget, authors, such as Leiser et al. (1990) can investigate the effects of these developmental stages on economic socialization. This type of study speculates that adults have a fully developed knowledge and understanding of the economic world. Authors such as Harrah and Friedman (1990) in the USA, Kirchler and Praher (1990) in Austria, or Wosinki and Pietras (1990) in Slovenia, have investigated children's understanding of buying and selling, as well as children's concepts of economic value of objects, by comparing children of different ages, such as 4 to 5 (pre-operational stage), 7 to 8 (stage of concrete operations), and 10 to 12 year old children (early beginning of the stage of formal operations). Studies, whether they refer to experiments, interviews or questionnaires, illustrate that in order to study abstract economic notions it is important to ask children to solve the kind of economic problems they are faced with in their everyday lives. In these cases, it seems necessary to put the child in a situation that might be meaningful; one of the best solutions is then the use of a combination of attractive materials which can, during the study, be manipulated by the child in order to help him/her express elements about notions which s/he already possesses. The second best option is to focus on how children understand and solve the economic problems they are faced with, rather than considering economic socialization as a steady process of adaptation to the economic behaviour and concepts of adults. This implies being more concerned with the child, and as Webley and Lea observed: 'only a determined effort of observation, empathy and imagination will enable us to enter children's own economic world and assess the relative importance of the events that happen in it' (1993: 466).

In combination with interviews, observation is also often used either as participant observation, as described in Willis (1977), or as direct observation of a child's behaviour in a particular environment. For example, Watiez (1987) observed children visiting small supermarkets in order to study their behaviour in a store. The observations were based on 'behaviour episodes' as a combination of actions or speech. At the end of their shopping excursion the children were interviewed about 'the different things that they found interesting in the supermarket'. Whereas, in most cases there are no gender differences in terms of economic knowledge, it is interesting to note that in this particular study girls seemed somewhat more knowledgeable in terms of product prices and qualities. One of the possible explanations for this arose from the observations of behaviour: girls seemed to be more 'at home' in stores than boys, and adopted a behaviour very similar to that of adults when shopping.

Another innovative study using observation was conducted in a school playground and involved observing children's games of marbles (Webley and Webley, 1990). Here the authors showed that children in a game reproduce the same economic behaviour as adults. In the playground, children appeared to have excellent economic thinking which was well adapted to their economic world; within this, it was possible to analyse how children could solve economic problems around complex rules in marble games, e.g., the value of each kind of marble, the importance of exchange, the role and the social position of a good player who can become 'rich' and acquire a high social status, as well as the one who is not so good and will have to 'work' in order to reimburse their debts, and so on. This can, potentially, be easily transferred to the real world of economics.

Differentiating factors

Not all children acquire the same knowledge and understanding of notions and the same types of values about money and other economic concepts at the same time. In fact, when investigating how children observe and perceive economic conditions, researchers tend to present their results in terms of differentiating factors such as age, gender, social class and cultural background.

- *Age* Most studies based on Piaget's theory remain descriptive and demonstrate that conformity and consistency increase as children get older. There are some significant differences according to age groups: the older the children are, the more abstract are the conceptions they seem to have of money.
- *Gender* Studies of economic thinking have found no fundamental differences between boys and girls. Gender differences do appear when dealing with economic knowledge: girls are sometimes more mature, as for example with topics related to buying and selling, and this may be explained, as in Lassarre and Roland-Lévy (1989), by the fact that girls still participate more in activities related to consumption such as shopping (see also Watiez, 1987).
- *Social class* One of the most frequently investigated factors in studies of economic knowledge is connected to the comparison of different social groups. These studies reveal that middle-class children are more familiar with banking vocabulary and professional prestige, while those who come from the working class seem to understand more about industrial relations. It should be emphasized that, in many cases, the observed differences cannot be directly related to the economic level of the family, but rather to the type of occupation or the educational background of the parents, especially the mother. For example, Jahoda (1981) found that children whose fathers were workers in large factories had a thorough knowledge and understanding of the world of manufacturing and production.
- *Social and cultural background* The last main differentiating factor seems to be the combination of the children's social and cultural background. It appears that children in each country have more or less the same knowledge and understanding of economic phenomena at approximately the same age, except when there are strong differences in terms of education, social class (see Vignette 2) and cultural backgrounds. In fact, where there are differences the social, economic and political situations of the countries should be taken into account. This is especially verified when comparing children from different countries. For example, French and Algerian children produce different answers to questions which clearly relate to their culture: in order to increase the amount of money they have, French children would 'invest the amount in a bank', whereas Algerian children – deeply influenced by the words of the Koran forbidding the practice of usury and interest – would say that they should 'work more'. Such findings illustrate the importance of collective cultural representation in the construction of knowledge and practices related to the economy (Roland-Lèvy, 1990).

Vignette 2: Using projective techniques to examine children's economic socialization

Occasionally, a projective approach is also utilized. For example, Lassarre and Roland-Lévy (1989) used pictures in a projective test concerning economic situations as part of a longer interview with children from different cultural communities (French, Portuguese, Algerian, Moroccan, and Antillean). Four hundred 11 to 12 year old children were shown four simple drawings: two of potential consumerism (a woman looking at a shop window, and a view of an open-air market), and two that present different employment situations (one male and

(Continued)

(Continued)

one female). For each scenario the children were asked to tell the story that the picture evoked and then expand on it. It was found that information acquired in the family was most important in the participants' discourse. Only 28 per cent of the children perceived a job situation in the picture of the two women while the majority of the French children perceived the women to have complementary roles, whereas children from other communities perceived the relationship to be a hierarchical one. But in both groups, the story appeared to be non-conflictive, and sometimes there was even a happy ending: 'She has been looking for a job and the lady behind the desk tells her that she has just got one for her'. Only 25 per cent of the children saw a job situation in the picture of the two men; a majority of those children were migrant children. Only the Portuguese children were quite prone to imagine a conflict: 'He didn't wash the stairs; his boss tells him he must find another job'. It appeared rather obvious that the family context *made* the children more or less sensitive to employment problems. This projective approach allowed the children to talk about themselves and their relations with the economic world, and thus demonstrated their capacity to describe complex situations in a very natural way.

Children's understanding of more abstract topics in the field of financial behaviour

This section looks at children's understanding of saving versus credit and taxes and taxation.

Savings versus credit

In this section the focus is on economic behaviour and how children solve the economic problems they are faced with in relation to savings and credit. In an attempt to examine the real economic behaviour of childhood, the new trend involves experimenters who organized a variety of creative and ingenious laboratory studies.

Webley et al. (1991) studied children in what they initially identified as a 'play-economy'. For example, in an experimental setting children (age 6 and 7) received money (in the form of tokens) and were put in a setting which consisted of different rooms in which they could either save their money in a bank or spend some – as little or as much as they wanted – on various activities. Some of the activities were free while others were not. Over a period of time the children had to find ways of spending as little money as possible, of saving some, in order to buy a toy that they wanted. Since then many authors have constructed other artificial economies for children, within which they can work and earn tokens which they can either save or spend (Sonuga-Barke and Webley, 1993). Abramovitch et al. (1991) also organized a laboratory experiment with children aged 6, 8 and 10; this study dealt with differences in children's behaviour toward money, especially credit versus cash. The children received $4 either in cash or in the form of a credit card to spend in an experimental toy store; what they did not spend in the store could be taken home. The observers noted what they did, how much they spent, what they spent it on, and so on. The results showed that the children who did not ordinarily receive pocket money spent more than those who were given a regular allowance.

In all these studies, the general conclusion shows a clear link between knowledge of economic notions and the regular use of money. The results demonstrate that the children who did not ordinarily receive pocket money knew less about the making of a budget, involving credit and savings, as well as about all related notions, including the bank, than those who were given a regular allowance.

Taxes and taxation: the understanding of issues around taxation

Children's understanding of taxation is an interesting topic when studying children and money (see Vignette 3). Taxation is related to money but is not directly connected to the world of children themselves since they do not, in principle, pay taxes! Researchers looked at taxation with children aged between 8 and 14 years old from a number of countries, included in a special issue on economic socialization in the *Journal of Economic Psychology* (Leiser et al., 1990).

Lyck (1990), who interviewed Danish children, found that 11 per cent of 8 year olds, 30 per cent of 12 year olds, 86 per cent of 14 year olds and all the parents interviewed understood the concept of tax. Almost all of the small children thought 'tax' always meant 'treasure', and some 'favourite things'. Older children explained that it was connected to rent or other expenses. Among the few children with a knowledge of taxes, an overwhelming majority found tax rate reductions to be bad because less public goods would be available.

Among Austrian children, from the same three age groups, one third thought that abolishing all taxes would not be a good thing. Some of the older children (aged 14) were especially aware of the utility of taxes and said that abolishing them would either be negative or would lead to both negative and positive consequences. Older children were also able to discuss the problem from both the individuals' and from the state's point of view, whereas young children identified with the isolated citizen. Taxes appear to be a complicated abstract topic, thus it is not surprising that half of the young children were unable to answer this question. Over one third said that abolishing taxes would be good (Kirchler and Praher, 1990).

In America, 56 per cent of 8 year olds did not know what would happen if there were no taxes, while 44 per cent thought that it would be a positive decision. In the 11 year old group, one fifth of the children did not know, while almost half believed that it would be good for people not to pay taxes, and one third agreed that it would have some negative consequences for the country. Most of the 14 year olds (60 per cent) agreed with this last response, while one third were aware of both the positive and negative aspects involved in not paying taxes (Harrah and Friedman, 1990).

Wosinski and Pietras (1990) found Polish girls tended to have less knowledge and understanding about taxes and their purposes. When asked about the economic consequences of tax abolition, none of the girls, and only one quarter of the boys, from the youngest age group was able to give an answer. The remaining boys pointed out both positive consequences (people would have more money: 33 per cent), as well as negative consequences of tax abolition (e.g., fewer public services: 40 per cent). The middle group also thought about positive (33 per cent) as well as negative (35 per cent) consequences of tax abolition. In addition, they pointed out some disadvantages for the government and for the whole nation (59 per cent). Similar explanations were found among 37 per cent of the older children. Additionally, 43 per cent of the 14 year old subjects mentioned positive but short-term consequences, such as the abolition of tax for people.

Zabukovec and Polic (1990), who analysed data from Slovenian children, also observed that knowledge about taxes was very poor for the two youngest groups (over half of the 7 to 8 year olds and 10 to 11 year olds responded with 'don't know' answers). Even for the oldest group (age 14) the problem was not quite clear. Children from all groups produced answers around this topic, but these answers were diverse and not in any way precise.

Vignette 3: Researching economic socialization in children

In order to study all the different aspects of the socialization of the child, investigations are frequently carried out with different kinds of semi-structured interviews. This technique is very convenient for young children, especially for those under 10 or 11; in this study, interviews were conducted in schools and each child was interviewed individually for about half an hour, allowing enough time for the children to discuss and explain different concepts in their own words. The project, which was conducted in many different countries with children from different age groups, included one question (out of 20) on the purpose of taxes. The formulation of the question was as follows. 'What would happen if there were no taxes?' The answers were coded according to the following options: (a) Don't know; (b) Good, people would have more money; (c) Bad, no public services; and (d) Aware of both positive and negative aspects. From this question on the topic of taxation, some contrast among the children from different countries emerged.

Source: Leiser et al., 1990

During the same period, the responses of comparable groups of 8 and 11 year old Algerian and French children were analysed. It appears that the French children understand slightly better the purpose of taxes, and they have a more mature economic reasoning on this topic, since 30 per cent of them pointed out both aspects: 'It is good for the individual but it will have some horrible consequences for the country'. The results highlighted interesting cultural differences: for example, the comparison of French and Algerian children showed that the latter have a better understanding of prices, monetary exchanges and the general economic mechanism of production and profit, as well as of their social-economic system – particularly of their government's role in the problem of employment versus unemployment. On the other hand, French children more often fail to answer the questions, but when they do answer they give a wider range of responses. They seem to have a better understanding and ability to reason about the purpose of taxes, seeing them both from the point of view of the individual and from that of society (Roland-Lévy, 1990).

These findings demonstrate that, when comparing different age groups, the older the children are, the more precise and accurate their knowledge is about abstract notions related to the economy. The second interesting result is that this gradual evolution of the knowledge also varies according to the general environment of the children, including social, political and economic contexts. In the last example, the differentiating factor, which appears to be most important, was based on the culture and religion of the children.

Conclusion

In today's research context, two fundamental theoretical orientations constitute the basis of research in the field of economic socialization: the analysis either centres on children's understanding of the economic world of grown-ups (e.g., on the topic of children's understanding of taxation various authors, when studying children and money, include taxation which is related with money but is not directly connected to the world of children themselves), or on how children solve the economic problems of their own world (cf.

Webley, 1986; Roland-Lévy, 1998). Webley and Lea (1993) argue that research in economic socialization is unsatisfactory when it adopts an adult-centred view of the economic world. These authors believe that researchers should be more concerned with the real economic world of childhood and suggest several lines of investigation focusing on how children solve the economic problems that face them. With that aspect in mind, they provided stimulating ways of dealing with the question via what is described as a 'play-economy' (Webley, 1986; Webley and Webley, 1990; Webley et al., 1991; Sonuga-Barke and Webley, 1993). In fact, we agree that more studies should take that direction in order to better understand how children can really apprehend and resolve economic problems of their own world (e.g., in the playground with marbles). Later this will also allow us to better grasp an understanding of the economic world of adults.

Direct consumption is only possible for those who have pocket money and this allows them to be active in handling money and to have a better understanding of the roles and functions of money. We would like to suggest that both parents and teachers try to introduce a more systematic education oriented towards a better understanding of money in the economic world. A good way of assuring an early economic education is via the introduction of pocket money, given on a regular basis and starting early in childhood; this money-giving should be accompanied by regular discussions about what it stands for, how it is earned, how it can be saved in order to accumulate and later buy something more expensive, how money can be borrowed, and particularly the consequences of borrowing money (Roland-Lévy, 1994). Lautrey (1980) has shown that a consistency between the parents' educative behaviour and the cognitive structures expected in schools is very important. He demonstrated that parents' educational style directly influences the quantity, type, and diversity of economic information known by children; this is reinforced by the sound effect of informal socialization through discussions about, for example, the family's consumption habits.

In conclusion we should stress the fact that not all children will possess the same notions or attitudes towards money at one specific time throughout the world. The more direct experience children have with money, the better they understand its use, the advantages of saving, the necessity of budgeting, and so on.

Future research directions

Children have to acquire the appropriate consumer-related skills, behaviour orientations, knowledge and attitudes to participate effectively in the adult marketplace. Pre-adult consumer socialization is also necessary for children to deal with practical problems in their childhood market. Research on consumer socialization has been carried out mainly from a psychological or a marketing perspective. Both approaches have inherent faults in terms of their ability to provide a full picture of children's consumer socialization, particularly with respect to children's cultural milieu (Cram and Ng, 2007).

Even though the two major developmental theories, the Piagetian developmental-cognitive approach and the environmental learning theory (Bandura), are still often used in the context of the study of consumer socialization and money, the field of economic socialization is today taking a new direction with more studies focusing on the influence of parents' lay conceptions of the economy and on the links between social representations of economic phenomena and economic behaviour (Roland-Lévy, 2002). It is now clear that several variables are important in differentiating the degree of understanding of economic concepts among children. Among these, one should note the differences based on the political and economic contexts, as Fülöp (1999) showed when comparing the perception of competition with students from Japan, Hungary and the USA. Culture, specific religious backgrounds and local social diversity are also important, such as Roland-Lévy (1990) showed in her cross-national comparison of Algerian and French children's economic socialization. In this study, French and Algerian children produced different answers to questions which clearly related to their culture. Such findings illustrate the importance of collective cultural representation in the construction of knowledge and practices related to the economy. Other studies, such as Ng (1983, 1985) have shown, for example, that the extreme maturity of Hong Kong children in terms of money, profit and banks, when compared to New Zealanders for example, is due to the specific environment in which consumption and economy represent essential values. In conclusion, more intercultural comparative studies should be carried out on economic socialization in order to better understand the differences among children from different socio-economic and political environments.

Discussion questions

1 What do you understand by the term economic socialization and what are the main challenges facing researchers working in this area of children's consumption?
2 Discuss the two main theoretical approaches to understanding children's economic socialization.
3 To what extent do you believe children are 'naïve' in relation to financial matters?

Further reading

Berti, A.E. and Bombi, A.S. (1981) 'The development of the concept of money and its value: a longitudinal analysis', *Child Development*, 52(4): 1179–82.

Dickins, D. and Ferguson, V. (1957) 'Practices and attitudes of rural white children concerning money', *Technical Support*, 43. Mississippi State College.

Furnham, A. and Argyle, M. (1998) *The Psychology of Money*. London: Routledge.

Godfrey, N. (1996) *A Penny Saved*. New York: Fireside.

Lewis, A. (1982) *The Psychology of Taxation*. Oxford: Martin Robertson.

Strauss, A. (1952) 'The development and transformation of monetary meaning in the child', *American Sociological Review*, 17: 275–286.

Takahashi, K. and Hatano, G. (1989) 'Conceptions of the bank: a developmental study', *JCSS Technical Report*, 11.

References

Abramovitch, R., Freedman, J.L. and Pliner, P. (1991) 'Children and money: getting an allowance, credit versus cash, and knowledge of pricing', *Journal of Economic Psychology*, 12 (1): 27–45.

Bandura, A. (1986) *Social Foundations of Thought and Action: A Social Cognitive Theory*. Englewood Cliffs, NJ: Prentice-Hall.

Berti, A.E. and Bombi, A.S. (1988) *The Child's Construction of Economics*. Cambridge: Cambridge University Press.

Boyer, R. and Coridian, C. (eds) (2000) *Modes de vie des collégiens et lycéens*. Paris: INRP.

Cram, F. and Ng, S.H. (2007) 'Consumer socialisation', *Applied Psychology*, 48 (3): 297–312.

Fülöp, M. (1999) 'Students' perception of the role of competition in their respective countries: Hungary, Japan, USA', in A. Ross (ed.), *Young Citizens in Europe*. London: University of North London. pp. 195–219.

Harrah, J. and Friedman, M. (1990) 'Economic socialization in children in a mid-western American community', *Journal of Economic Psychology*, 11 (4): 495–513.

Jahoda, G. (1979) 'The construction of economic reality by some Glaswegian children', *European Journal of Social Psychology*, 9 (2): 115–127.

Jahoda, G. (1981) 'The development of thinking about economic institutions: the bank', *Cahiers de Psychologic Cognitive*, 1: 55–73.

Kirchler, E. and Praher, D. (1990) 'Austrian children's economic socialization: age differences', *Journal of Economic Psychology*, 11 (4): 483–494.

Lassarre, D. and Roland-Lévy, C. (1989) 'Understanding children's economic socialization', in K.G. Grunert and F. Olander (eds), *Understanding Economic Behavior*. Dorecht: Kluwer Academic.

Lautrey, J. (1980) *Classe sociale, milieu familial, et intelligence*. Paris: PUF.

Le Bigot, J.-Y., Lott-Vernet, C. and Porton-Deterne, I. (2004) *Vive les 11–25 ans*. Paris: Editions d'Organisation, Eyrolles.

Leiser, D., Roland-Lévy, C. and Sevòn, G. (eds) (1990) Special issue on Economic Socialisation, *Journal of Economic Psychology*, 11 (4): 467–468.

Lyck, L. (1990) 'Danish children's and their parents' economic understanding, reasoning and attitudes', *Journal of Economic Psychology*, 11 (4): 583–590.

Ng, S. (1983) 'Children's ideas about the bank and shop profit', *Journal of Economic Psychology*, 4 (3): 209–221.

Ng, S. (1985) 'Children's ideas about the bank: a New Zealand replication', *European Journal of Social Psychology*, 15 (1): 121–123.

Piaget, J. (1932) *Le jugement moral chez l'enfant*. Alcan.

Piaget, J. (1967/1947) *La psychologie de l'intelligence*. Paris: Colin.

Roland-Lévy, C. (1990) 'A cross-national comparison of Algerian and French children's economic socialisation', *Journal of Economic Psychology*, 11 (4): 567–581.

Roland-Lévy, C. (1994) 'Savings and debts: the impact of the family structure on the processes of money management', in *Integrating Views on Economic Behavior*, Rotterdam, The Netherlands (Abstract, p. 580).

Roland-Lévy, C. (1998) 'Economic socialization', in P.E. Earl and S. Kemp (eds), *The Elgar Companion to Consumer Research and Economic Psychology*. Cheltenham: Edward Elgar. pp. 174–181.

Roland-Lévy, C. (2002) 'Economic socialisation: how does one develop an understanding of the economic world?', in M. Hutchings, M. Fulop and A-M. van Den Dries (eds), *Young People's Understanding of Economic Issues in Europe* (CiCe Series: *European Issues in Children's Identity and Citizenship*, vol. 2, Trentham Books, UK) pp. 17–30.

Roland-Lévy, C. (2005) 'L'argent de poche comme révélateur du processus de socialisation de l'enfant consommateur', in V.-I. de La Ville (ed.), *L'enfant consommateur: Variations interdisciplinaires sur l'enfant et le marché*. Paris: Vuibert. pp. 51–71.

Sonuga-Barke, E.J.S. and Webley, P. (1993) *Children's Saving: A Study in the Development of Economic Behaviour*. Hillsdale, NJ: Erlbaum.

Watiez, M. (1987) 'Comportements économiques sur les lieux de vente: observations et questionnaires dans des supermarchés', in D. Lassarre (ed.), *Éducation du jeune consommateur*. Université René Descartes, Laboratoire de Psychologie sociale. pp. 57–88.

Webley, P. (1986) 'Playing the market: the autonomous economic world of children', in P. Lunt and A. Furnham (eds), *Economic Socialization*. Cheltenham: Edward Elgar. pp. 149–161.

Webley, P. and Lea, S.E.G. (1993) 'Towards a more realistic psychology of economic socialisation', *Journal of Economic Psychology*, 14 (3): 461–472.

Webley, P., Levine, R.M. and Lewis, A. (1991) 'A study in economic psychology: children's saving in a play economy', *Human Relations*, 44 (2): 121–146.

Webley, P., Robben, H., Elffers, H. and Hessey, D. (1991) *Tax Evasion: An Experimental Approach*. Cambridge: Cambridge University Press.

Webley, P. and Webley, E. (1990) 'The playground economy', in P. Webley and S.E.G. Lea (eds), *Applied Economic Psychology in the 1990s*. Exeter: Washington Singer.

Willis, P. (1977) *Learning to Labour: How Working Class Kids Get Working Class Jobs*. London: Saxon House.

Wosinki, M. and Pietras, M. (1990) 'Economic socialization of Polish children in different macro-economic conditions', *Journal of Economic Psychology*, 11 (4): 515–529.

Youniss, J. (1978) 'The nature of social development: A conceptual discussion of cognition discussion of cognition', in H. McGurk (ed.), *Issues in Childhood Social Development*. London: Methuen.

Zabukovec, V. and Polic, M. (1990) 'Yugoslavian children in a situation of rapid economic changes', *Journal of Economic Psychology*, 11 (4): 529–543.

Zigler, B. and Child, I. (1968) 'Socialization', in G. Lindzey and E. Aronson (eds), *Handbook of Social Psychology* (vol. 3) (2nd edition). Reading, MA: Addison-Wesley. pp. 450–555.

Part III
Kids' Stuff

10 Children and Food

David Marshall and Stephanie O'Donohoe

Chapter aims

- To trace the emergence of a distinct children's food culture.
- To identify growing concerns over children's diet and the role of marketing and promotion in shaping children's food preferences.
- To explore family socialization issues surrounding children's food consumption.
- To incorporate children's own perspectives and accounts into debates about food marketing.
- To identify emerging issues and suggest future research directions in the area of children's food marketing and consumption.

Vignette 1: A child's daily intake …

In this extract the author highlights the emergence of a children's food culture that is separate from that of adults and populated by highly processed foods. She argues for the need to socialize children into good eating habits by introducing them to adult eating patterns and a wide range of tastes from an early age.

… might start with a bowl of highly refined cereal stuck together with sugar in one form or another, followed by a sweet drink and a packet of crisps for morning snack. Chips and custard might be the most popular canteen choice at lunchtime, or a protein and fat-based, vegetable-free sandwich in the lunchbox, accompanied by sweets, a token apple (if you're lucky) and often yet another packet of crisps. In the starving after-school interval, biscuits and more crisps fill the gap until the 'children's teatime', when out come frozen Kievs, fish fingers, pizzas and burgers, destined to be scoffed with chips and copious

(Cont'd)

amounts of ketchup and washed down by something sweet and fizzy. For pudding there's the sickly-sweet 'kiddie' yogurt with its lovable cartoon characters and child friendly synthetic flavours. Not surprisingly, by bedtime they're hungry again and it's time for supper. That packet of cereal beckons once more, as do the biscuits.

Source: Blythman (2005: xi)

Introduction

Food marketers have clearly noticed the value of the children's market and developed distinctive market offerings for this segment. The 'Big Five' children's food products – fast food, pre-sugared breakfast cereals, crisps and savoury snacks, soft drinks and confectionary are a regular feature of many children's diets (see Vignette 1). Blythman's concern over the emergence of a distinct category of 'children's foods' and the growing chasm between what children and adults eat revolves around the promotion and marketing of food – much of it high in fat, salt and sugar (HFSS), which has significant health implications. Such concerns sit within a wider debate about children's food habits and obesity in many developed economies and are often based on a view of children as vulnerable to manipulation by unscrupulous marketers. In this chapter we examine growing concerns about childhood obesity and look at the emergence of a distinct children's food culture, aided by a range of child-targeted marketing practices. We argue, however, that these issues must be considered in the context of family socialization, eating practices and routines, as well as children's own perspectives as food consumers.

Children's food and the obesogenic environment

Although children's increasingly sedentary lifestyles receive some of the blame for what has been termed their 'obesogenic' environment, food marketers have been accused of contributing to it by cultivating young consumers. They are lambasted for promoting 'energy-dense, low-nutrient food and beverages', such as the Big Five listed above, and encouraging children to pester their parents to buy these items (WHO, 2006). In 2002, concerns about food marketing in Britain reached a new level with the publication of the Government Chief Medical Officer's report of increasing child obesity levels. This led to the Food Standards Authority commissioning a systematic review of international studies on food promotion to children (Hastings et al., 2003: 13), which concluded that:

1   There is a lot of food advertising to children.
2   The advertised diet is less healthy than the recommended one.
3   Children enjoy and engage with food promotion.
4   Food promotion is having an effect, particularly on children's preferences, purchase behaviour and consumption.
5   This effect is independent of other factors and operates at both a brand and category level.

In response to these reports, the British Government required Ofcom, the communications regulator, to tighten the code for HFSS food advertising to children and to commission a nutrient profiling model so that advertising for these foods could be identified. Such regulatory activity was given extra impetus by the broader moral panic surrounding children's diets, and this in turn was fed by media interventions such as the TV series *Jamie's School Dinners*, documenting celebrity chef Jamie Oliver's battle against unhealthy school meals. During this time, Ofcom engaged in a major programme of consultation and research itself. Although the evidence it gathered indicated a small *direct* effect of food advertising on children's preferences, concerns about the potential *indirect* effects led to a ban in 2007 on the television advertising of HFSS foods targeting children under 16 years old (Ofcom, 2007).

Ofcom's measures were more draconian than anticipated, particularly since they applied to under 16 year olds rather than under 12 year olds, but even so critics argued that children were still exposed to HFSS food advertising as well as a host of other marketing 'tricks' and 'ploys'. Various organizations have published 'exposés' of promotional practices, such as featuring licensed cartoon, television and movie characters on packaging, developing campaigns for mobile phones, creating dedicated websites and video games, and sponsoring events or tourist attractions suitable for children (*Which?*, 2006). Perhaps one of the best known tactics is positioning confectionary at supermarket checkouts, a practice abandoned by several retailers but still evident in stores operated by some of the market leaders.

There is incontrovertible evidence that childhood obesity is increasing in much of the developed world (WHO, 2006), and a widespread belief that this is related to children's increasingly sedentary lifestyles and diets favouring high-energy foods as part of a 'fast food culture'. The moral panic surrounding sedentary lifestyles and fast food can be understood in the broader context of the risk society, leading Kline (2005) to argue that children must be educated about the role of marketing in their lives and the long-term risks associated with their consumer choices. One prominent theme in food marketing to children concerns food as fun, and this is discussed in the following section.

Children's (fun) food culture

Fun has long been part of children's food culture as is evident in the marketing of sweets and confectionery. How children talk about sweets reveals some of the distinct boundaries between child and adult worlds. For example, children in the north of England call the sweets they buy themselves 'kets', a term that translates as 'rubbish' for adults and reflects the difference between adult and child perceptions (James, 1982). Products with names like 'jelly babies', 'white mice', 'gobstoppers', 'sherbert dib dab' and 'winders' playfully challenge adult notions of what is edible. Confectionery is not food in the adult sense; if anything it is anti-adult, a rebellion against the dull restrictive world of adults with their rules about 'proper eating' and 'nutritional correctness'. The pleasures and independence offered by sweets should not be overlooked or devalued, even as we seek to protect children from (nutritional) harm. As Richardson (2005) argues, far from being 'empty' the calories derived from sweets are actually full of fun.

While the world of sweets and confectionery is seen as distinctly childlike, this fun theme has spread across a wide range of food categories (the *cereal-ization* trend), and includes provisions for special occasions such as birthday parties (the *deseasonalization* trend) (Elliott, 2005, 2008). The use of vibrant primary colours – greens, reds, blues and yellows – and graphics with anthropomorphized characters, cartoons and pictures of children (many engaged in some physical activity) are used in packaging that emphasizes this fun theme. Reinforcing the idea of food as edible entertainment brings with it some creative and 'unique' product descriptions emphasizing its interactive or transformative qualities and food that can be stretched, stacked, peeled, shredded, and, of course consumed on the go (see Vignette 2).

Vignette 2: Fun foods

Food manufacturers are targeting children with an increasing range of strangely named products that emphasize fun. Consider the following examples from Canada.

- Heinz E-Z Squirt Stellar Blue ketchup or Heinz E-Z Squirt Funky Purple ketchup.
- Parkay's Shocking Pink Fun Squeeze margarine.
- Kellogg's Mickey's Magix cereal (which 'magically' turns milk blue).
- Quaker Oats' Dinosaur Eggs oatmeal (in which dinosaur eggs 'hatch' with the addition of hot water) or Quaker Oats' Treasure Hunt oatmeal (whereby the 'treasure chest' melts into green, red and gold coins when hot water is added).
- Saputo's Cheese Heads Play Cheese Snacks.
- Ore-Ida's Funky Fries (coloured Kool Blue).
- Yoplait Yumsters or Yoplait Go-GURT.
- Kraft Macaroni & Cheese *Sponge Bob Square Pants*; Kraft Macaroni & Cheese *Scooby Doo*; or Kraft's *Blue's Clues* Macaroni and Cheese (with blue colured paw prints).
- Mott's *Blue's Clues* Berry Flavored Apple Sauce (tinted blue).

- Kool-Aid Magic Twists Switchin' Secret (which turns into 'a secret color and flavor').
- Frito Lay's Mystery Colorz Snack Cheetos (which 'dye' consumers' tongues either blue or green).
- Pepperidge Farm's rainbow-coloured Goldfish.

Source: Published in the *Journal of Family and Consumer Sciences Education*, 23(1) (Spring/ Summer): 48–49. National Association of Teacher Educators for Family and Consumer Sciences (NATEFACS), an affiliate of Association of Career and Technical Education.

Such practices are clearly not unique to North America. Ever since McDonald's test-marketed Happy Meals in 1977, children's packs have become a staple in fast food restaurants around the world; these typically feature toys (often part of a collectible range tied in to popular children's films or TV series) alongside food and a drink, presented in a fun-themed box. British marketers use packaging adorned with games and linked to interactive websites in an attempt to build 'play value' into a wide range of food brands (BHF, 2008). In Italy, De Iulio and Diasio (2006) have examined the appeal of *Kinder Sopresa* (Kinder Surprise), a thin milk chocolate egg encasing a self-assembly toy. They argue that fun food has become such an integral part of children's everyday diet, rewarding and reinforcing good behaviour, that its nutritional value becomes almost insignificant. Although the food industry sees this as a legitimate way of adding value, others have expressed concerns about how marketing food as fun increases children's demand for heavily promoted food brands which are overwhelmingly HFSS products. Furthermore, framing children's food primarily in terms of entertainment may distort their relationship with food, with potential long-term health consequences.

Family socialization and negotiated choice

As Ward (1974) discusses in detail, children acquire the skills, knowledge and attitudes that allow them to function as consumers in the marketplace through a process of socialization. Family socialization occurs partly through direct communication and deliberate training, and partly by a process of osmosis, whereby children observe and imitate other family members from an early age. Since children come to like what is familiar, their food preferences and acceptance will reflect the food environment that they are exposed to when young. In many households, parents (particularly mothers) act as gatekeepers, determining what food is 'allowed' inside and outside the home (Davis and White, 2006; Hughner and Maher, 2006). Children also pick up important cues about food from how their parents and other family members talk about and endorse particular practices, such as dieting or finishing everything on the plate. Some well-intentioned parental strategies can be counterproductive, however. Attempts to restrict children's intake of HFSS foods, for example, or to frame these as rewards for good behaviour (such as eating up healthier food) might actually increase the appeal of HFSS foods. Furthermore, adding such symbolic value to these foods may distract children from realizing when they are hungry or full (Birch and Fisher, 1998). Moreover, resisting parental guidance on food may be one way for children to assert their independence, so presenting a food as healthy may actually lead to it being rejected and 'junk food' may be valued precisely because it meets with parental disapproval (Davis and White, 2006). When asked what they associated with the term 'junk food', some American children laughed and offered many examples, commenting that these were 'good to eat' (Neely, 2006). From the child's perspective, then, 'good to eat' may have little to do with nutritional status or health[1] (see Vignette 3).

Vignette 3: 'You've gotta be crazy to eat a Big Mac'

The website for Adbusters, the counter-culture consumer organization (www.adbusters.org), recently offered some speculative print ads critiquing a range of advertisers and their practices. Visitors to the website were invited to comment on or improve the ads, and Adbusters hoped to place the revised versions in mainstream media alongside the very advertising they critique. Under the heading 'Parents Versus the Fast Food Industry', Adbusters proposed an anti-fast food campaign, making some visual and verbal references to McDonald's. The campaign, designed for parenting magazines attracting fast food advertising, aimed to encourage parents to question the nutritional value of fast food and the nature of marketing practices within the industry; the hope was that parents would pass on these critical perspectives to their children, and that this in turn would enable children to make more informed dietary decisions. Given the costs of advertising in mainstream media, however, and the reluctance of magazines to bite the hand that feeds them, the chances of these ads seeing the light of day were extremely slim. To raise the profile of the campaign, Adbusters also posted artwork for a sticker declaring 'You've gotta be crazy to eat a Big Mac'. This featured the McDonald's golden arch rotated to replace the 'z' in crazy, and small print claiming that 50 per cent of the calories come from fat – a fact, we are told, coming from McDonald's own literature.

Source: originally available at http://www.adbusters.org/memewars/viewtopic.php?t=5 (no longer active)

Young children rely on their parents for most things, and although they become more self-reliant with age their limited purchasing power means they depend on parents to buy what they want (see Ekström, Chapter 3 in this book). It is hardly surprising, therefore, that they request particular foods they like or think they might like. 'Pester power' is nonetheless a highly-loaded term. Critics accuse food marketers of manipulating children into making persistent requests of their parents to buy particular brands, whilst marketers point in their defence to advertising codes that explicitly ban 'pester power' appeals (McDermott et al., 2006). Others challenge the notion of passive, defeated parents, noting that they don't always give in to their children's demands and take other factors into account when deciding what to buy (Spungin, 2004).

There is some evidence that children who watch more television make more requests for heavily advertised products like cereals, snacks and takeaway foods, but parental yielding to those requests appears to depend on their nutritional knowledge and the degree of their 'child centeredness' (Berey and Pollay, 1968). Parents generally seem more willing to take children's preferences into account for products like breakfast cereals, takeaway food and snacks – all categories that are heavily advertised, but it is unclear if this is related to the weight of advertising spend or reflects something else specific to these product categories. A recent Danish survey of families with 10 to 13 year olds found that children's influence was greatest for small meals, easily prepared food and unhealthy categories, and that their preferences were taken into account for fruit more than vegetables (Nørgaard et al., 2007). The extent to which children's views and desires are taken into account also depends on their age and gender as well as family communication styles. Many family decisions have been 'democratized'; parents increasingly seek to accommodate their children's preferences, not least in relation to food (Carlson et al., 1993; Cook, 2007; Nørgaard et al., 2007). In many cases parents will buy food that offers variety and pleasure rather than prioritizing health and nutrition. This may be because their nutritional knowledge is poor or traded off against the desire to give their children what they like or what allows them to fit in with their friends (Hughner and Maher, 2006).

Snacks vs 'proper meals'

Concerns about children's food do not simply relate to *what* children are eating, but also *how* and when they are *eating*. In this respect family meals play an important role in the socialization process, since they teach children what constitutes a 'proper meal', and also introduce them to adult rules and elaborate social codes regarding 'table manners'. This socialization role of family meals is threatened by increasingly individualized patterns of eating, as family members sit down to different meals, at different times, based on their individual preferences, without necessarily relying on someone else to prepare and cook what they want (see Chitakunye and MacLaren, 2008). For Blythman (2005), the decline of the collective family meal in Britain[2] is at odds with practices in other European countries where it remains sacrosanct – children continue to eat as part of the family unit and become socialized into adult eating patterns. Research among Italian families suggests that they tended to use 'a combination of "proper meals" all together and alternative, separated meals for parents and children reflecting their tastes' (Romani

2005: 8). Such a pattern allows children to exercise some agency over what they eat, and still participate in and learn from traditional family meals. Rather than having their tastes subordinated to fit with the adult world of mealtimes children are allowed greater autonomy, to such an extent that their preferences play an important role in shaping family food choice (Cook, 2007).

But how is this manifest in the case of snacks and snacking? These eating occasions are typically located at the periphery of the meal system and tend to be more informal and individualistic than the collective 'proper meal'. Although fruit may be eaten as a snack, the typical snack involves processed foods. Snacks require little time or expertise to prepare, thus freeing up time for other activities. Morover, they can be eaten on the move rather than seated at a table and with fingers rather than cutlery. Filling the gaps between meals snacking and snack foods are associated with fun, informality and freedom from the normal eating conventions (Marshall, 2005). With the (adult) rules of 'proper' eating relaxed this may be at the heart of their appeal to children.

Snacks appear to have moved from occasional treats to a regular feature in many children's diets; they are often used to express love and also closely related to family systems of reward and punishment (Curtis and Fischer, 2007). A recent survey of British 7 to 14 year olds found 82 per cent did not think of crisps as a treat, and over half did not see sweets as a treat (BHF, 2008). In another study, two-thirds of Scottish parents agreed that they gave in to their children's demands, and admitted to buying unhealthy foods as treats. At the same time, many claimed to be aware of health issues and trying to buy healthy foods for their children as well as refusing to give in to pester power (Turner et al., 2006). These authors suggest that such an ambivalent stance may reflect feelings of guilt and attempts to compensate for time lost with children due to work commitments.

Having reviewed the key debates and evidence regarding children's food marketing and food socialization, the chapter now turns to children's own accounts of their food consumption and food marketing experiences. The discussion below focuses on snacking, since this is an area where children are thought to have more influence on family purchases, and is also one where the role of food marketing is particularly controversial.

Children's own accounts of snacking

Amidst concerns over childhood obesity and the promotion and marketing of HFSS foods, we might ask what do children make of all of this? Our work[3] with 8 to 12 year olds in New Zealand, Scotland and Canada included looking at children's own accounts of advertising, and their experiences with food. The following section draws on surveys undertaken with 95 New Zealand children, 107 Scottish children, and 153 Canadian children, supplemented by focus group discussions. The research was undertaken in schools which attracted broadly middle-class families, and so may not be representative of other socio-economic groups. This section reviews key findings from these studies, reporting on children's response to food advertising, their categorization of snacks and the degree of control they had over what they ate as snacks.

While advertising for fast foods, cereals and confectionary featured amongst their favourite ads, the vast majority of these were for non-food products. Around three-quarters of the New Zealand children claimed that seeing a television commercial made them want to buy the product and around two-thirds claimed that food advertisements made them feel hungry 'sometimes' or 'often'. Only around one in ten said it had no effect on them. Two-thirds reported that ads, in general, made them pester their parents 'sometimes' or 'often', with around one in five claiming that ads 'never' had that effect on them. Very similar results were found in Canada, but in Scotland just over half the children said advertising for food made them feel hungry. One in three Scottish children 'sometimes' or 'often' pestered their parents after seeing advertising on television, but most claimed they 'never' or 'rarely' did so; the main reason given for this was that they didn't expect their parents to give in to pestering.

We found that children did not have a narrow or restricted notion of snacks (centred on the HFSS items such as crisps, confectionery, carbonated soft drinks, sugary breakfast cereals and fast food), but used a wide categorization and included savoury snacks such as beans on toast and bacon rolls as well as the healthier options of fruit and vegetables. In the New Zealand survey, for example, the children reported liking chocolate, chips (crisps), and fruit to a lesser extent, whereas proportionately more of the children said they did not like bread and jam and vegetables. A similar picture emerged in Canada, although fruit and vegetables were rated more positively and no food category was particularly disliked. In Scotland fruit was highly rated and over half the respondents liked vegetables, although fewer of the children claimed to like chips and ice cream compared to the Canadian and New Zealand sample. Even in the case of TV snacks, which are often associated with unhealthy eating, the picture that emerged was not necessarily bleak. Almost two-thirds of the children in New Zealand but less than half of those in Scotland and just one in four of the Canadian children reported snacking in front of the television 'often' or 'most days'; only one in ten in each country claimed they 'never' snacked while watching television. In terms of what was eaten in front of the TV, healthy items featured alongside the usual HFSS suspects. In the Scottish study, for example, fruit and vegetables (28 per cent) were the most common TV snack, followed by crisps (18 per cent) and biscuits/cakes (14 per cent). The most popular options among the New Zealand children were potato chips/crisps (23 per cent), followed by fruit/vegetables (17 per cent) and biscuits/cakes (15 per cent).[4] In the Canadian study around half the foods eaten while watching television were healthy.

Most of their accounts of eating focused on snacking at home or during break or lunchtime at school. It was clear that for these children snacking was closely aligned with the family meal system in the sense that snacks were often organized around other eating events. Yet snacks were seen as distinctly different from meals and associated with informality and fun. Rather than being seen as occasional treats, snacking appeared to be incorporated into their everyday dietary repertoire and lifestyles. Their consumption of snacks, however, appeared to be monitored and mediated by parents. Some of the children could access snacks independently, but many had to ask their parents for snacks or seek permission before choosing something from the kitchen cupboard. Some children reported that their parents hid snacks so that they could only be accessed through them, and others described the snacking rules in their homes. For example, one 11 year old Scottish boy explained that 'Practically every day when I come home from school I have a piece of toast and marmalade, or just toast and butter. And if I'm going to have something that's got sugar in it I have to ask for it, in case I'm not allowed it – but if it's like something that's good for you then I just take it'.

Of course various strategies were reported for the occasions when access was denied, such as locating secret hiding places or occasionally helping themselves to 'treats'. A 10 year old New Zealand girl described how she tried to work around her mother's restrictions: 'I sneak lollies and you know go into the fridge and take a piece of cheese …. Normally when I come back from school she [mum] does it [gets her a snack] and if not I will just go into the fridge [a snack] or get it [candy lollies] out of the cupboard and I sometimes never told her that I snack on lollies, I only told her I had a piece of cheese or something. In fact I never told her about the lollies'.

Most of the children were aware of healthy eating messages and included healthy products among their favourite snacks, suggesting the importance of the domestic environment in shaping individual food preferences. Parental monitoring or control also extended beyond the home; for example, the Scottish and New Zealand[5] children talked about how their parents decided what they got in their school lunchbox and often checked what they had eaten at the end of the school day.

Much of what we regard as food socialization is about teaching children how to eat 'properly' at the dining table. Here, rules are explained and enforced, explicitly and implicitly, leading to children's gradual immersion and inclusion in the family meal. What does appear to be changing is parents' willingness to empower their children and include them in family decisions about food. This is evident in their accounts of negotiations with parents over the content of their school lunchbox and what goes into the shopping trolley. Children's own accounts of their favourite foods, their discussion about (un)healthy eating and reference to a wide range of food advertising, all point to a generation that is versed in a food culture extending beyond sweets and confectionery. For example, one of the favourite ads for the Scottish children was the Marks and Spencer's 'Simply Food' campaign which features a 'food as indulgence' theme. While not disagreeing that food promotion and television advertising can have an influence our research findings led us towards a 'limited effects' perspective on advertising's influence (Livingstone and Helsper, 2004).

What children snack on appears to be regulated and controlled by parents, to varying degrees, as indicated in Table 10.1 and reflected in their discussion of restricted access to certain types of food at home. Across the three countries, we found that while items like fruit were quite readily available, less healthy items such as crisps, sweets or fizzy drinks were often restricted by parents. Moreover, many of the children in our research had relatively limited opportunities for discretionary spending on food, so most of their food consumption was mandated or negotiated through their parents. Many children learned about healthy eating in school as well as from the media and in the home, and could distinguish between 'good' and 'bad' foods, with junk food and confectionery clearly understood as being in the latter category.

Table 10.1   Children's reports of parental limits on snacking in the home and responsiveness to requests for snack foods in Scotland, New Zealand and Canada studies

| | Do your parents limit what you snack on in the house? (%) | | | If you ask for a snack food will your parents buy it? (%) | | |
| | Scotland | NZ | Canada | Scotland | NZ | Canada |
Country (n)	(100)	(96)	(146)	(100)	(94)	(145)
Never	2.9	7.3	12.2	4.0	8.5	10.3
Rarely	13.5	15.6	17.7	12.0	14.9	24.1
Sometimes	27.9	44.8	41.5	66.0	56.4	51.0
Often	25.0	11.5	28.6	11.0	13.8	14.5
Almost every day	30.8	20.8	–	7.0	6.4	–

Conclusion

Food offers a fascinating lens for studying children's consumption and their changing role in contemporary society. There appears to be a distinct children's food culture centred on eating as fun. Yet children's food experiences extend beyond sweets and snacks to embrace a broader range of eating occasions that reflect their integration into the family food system. As children become more actively involved in family food decisions, there are questions over the extent of their influence across different occasions and product categories, their competencies as food consumers, and, of course, the impact of food promotion on their preferences and choices. They appear to have some agency in relation to less formal snacking occasions but as one moves from snacks, at the periphery of the meal system, towards more formal meal occasions, children appear to have less autonomy. As the children's own accounts attest, parents continue to regulate their food consumption, restricting certain foods and permitting others, usually based on the nature of the eating occasion and some lay notion of what constitutes a healthy diet.

Debates about childhood obesity may well show a heightened awareness of healthy eating amongst both children and parents, yet both parties seem to struggle when it comes to putting this into practice. Parents seem to know what is good for their children but will still provide less healthy options reflecting what Noble et al. (2007) have called the paradox of modern parenting. This is partly explained by the perceived shortage of time and skills but also reflects broader tensions around notions of 'good parenting' and 'quality time'. Consequently, any attempts to change behaviour should reflect the complexities in modern family life (Noble et al., 2007). Parents must clearly take responsibility for feeding their children, but while they may benefit from further support and guidance in the area of nutrition and healthy eating there is always the danger that these are provided in ways that are perceived as patronizing, interfering or alienating. If the focus is on reducing obesity, diet alone cannot be the focus of interventions, since the consensus is that a more holistic approach is required. This may include improving access to affordable healthy food for less affluent families and finding ways to encourage more physically active lifestyles. Finally, whilst raising awareness of childhood obesity is important, there is a danger that a moral panic might distort children's relationship with food, feeding a heightened sense of risk and replacing enjoyment with guilt and anxiety (see Kline, Chapter 14 in this book).

Future research directions

Several recent studies have demonstrated the value of listening to children on their own terms and there is undoubtedly scope for more qualitative ethnographic studies to elicit children's understandings, experiences and negotiations in relation to food. We also need to examine further the extent to which children can have any real discretion in terms of what they eat. Young children, like the 8 to 12 year olds in our research, are, for the most part, still dependent on their parents to make decisions about what foods they encounter and are encouraged to eat. There is certainly scope for a more nuanced and contextualized understanding of the balance between what we have called mandated, negotiated and discretionary food consumption in children's lives, and indeed on how parents and children use their persuasion knowledge in food negotiations (Marshall et al., 2007). Greater understanding of the interactions between multiple socialization agents is also required to unpack the complexities involved (Ekström, 2006).

As food marketers come to realize the pressure on parents to provide healthy options for their children, some are improving the nutritional content of their products and removing certain additives. Such strategies, and how they are perceived by parents, also merit research attention. Several UK initiatives to promote healthy eating borrow from commercial marketing strategies. These include the Food Standards Agency's use of the Bash Street Kids, cartoon characters from the *Beano* comic strip, to promote healthy eating messages in primary schools, and the Food Commission Research Charity's 'Chew on This' website which targets secondary school children with information on healthy eating and a range of food marketing tactics. The UK government's 'Change 4 Life' also attempts to encourage families to 'eat well, move more, and live longer'. Other innovative private initiatives to develop children's nutritional literacy include the preschool TV programme *Lazy Town*, which encourages children to be active and to eat fruit and vegetables, re-branded as 'sports candy'. A systematic international review of such initiatives would also be worthwhile.

Finally, the opening vignette of this chapter exemplifies a growing concern over what children are eating and raises questions about how children, and their parents, are being targeted as a distinct market segment. More broadly it raises issues about the commercialization of childhood and the legitimacy of treating children as consumers. Irrespective of whether one sees children as vulnerable to commercial persuasion or sufficiently competent to deal with it, they are clearly considered a viable, valuable segment of the food market. Rather than being subsumed and merged into the adult world, children's food has a distinct identity that is increasingly commercialized and shaped by the food industry. Children have retained a unique link with food through sweets and snacks but these remain juxtaposed against an adult meal system that stresses rationality, health and eating properly. While obesity trends are clearly worrying, it is important to recognize that children's eating is about much more than nutrition. Over a quarter century ago, Postman (1994) raised concerns over what he saw as the disappearance of childhood. As he noted, it is children who recognize and acknowledge the distinction between adults and children, and the value in being different.

Discussion questions

1 Explain why children's diet has become such an important issue in contemporary industrialized economies.
2 To what extent does marketing actively encourage children's consumption of unhealthy foods?
3 Suggest some reasons for the segregation between children's food and adult diets.
4 How important is the family in shaping children's food choices?
5 Should policy makers further regulate food marketing directed at children?
6 Can marketing be part of the solution to the childhood obesity crisis? Identify cases where marketing has been used to promote healthy lifestyles among children.

Further reading

Atkin, C. (1978) 'Observation of parent–child interaction in supermarket decision-making', *Journal of Marketing*, 42 (4) (October): 41–45.

BMA (2005) 'Preventing childhood obesity: A report from the BMA Board of Science'. London: BMA. Available at http://www.bma.org.uk/ap.nsf/AttachmentsByTitle/WordChildhoodobesity/$FILE/ChildhoodObesity.doc (last accessed 30 October 2007).

Caruana, A. and Vassallo, R. (2003) 'Children's perception of their influence over purchases: the role of parental communication patterns', *Journal of Consumer Marketing*, 20 (1): 55–66.

Clark, B. (2002) 'Eating trends: adapting to kids' lifestyles', *International Journal of Advertising and Marketing to Kids*, 3 (2): 33–37.

Coon, K.A. Goldberg, J., Rogers, B.L. and Tucker, K.L. (2001) 'Relationships between use of television during meals and children's food consumption patterns', *Pediatrics*, 107 (1) (January): 1–9.

Dixon, J. and Banwell, C. (2004) 'Heading the table: parenting and the junior consumer', *British Food Journal*, 105 (3): 182–193.

International Obesity Task Force (2004) 'Childhood obesity out of control'. Extracts from *Childhood Obesity Report*, May, 2004. Available at http://www.iotf.org/media/IOTFmay28.pdf (last accessed 8 September 2007).

Young, B.M. (2007) 'Advertising literacy revisited: fat children and other things', in M. Saren, P. Maclaran, C. Goulding, R. Elliott, A. Shankar and M. Catterall (eds), *Critical Marketing: Defining the Field*. London: Butterworth-Heinemann. pp. 113–124.

References

Berey, L.A. and Pollay, R.W. (1968) 'The influencing role of the child in family decision making', *Journal of Marketing Research*, 5 (1) (February): 70–72.

Birch, L.L. and Fisher, J.O. (1998) 'Development of eating behaviors among children and adolescents', *Pediatrics*, 101 (3) (March): 539–549.

Blythman, J. (2005) *The Food Our Children Eat: How to Get Children to Like Good Food*. London: Harper Perennial.

British Heart Foundation (BHF) (2008) Protecting Children Report (accessed 14 February 2008 at http://www.bhf.org.uk/news_and_campaigning/our_campaigns/food4thought/food4thought.aspx). See also http://www.bhf.org.uk/news_and_campaigning/press_office/latest_news_views/food4thought.aspx.

Carlson, L., Grossbart, S. and Stuenkel, J.K. (1993) 'The role of parental socialization types on differential family communication patterns regarding consumption', *Journal of Consumer Psychology*, 1 (1): 31–52.

Chitakunye, D.P. and MacLaren, P. (2008) 'The everyday practices surrounding young people's food consumption', *Young Consumers: Insights and Ideas for Responsible Marketers*, 9 (3): 215–227.

Cook, D.T. (2007) *Semantic Provisioning of Children's Food: Commerce, Care and Maternal Practice, Childhood*, 16 (3): 317–334.

Curtis, P. and Fisher, P. (2007) *Bringing it all back home: families with children with obesity* (ESRC Seminar Series: Obesity – understanding the role of the social and physical environment, 17 January). London: The Kings Fund.

Davis, T. and White, L. (2006) 'Children and snack foods: is there a relationship between television viewing habits and nutritional knowledge and product choice?', *Asia-Pacific Advances in Consumer Research*. Sydney: Association for Consumer Research.

De Iulio, S. and Diasio, N. (2006) 'A world to eat: marketing and advertising strategies of fun food: the case of *Kinder Sorpresa'*. 2nd international conference on pluridisciplinary perspectives on child and teen consumption, Copenhagen Business School, 27–28 April.

Ekström, K. (2006) 'Consumer socialization revisited', *Research in Consumer Behavior*, 10: 71–98.

Elliott, C. (2005) 'Childhood obesity and our "toxic environment": suggestions for future research', *Journal of Family and Consumer Sciences Education*, 23 (1): 47–51.

Elliott, C. (2008) 'Assessing fun foods: nutritional content and analysis of supermarket foods targeted at children', *Obesity Reviews*, 9 (4) (July): 368–377.

Hastings, G., Stead, M., McDermott, L., Forsyth, A., MacKintosh, A., Rayner, M., Godfrey, C., Caraher, M. and Angus, K. (2003) *Review of Research on the Effects of Food Promotion to Children*. Food Standards Agency, September (accessed 14 February 2008 at http://www.foodstandards.gov.uk/multimedia/pdfs/promofood childrenexec.pdf). For a full report see http://www.food.gov.uk/multimedia/pdfs/foodpromotion-tochildren1.pdf.

Hughner, R.S. and Maher, J.K. (2006) 'Factors that influence parental food purchases for children: implications for dietary health', *Journal of Marketing Management*, 22 (9/10): 929–954.

James, A. (1982) 'Confections, concoctions and conceptions', in B.Waites, T. Bennett and G. Martin (eds), *Popular Culture: Past and Present*. London: Croom Helm/Open University Press. pp. 294–307.

Johansson, B. (2006) 'Children and their money', *European Advances in Consumer Research*, 7: 327–332.

Kline, S. (2005) 'Countering children's sedentary lifestyles: an evaluation study of a media risk education approach', *Childhood*, 12 (2): 239–258.

Livingstone, S. and Helsper, E. (2004) 'Advertising foods to children: understanding promotion in the context of children's daily lives: review of the literature prepared for the Research Department of OFCOM'. Available at http://www.ofcom.org.uk.

McDermott, L., O'Sullivan, T., Stead, M. and Hastings, G. (2006) 'International food advertising, pester power and its effects', *International Journal of Advertising*, 25 (4): 513–539.

Marshall, D. (2005) 'Food as ritual, routine or convention?', *Culture, Markets and Consumption*, 8 (1): 69–85.

Marshall, D. and Pettinger, C. (2009) 'Revisiting British meals', in H. Meiselman (ed.), *Meals in Science and Practice: Interdisciplinary Research and Business Applications*. Oxford: Woodhead. pp. 638–664.

Marshall, D., O'Donohue, S. and Kline, S. (2007) 'Families, food, and pester power: beyond the blame game?', *Journal of Consumer Behaviour*, 6 (4) (July/August): 164–181.

Neely, S. (2006) 'Seeking insight into adolescents' nutrition understanding, inferences, and food choices'. Paper presented at the 2nd international conference on pluridisciplinary perspectives on child and teen consumption, Copenhagen, 27–28 April, Copenhagen Business School, Denmark.

Noble, G., Stead, M., Jones, S., McDermott, L. and McVie, D. (2007) 'The paradoxical food buying behaviour of parents: insights from the UK and Australia', *British Food Journal*, 109 (5): 387–398.

Nørgaard, M., Bruns, K., Christensen, P. and Mikkelsen, M. (2007) 'Children's influence on and participation in the family decision process during food buying', *Young Consumers*, 8 (3): 197–216.

Ofcom (2007) *Television Advertising of Food and Drink Products to Children: Final Statement*, 22 February 2002. Available at http://www.ofcom.org.uk/consult/condocs/foodads_new/statement/statement.pdf (last accessed 3 March 2008).

Postman, N. (1994) *The Disappearance of Childhood*. New York: Vintage.

Richardson, T. (2005) 'Let them eat sweets', *The Guardian*, 6 August. Available at http://www.guardian.co.uk/weekend/story/0,,1542389,00.html#article_continue (accessed 9 October 2007).

Romani, S. (2005) 'Feeding post-modern families: food preparation and consumption practices in new family structures', *in European Advances in Consumer Research* (Volume 7), K.M. Ekström and H. Brembeck. Goteborg, Sweden: Association for Consumer Research. pp. 250–254.

Spungin, P. (2004) 'Parent power, not pester power', *International Journal of Advertising and Marketing to Children*, 5 (3) (April–June): 37–40.

Turner, J.J., Kelly, J. and McKenna, K. (2006) 'Food for thought: parents' perspectives of child influence', *British Food Journal*, 108 (3): 181–191.

Ward, S. (1974) 'Consumer socialization', *Journal of Consumer Research*, 1, (September): 1–16.

WHO (2006) 'Marketing of food and non-alcoholic beverages to children: report of a WHO Forum and Technical Meeting', Oslo, Norway, 2–5 May.

Which? (2006) 'Childcatchers: the tricks used to push unhealthy food to your children'. January (see http://www.which.co.uk/about-which/press/campaign-press-releases/food/2006/01/junk-food-tricks.jsp).

Websites

Food Standards Agency 5-a-day the Bash Street way archive at http://www.food.gov.uk/archive/nutritionarchive/schoolsarchive/teachingtoolsarchive/bashstreetdiet/

Food Commission Research Charity Ltd. 'Chew on This' at http://www.chewonthis.org.uk/

UK Department of Health Change 4 Life at http://www.nhs.uk/change4life/Pages/Default.aspx

Notes

1 But how much do children know about what is 'good' for them? Nutritional knowledge underpinning children's food choices has not received sufficient

attention in the marketing literature. Some recent studies offer insights into the gaps in children's nutritional literacy. For example, the 7 to 12 year old American children had a very simplistic understanding of the term 'nutrition'. They generally demonstrated some basic knowledge of the food pyramid and knew they should eat fruit and vegetables but limit sweets and their calorie, fat and sugar intake. They tended not to read nutrition labels, making inferences from a pack's visual cues instead, and when asked to read some labels expressed both scepticism and confusion. Parents and other family members are seen as the source of nutritional knowledge, although formal education also has a role to play. In this context, one child noted that her teachers used games and activities to make nutrition lessons fun, and offered candy as prizes! (see Neely, 2006).

2 There is something of a resurgence of interest in families eating together and 'cooking from scratch' (Marshall and Pettinger, 2009).

3 This is an on-going collaboration with Professor Steve Kline at Simon Fraser University, Canada.

4 The relationship between watching television and snacking is not entirely clear. In both our New Zealand study and Scottish (unpublished) studies, with children in the same age group, those who reported watching television never/sometimes were just as likely to eat healthy or unhealthy snacks as children who watched television often/almost everyday.

5 One of the New Zealand schools ensured that any uneaten items were returned home at the end of the day so that parents could see what their children had eaten.

11 Children and the Internet

Birgitte Tufte and Jeanette Rasmussen

Chapter aims

- To look at the development of the internet as a medium for marketing communication.
- To focus on the relationship between consumption and media use from national and international studies.
- To consider tweens' media consumption.
- To outline some of the concerns over children and use of the internet.
- To identify future research challenges around children's use of new media and the internet.

Vignette 1: Kids online

Symantec tracked the search activity of 3.5 million users of their Onlinefamily. Norton service between February and July 2009 and identified the Top Ten most frequently searched terms. To be included a term had to be submitted at least 50 times by a registered user of their service, which allows parents to monitor their children's online activity and Web searches, as well as managing their computer time. The service, geared towards 8 to 13 year olds' activity, revealed the Top Ten most popular searches.

1 YouTube
2 Google
3 Facebook
4 Sex
5 MySpace
6 Porn

7 Yahoo
8 Michael Jackson
9 Fred (a popular fictional character whose YouTube channel has become a
   hit among kids)
10 eBay

The popularity of video sites, search engines' sites and social networking sites
is apparent and with 'porn' and 'sex' making it into the top search terms it
provides some insight into what children are searching for online. The fact that
they will search for sites, such as YouTube, rather than typing them directly into
a browser also gives us some insights into the ways in which they navigate
towards sites. While the sample relates only to those parents who have already
subscribed to the service it does raise some interesting questions over the extent
to which parents feel they need to moniter their children's behaviour online.

Source: adapted from CNET News (http://news.cnet.com/8301-10797_3-10306357-235.
html) and the Norton website for the Top 100 searches (http://onlinefamilyinfo.norton.com/
articles/schools_out.php)

Introduction

There is a view on children which could be called 'the strong child-paradigm' –
i.e. an emphasis on no longer considering the child as mainly a vulnerable
creature who ought to be protected, a 'becoming', but as a human 'being'
who is acting in her/his own life and has a say in the decisions of the family, not least in relation to media consumption. The opening example
(Vignette 1) offers us some insights into the online search activities of one
group of young consumers but also raises this issue of how much we should
protect and monitor what children do online. This chapter will look at the
development of the internet as a communication medium and the way in
which children use it as part of their everyday consumption. It reports on
research with children in the Nordic countries and international studies and
provides an insight into their online activities.

What is the internet?

The internet is a global high-speed network, consisting of a set of network
computers, which is simply a vast number of computer networks linked
around the world. The explosion of the internet has occurred during less
than two decades all over the world. As a matter of fact the internet has been
available since the early 1960s when it was developed for military purposes.

However, it was not until the 1990s when a new generation of software – the World Wide Web (WWW) browsers – was developed that the internet became widespread. It delivers an enormous amount of information, which according to the American researchers Victor C. Strasburger and Barbara J. Wilson (2002) could be described as follows:

- *Email for electronic communication*   Many would agree that this is certainly one of the most popular forms of communication in today's society. Even this simple and everyday form of technology has changed in recent years, with the ability to send voice, video, and other forms of attachments around the world in an almost instantaneous manner.
- *Bulletin board systems*   These are for posting information on almost any topic one could imagine.
- *Chat groups*   These can be used for real-time conversations. For many adolescents, it is the global equivalent of a 'free' conference call. However, unlike the traditional conference call, you can choose your topic, person and time in any manner you desire.
- *The World Wide Web*   This combines visuals/sound/text together in a manner that allows linkages across many sites that are related to a particular topic. These topics obviously can be those related to sex, violence, drugs, or any other content about which we have concerns. (Strasburger and Wilson, 2002: 304)

The latest phenomenon discussed among parents, teachers, politicians and others interested in children's use of the internet is Web 2.0, which is both new and the common name for user-created content and new web technologies such as the podcast, vodcast, weblog, wiki, and RSS-feeds. The idea behind Web 2.0 is that as a user you can operate in an open and interactive universe, whereas in Web 1.0 – the sites used so far – there is a higher degree of closeness and one-way communication. This new way of discussing the internet is described as the 'open source' movement (www.opensource.org). Young people can create their own digital portfolios and there is indeed evidence that they are engaging with this new medium at home in social and creative ways but there is an increasing divide between those who are web-confident and those who simply use the web for content retrieval (Green and Hannon, 2007; Sharples et al., 2009). Evidence from the USA shows that teenagers in particular regularly update their social networking web pages (Nielsen, 2009).

What do we know about children, the internet and consumption?

Media play an important role in the daily life of children all over the world although there are differences depending on where children live. The internet is the newest member of the global family of media technology. Compared to other media the internet is, as already mentioned, highly interactive. Unlike traditional media it allows children and adolescents access to different kinds of content, and a specific characteristic is that this can be done in privacy, without the knowledge of parents. The most influential sources of information for children today making decisions and keeping contact with peers are media, meaning that children receive far more information from media than from parents and schools. This phenomenon has been called 'the parallel school of media', which means that children and adolescents will daily use up several hours on various media.

A report on media use among young Europeans shows internet (broadand) penetration is 60.7 per cent for the EU27 and this ranges from 23.5 per cent in Malta up to 83.0 per cent in Finland. Children's internet usage continues to grow, most notably among younger children aged 6–10 years old with 60 per cent online in 2008. Figures for the 11–14 year olds and 15–17 year olds are 84 per cent and 86 per cent respectively across the EU. Use increases with age but today plateaus at around 10–11 years old.

One of the developments since 2005 is that as many parents are now on-line as children and there is evidence that parental mediation of internet use varies by country (Nordicom, 2009). The international project 'Mediappro – A European Research Project: The Appropriation of New Media by Youth', which compared use of the internet and mobile phones among 12–18 year olds (www.mediappro.org), shows some similar trends in nine European countries, such as:

- A gap between the use of media at home and in school.
- Differences in media use related to age, gender and generation. Internet use increases with age – the older you get between 12 and 18 years, the more you use the internet. Girls are using the internet for chatting more than boys, whereas boys spend more time than girls playing games.
- The increasing importance of the internet as a commercial marketplace: for example, young people will sometimes buy things online, using their parents' credit cards (and with their permission), and they are convinced that when they grow up they will shop much more online than their parents do today. Parents have a rather liberal attitude towards their children's media use.
- A need for the schools to teach the students a critical approach to the internet. Children would like to have some tools to find out if they can trust the articles they find for their school work when they 'google' a theme for an essay for example.
- Young people are aware of the risks online and do take appropriate action but do not feel unduly at risk.

Source: some of the results from the Danish part of the Mediappro project

In Denmark, 96 per cent of families with children have internet access, whereas the average for Danish households is 78 per cent. This means, how-ever, that almost all children and adolescents have internet access at home (Forbrugerredegørelsen, 2008). In the Mediappro survey 96.7 per cent of the children claimed to have internet access (at home and/or school) and

79.1 per cent considered themselves competent users. At home Danish children mainly used the internet to communicate by using email and Messenger or listened to music or played online games: few used blogs. When they were online they spent most of the time playing games, chatting and emailing, and as far as the latter activities are concerned the girls spend more time doing so than the boys, whereas the boys to a greater extent are downloading music and programmes (Tufte et al., 2009).

We know from the European Project Mediappro (www.mediappro.org) and other studies, that children use search engines, send emails and communicate with their peers through sites such as MSN Messenger and Facebook (see Table 11.1) as well as playing games online (Tufte, 2007). Interestingly, creating their own web content did not feature heavily in the Mediappro study with only 18 per cent of the children reporting having their own personal website or blog. Having an internet profile (for example, on a web community, virtual world, game site, or photo share) increases with age and in Denmark while just over a quarter of 9–10 year olds had an internet profile, 61 per cent of 11–13 year olds and 86 per cent of 14–16 year olds claimed to have their own internet profile (Danish Media Council, 2009). In the USA around 64 per cent of children aged between 5 and 14 years old who access the internet do so to play games (USDE, 2003).

Table 11.1   Children's activities online

Internet activities (sometimes+often+ very often) %	Search engines	Email	Instant Messenger	Chat rooms	Downloading
Belgium	95	74	81	28	58
Denmark	92	66	87	26	50
Estonia	90	69	88	33	73
France	94	67	69	32	49
Greece	81	46	39	41	65
Italy	86	59	49	33	59
Poland	91	62	75	34	67
Portugal	95	69	77	38	60
UK	98	81	78	20	60
Average	**91**	**66**	**71**	**32**	**60**

Source: www.mediappro.org. With kind permission

New Danish figures regarding 8–18 year olds' use of media show that on average they spend about five hours per day on media. This seems impossible as they are spending 6–7 hours in school, on leisure activities, eating, sleeping, being together with friends, etc. The fact is, however, that children are great multi-taskers – watching TV while surfing on the internet for fun or doing schoolwork at the same time as listening to the sound of the mobile phone telling them that text messages are coming in (see Vignette 2). There is definitely a tendency among children and young people to spend less time on TV and more on the internet when compared to some years ago. For instance, Danish 8–12 year olds spend 52 minutes per day on average on the internet, up from 25 minutes per day in 2003 (Tufte et al., 2009). Teenagers in the USA spend around 11 and a half hours per month on the internet, less than half the US average, but are watching more television than ever with viewing up 6 per cent in the last five years (Nielsen, 2009).

Vignette 2: The multimedia generation

A normal situation for a 12 year old girl in Denmark is that she comes home from school at around half past two. She is alone in the house, as her parents are working and her younger siblings are still in kindergarten or at other day care institutions. So she turns on MTV, opens up her laptop, places her mobile phone on the table and starts doing her homework for the next day or maybe just checking Facebook. She is multitasking, and when her parents come home they will yell at her, worried about all the time she spends on such media, and also worried about her – in their minds – far too extensive use of chatrooms and computer games. However, she is not spending as long a time playing computer games as do her male peers, although some games appeal to her, as in general boys spend more time on games.

Danish research shows that children learn a lot of things through media which are not taught at school – and in a way which is different from the way they are presented with knowledge in school. They develop competencies about how to use the computer by 'hands on pedagogy', obtained by themselves or taught by peers, aquiring information about new sites, games and the like from friends and older siblings. And being a 12 year old having a profile on Facebook for instance you learn a lot about communication and social relations, you make a lot of acquaintances and maybe friends. Children definitely distinguish between having a huge number of contacts via these sites, which gives a certain status, and having real friends, which is normally limited to just a few. All this suggests that many children and young people are competent navigators in the new media landscape. This new media landscape is also increasingly mobile and children will have mobile phones from an increasingly young age, even down to 6 or 7 years old. The main reason given for buying mobile phones for very young children is that parents want to control their children, to know where they are. Older children (10–14 year olds) primarily use their mobile to be in contact with their peers sending and receiving text messages. The data of one study show that in 2000 17 per cent of 8–12 year olds had a mobile phone, whereas the percentage in 2007 was 75 per cent – and is probably even higher today (Tufte et al., 2009). Despite attempts to market directly to children on this medium there appears to be some resistance from them (Grant, 2007).

Gender differences in media use

The gender difference in media use is very striking and stronger than age and social background, a fact emphasized by the Danish researcher Kirsten Drotner (2001). This is especially true for computer games where 9–16 year old boys report spending four times as long playing games as girls. Girls use the computer for schoolwork more than the boys and tend to read more books than boys. While 52 per cent of boys and 49 per cent of girls use the internet they use it for different purposes. The girls mostly use the internet for surfing, chatting and email, whereas the boys use it for seeking information, the production of websites and downloading software. Similar trends can be seen among Swedish 15–24 year olds' use of the internet: 'Both boys and girls were of the opinion that television was the most important medium for entertainment/pleasure. As to knowledge and information the boys gave priority to the Internet in the first place and television in the second. The girls chose books first and television second' (Feilitzen, in Hansen et al., 2002: 108). However, today such a distinction may not be valid, as the distinction between TV and the internet is becoming blurred, as you can now watch TV programmes on your computer and go on the internet by means of your mobile phone. These gender difference are reflected in the time spent on line with 13–18 year old boys spending about 24 minutes more time on the internet each day than girls (Tufte et al., 2009).

The gap between school and home

We know that media play a very important role in children's spare time, for entertainment and for learning, and that they obtain various skills through media in general and though their use of computer games. We also know from the Mediappro study that media and games are rarely used in schools in relation to learning and this is where the gap between school and home emerges. There are various reasons for this such as a lack of technology in schools, a lack of training for teachers, and let us not forget the cultural capital of the teachers, which is mainly based on the written and spoken language, as expressed by a 12 year old boy in the Mediappro project: 'The teachers do not know very much … most of them are old'. But there are also constraints imposed by local authorities and school governors, in an increasingly 'risk averse' environment around fears of exposure to inappropriate content or online abuse or 'cyberbullying'. One question is what role should schools have to play in educating children on how to use the internet (Sharples et al., 2009)?

This is in accordance with the opinion of researchers interested in and working with media education, as Buckingham (2003: 176) notes: 'We may be seeing a widening gulf between the styles of learning that are cultivated by formal schooling and those that characterise children's out-of-school experiences'. There is a need for media education, to give children competencies that they do not gain through their present use of media, and as he goes on to say 'It would be quite false to pretend that young people are already competent users of these new media, or that they necessarily know all they need to know' (ibid., p. 176).

Media education has, during the last decade, gradually gained a foothold in school curricula within many countries. For instance, in the UK Buckingham has pioneered the development of broad media and information competencies in media education, enabling people to communicate, search for information, share knowledge and use this new media in several ways. In Finland this has been described as a necessity, i.e., that such a broad media concept must be implemented in the overall educational system as a cross-disciplinary dimension (Vettenranta, 2007). In Denmark we have also for many years tried to integrate media education into the curriculum in primary and secondary schools, based on a pedagogy which combines media analysis with the children's own media production (Tufte, 1995; Christensen and Tufte, 2001).

While some adults appear to be impressed with children's 'technical' competencies in surfing and playing on the internet, there is still the question of guidance in relation to finding relevant information. What they often get are random, fragmented pieces of information, with blurred and contradictory messages. This makes it difficult to distinguish fact from fiction – or information from a commercial message – and raises the issue of children's ability to distinguish between the two. Research also suggests that children do not trust all the information they receive online (Tufte and Rasmussen, 2005). One role for grown-ups, be it a teacher or a parent, is to guide and explain. So on the technical side we have a generational gap, where the net generation is competent, but from a cultural and learning point of view we have another kind of gap where it is the grown-ups who are competent. Teachers have their professional background, be it mathematics, English or history, and there will be a set curriculum in relation to the different subjects that they have to follow and so media education is gradually finding its place in the curriculum of many countries (Kotilainen and Arnolds-Granlund, 2010).

Is it possible thesefore to bridge the generational gap? That such a gap exists, especially in relation to the internet, is expressed in the following conversation with a dad who had three sons aged 8 to 16:

Interviewer:	Do you think there is a generation problem in most families that the children are so competent (as to media)?
Dad:	You should not look at it as a problem before it turns into one. I don't use it for the same as the children, and I guess most adults use it today. By now I think that it is only a few adults that cannot use it moderately.
Interviewer:	What we have come upon is that the adults are more occupied by all the things the children can do compared to what they can do themselves?
Dad:	Well, I am envious of them for the many things they can do faster than I can ...

Source: unpublished material in the project 'Girls' and boys' everyday life and media culture' (the final results were published in Christensen and Tufte, 2001)

Tweens, media and consumption

As has already been mentioned, companies and advertisers to an increasing degree are showing an interest in children as consumers, and especially 'tweens',[1] i.e., those in-between childhood and teen-age. From 2004–2006 a research project regarding the media consumption of tweens, here defined as 10–12 year olds, was carried out at the Copenhagen Business School (Tufte, 2007). The aim of the project was to examine the role of the media in 10–12 year old children's consumer behaviour relative to other socialization factors such as family, school and friends. Quantitative and qualitative data were collected in schools in four different geographical areas in Denmark (i.e., one rural area and three others in the neighbourhood of Copenhagen) representing different social classes. The study began with questionnaires for one school in each region, covering three different age levels (i.e., 10–12 year olds). The pattern of internet use was rather similar in the four areas. It was mainly used at home, but also together with friends, at the school library and in school. The internet was not widely used at school except in one of the areas, where children used it often for schoolwork and sometimes were allowed to play online as well. The reason for this was undoubtedly that the school was situated in a municipality, where the local policy for many years had been to integrate media education in the schools in an attempt to improve children's media competence.

When it comes to questions about advertising the 10–12 year olds had a rather critical attitude towards advertising, with boys being slightly more critical than girls. Both boys and girls would 'zap' and 'zip' away from TV commercials and do not like pop-up ads on the internet. More boys than girls considered it a good idea not to have TV commercials at all.

The study ended by emphasizing that the 10–12 year olds in general were not extremely interested in consumption, although advertising and shopping were a part of their daily life. Girls were more materialistic and interested in fashion and jewellery and how they looked and were perceived by others. The pattern of their media use and consumption was very much influenced by their interests. If, for instance, you are interested in football you will probably watch football on TV, search for football websites on the internet and play football yourself. For girls this activity may be aimed for instance at a hobby like horse riding (or indeed football, which is gradually also becoming a sport for girls). Interestingly, they did not define themselves as tweens but alternated between kid and teenage behaviour, for example playing with their pets and toys but showing an interest in fashion, brands, etc. Their identity was not primarily based on consumption although they used commercial websites and spent time in shopping malls. Their sense of identity was based on a wide variety of factors such as family, friends and school, as well as advertising, websites and consumption. Younger children appeared to be more influenced by their parents and very dependent on them when it came to buying clothes and so an. When it came to influence from friends they were very conscious about the role of the trendsetters in their class. As one 12 year old girl, a trendsetter herself, noted: 'Yesterday I was wearing a new pair of jeans, a brand which is absolutely new, and I know that very soon the other girls will persuade their parents to buy the same kind of jeans for them'. This is very much in accordance with what Martin Lindstrøm (2003) has called:

- *The frontrunners*, i.e., the independent young people, who are rather and could be described as being 'avant-garde' when it comes to trendsetting.
- *The leading group of young people*, i.e., the kind of trendsetters that their peers are following to a higher extent than the frontrunners.
- *The followers who are the biggest group*, i.e., they are aware of the taste and style of the leading group and they listen to the frontrunners, but they never try things first.
- *The passive*, i.e., who are not belonging to any group but sometimes try to get into a group.

Source: Lindstrøm, 2003: 14–15

Children, money and digital marketing

There is no doubt that economy and money play an important role as well in the real world (see Roland-Lévy, Chapter 9 in this book) as in the digital world in which children navigate. A Nordic report regarding the 13–17 year olds' income (Lehmann Eriksen, 2007) shows that 55 per cent of the Danish young people in this age group have a job after school, whereas the percentage is much lower in the other Nordic countries (12 per cent in Finland, 23 per cent in Sweden and 30 per cent in Norway). There are gender differences as to what boys and girls are using their money for, with the girls using their money for make-up, clothes and books, whereas the boys are spending money on sport activities and the internet (see Table 11.2).

Table 11.2   Expenses – priority 1–5 for Nordic girls and boys

13–14 year old girls' expenses	*13–14 year old boys' expenses*
1 Accessories/make-up	1 Food/sweets
2 Amusements	2 Amusements
3 Clothes/shoes	3 Music/movie/games
4 Food/sweets	4 Clothes/shoes
5 Books/magazines	5 Holidays/travels
15–17 old girls' expenses	*15–17 year old boys' expenses*
1 Accessories/make-up	1 Food/sweets
2 Amusement	2 Amusement
3 Clothes/shoes	3 Music/movie/games
4 Food/sweets	4 Clothes/shoes
5 Books/magazines	5 Alcohol/tobacco

Source: Lehmann Erichsen, Nordea 2009. Used with kind permission. Survey carried out in 2007 and in 2009 by Synovate for Nordea

The interesting thing here is that more boys than girls are saving their money. Whereas boys spend their money on the internet and their mobile phones, girls use their money to buy clothes/shoes and cosmetics (Lehmann Eriksen, 2007).

Another Nordic study[2] looked at how 12–16 year olds were using the new types of marketing targeted at them via mobile phones, product placement and viral marketing (Busch, et al., 2006; Grant, 2007). The findings suggest that within the next three to five years a number of marketing strategies will be increasingly common:

- SMS-services on the mobile phone.
- Chat-fora: where children meeting on the net will see commercial messages.
- Viral marketing: where children are sending films and different commercial messages to each other via email.
- Search engines: where children's search activity can be tracked and used to target them in relation to their interests.
- Product placement and advergaming: where products and advertising are 'embedded' in films and computer games.
- Weblogs: where personal 'blogs' are posted on the Net and it can be difficult to distinguish whether the text is a 'normal' text or a commercial message.

As can be understood there are advantages as well as drawbacks in relation to children's everyday life with media. A number of children are competent navigators in cyberspace, communicating about new sites (music, films and jokes) and multitasking, using various sites on the internet, watching

TV and communicating on their mobile phones. These are competences that will probably be relevant in the future, one that will be characterized by a need to be able to adjust yourself to new conditions in relation to employment and the development of technology. Talking about the drawbacks that many grown-ups are worried about includes the content of the media such as violence in films and news programmes, pornographic sites, and the dangers for young people in meeting people they have been chatting with and who may be older than they admitted on the chat site. It seems, however, as if most young people are aware of many of these dangers but more often worried for their younger siblings about this. There is no doubt that within the coming years there will be increasing interest from business in targeting children via these new media, and when asked, many children and adolescents will say that when they grow up they will probably buy more online than their parents do today. As one 14 year old Danish boy commented 'I think that in the future a lot of things are going to take place on the Internet ... and people are going to buy many things – they already do. For instance I have bought a bicycle' (Ramaat et al., 2008).

Concerns about the internet

Livingstone and Haddon (Nordicom, 2009) identify a number of opportunities and risks for children as recipients, participants and actors online. These include education and learning, participation and civic engagement, creativity and self-expression, identity and social connections. Risks revolve around aggressive sexual values and commercial risks that include children's exposure to advertising and spam, the tracking and collection of personal information, and their involvement in gambling, illegal downloading and hacking.

While on the one hand many parents think that it is fantastic with all the information that children can receive, on the other hand they are worried about access to adult sites and violence on the internet and issues surrounding privacy. There are already a number of child-oriented sites with advertisements, and often it can be difficult to distinguish between information and advertisements on some of these or to identify the commercial message and sender (Kjørstad, 2000). A SIFO (The National Institute for Consumer Research) qualitative study of 12 year-old-children's understanding of different forms of advertising on the internet, found children were generally positive about commercial advertising on the internet and thought that they knew about most kinds of commercials that exist there. There were three types of internet commercials that seemed difficult for children to recognize – sponsoring, newsletters and chat-commercials. Regarding chat-commercials for instance, they thought it was not acceptable to interrupt what is considered a private conversation. While children understand the purpose of this kind of marketing 'they will probably have problems recognising it because of the fact that it is exposed in a medium in which they do not expect to find commercials. Most children are very negative towards this kind of marketing' (Kjørstad, 2000: 17).

Advertising sponsored video games, or advergames, created to promote branded products appears to be particularly appealing to children and the cause of some concern. Expenditure on online games was expected to reach $230m around 2007 (Mack, 2004). Moore and Rideout (2008) suggest that 'if children do not invoke their defenses when viewing television advertisements, they may be even less likely to do so when selling messages are embedded in on-line games' (2008: 203). Yet despite these concerns there is no government regulation of online marketing to children. Discussing on-line marketing practices in relation to food found that games were a prominent feature on a number of websites and questioned the capacity of children to understand the persuasive intent of these commercial activities. They also considered viral marketing and found a high proportion (64 per cent) of websites in their study encouraged some kind of viral marketing and brand advocacy. They argued that there are no restrictions, half of which had television commercials and the others video content. However, almost all the sites had information for parents, along with legal information and disclaimers, with around three-quarters having explicit statements about compliance with the Children's Online Privacy Protection Act (COPPA) 1999. Moore and Rideout raise important issues about children's privacy, the conditions of website membership, and obtaining parental consent. The most significant policy issues surrounding the marketing of food products online relate to the questionable nutritional profile of the promoted brands (many HFSS); the potential for tacit persuasion through games; the absence of limits on total ad exposure; the use of viral marketing; the lack of ad breaks; and the direct inducements to purchase (2008: 216).

Conclusion

To grow up in today's society means to be a child in a society offering a wide variety of possibilities and many risks. It is a consumer and media society which children and adolescents navigate and feel comfortable in, whereas the older generation will often feel insecure and will not have sufficient knowledge to guide children, especially in relation to media technology and the new media platforms. As these platforms continue to merge – for example, television companies now offer programmes via their websites – so the distinctions between television and the internet become blurred.

We have to admit that we find two groups on the leading edge regarding new media i.e., children and marketers. Children can very quickly adopt and use new media technology and companies and advertising agencies are extremely innovative and creative when it is a question of targeting children with commercial messages. Parents, teachers, researchers and politicians are lagging behind in trying to keep up and defend traditional cultures and norms. Many grown-ups are very concerned and have adopted a moralistic approach to children's use of the 'parallel school of the media'. This could be put forward and discussed as two different discourses – types of discourse which are actually often debated in the media in articles and in TV programmes focusing on children, media and consumption.

As will be understood from the above there are different approaches and opinions among grown-ups regarding children and the internet. On one hand we have the concept of the child who is on his/her way to 'becoming' a reasonable grown-up. In this way of thinking it is very important to guide and educate the child. The school represents this position with its aim of educating that child to become a good citizen in a democratic society, and this cultural capital is represented by books and traditional media. On the other hand we have the representatives of the free market sources who consider the child as a competent creature who is able to make choices and influence the members of the family. In this way of thinking the child is perceived as a competent consumer and user of new media. Between these two positions – which perhaps are a bit exaggerated – we have parents, teachers, politicians and others who feel that they have a foot in both camps, doing their best to educate children and take the appropriate pedagogical and legal action.

The child is on its way to 'becoming' a grown-up, but on the other hand the child of today is also a 'being', a competent person who is negotiating with parents and teachers. And in relation to their use and competencies regarding the internet, mobile phones and consumption, they are definitely more 'social beings' than 'social becomings', but of course this is not the case with very small children but children from about 7 to 8 years old. And obviously every human being is a citizen as well as a consumer, yet there is a trend today to focus more on the consumer perspective than on educating and influencing children to become critical citizens in a democratic society, a society where market forces have a growing influence on our daily lives as well as offline and online. It is important to emphasize that it is – of course – important to try to build a bridge between the representatives of the two sides, which may take place in the form of information, teaching, and initiatives by consumer organizations and politicians, not to forget self-regulations from the part of the industry itself. And this seems to be a trend which may develop in the future, as most of the companies who are marketing to children want to have a high ethical profile. Naturally this model (see Figure 11.1), which tries to illustrate the problems regarding different approaches to children, media and consumption, should not be interpreted as too narrow-minded, but there are different interests and opinions dominating the discussion. It is not simply a question of either/or, with parents, teachers and politicians standing in between the two discourses.

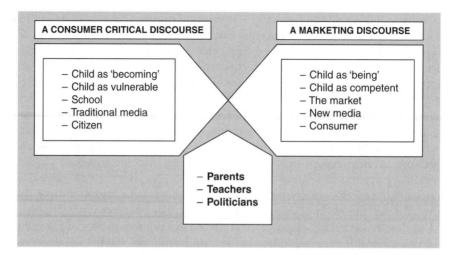

Figure 11.1 Children, media and consumption: two different positions

Future research directions

As this chapter has illustrated there are a number of interesting issues emerging around children's use of new media and the internet. We still have a lot to learn about how children interact and engage with websites and various marketing activities online and on mobile environments. Further work tracking and monitoring online marketing represents a major challenge and one that would benefit from some collaborative activity, such as that adopted in the Mediappro study, to examine cultural differences. The role of government in legislating online activity is at an early stage and we need to look more closely at issues of competence in this new interactive environment while areas where children are more vulnerable remain a key research challenge. Finally, the area of children online and new media calls for some innovative approaches to looking at how children engage online as they explore social networking sites, play games, and create their own cyber identities and avatars in a world facilitated by Web 2.0 and other emerging tools that seem to have captured their imaginations.

Discussion questions

1 Why is it important to relate children's use of media to their way of behaving as consumers?
2 What are the barriers if you want to create a dialogue between 'a consumer critical discourse' and 'a market discourse'?

3 Describe what you see as future trends in relation to children and media.
4 Discuss the possible legal actions to be taken in order to protect the influence of media on children.
5 What do you think about teaching children media and consumption at school?

Further reading

Buckingham, D. and Willett, R. (eds) (2006) *Digital Generations: Children, Young People and New Media*. Hillsdale, NJ: Lawrence Erlbaum.

Calvert, S.L. (2008) 'Children as consumers: advertising and marketing', *Future of Children*, 18 (1): 205–234. Available at http://www.futureofchildren.org/futureofchildren/publications/journals/article/index.xml?journalid=32&articleid=62

Feilder, A., Gardner, W., Nairn, A. and Pitt, J. (2007) 'Fair game? Assessing commercial activity on children's favourite websites and online environments', National Consumer Council, London. Available at http://www.childnet.com/downloads/fair-game-final.pdf (accessed 10 April 2009).

Drotner, K. and Livingstone, S. (eds) (2008) *The International Handbook of Children, Media and Culture*. London. Sage.

Livingstone, S. (2009) *Children and the Internet: Great Expectations and Challenging Realities*. Cambridge: Polity.

Stald, G. (2008) 'Mobile identity: youth, identity and mobile communication media', in D. Buckingham (ed.), *Youth, Identity and Digital Media*, The John D. and Catherine T. MacArthur Foundation Series on Digital Media and Learning. Cambridge, MA: MIT Press. pp. 143–164.

References

Buckingham, D. (2003) *Media Education: Literacy, Learning and Contemporary Culture*. Cambridge: Polity.

Busch, H., Knudsen, S. and Thim, M. (2006) *Markedsføringskanaler til børn og unge i Norden*. [Marketing Channels to Children and Adolescents in the Northern Countries]. TemaNord.

Christensen, O. and Tufte, B. (2001) *Familier i forandring – hverdag og medier i danske familier* [Changing Families – Everyday Life and Media in Danish Families]. København. Akademisk Forlag.

Cook, D. and Kaiser, S. (2004) 'Betwixt and between', *Journal of Consumer Culture*, 4, 2.

Danish Media Council (2009) *Digitalt børne- og ungdomsliv anno 2009* [Digital Childhood and Youth in the Year 2009]. Medierådet for børne og unge [Danish Media Council], København, Available at www.medieraadet.dk. (cited in Nordicom, 2009. op cit.).

Drotner, K. (2001) *Medier for fremtiden: børn og unge og det nye medielandskab.* [Media in the Future: Children, Young People and the New Media Landscape]. Høst & Søn: København.

Feilitzen, C.V. (2002) 'Times are changing and youth with them – on young people's media use in Sweden', in F. Hansen et al. (eds), *Children: Consumption, Advertising and Media.* Copenhagen: Copenhagen Business School Press.

Forbrugerredegørelsen (2008) *Forbrugerstyrelsen* [Annual Report from the Danish Consuming Agency], Copenhagen.

Grant, I. (2007) 'Why young consumers are not open to mobile marketing communication', *International Journal of Advertising*, 26 (2): 223–246.

Green, H. and Hannon, C. (2007) *Their Space: Education for a Digital Generation.* London: Demos. Available at http://www.demos.co.uk/publications/theirspace

Kjørstad, I. (2000) *Barn og internet-reklame* [Children and Internet Advertising]. Lysaker: SIFO.

Kotilainen, S., Arnolds-Grandlund, S-B., Lundgren, P., Högberg, L., Erstad, O. and Tufte, B. (2010) *Media Literacy Education: Nordic Perspectives.* Helsinki: Nordicom & The Finnish Society on Media Education.

Lehmann Erichsen, A. (2009) *Teenagerøkonomi – Teenager Economy – The 13–17 Year Olds' Income, Consumption, Dreams and Knowledge.* Copenhagen: Nordea. http://www.nordea.dk/1262302.html

Lindstrøm, M. (2003) *BrandChild.* Copenhagen: Markedsføring.

Mack, A. (2004) 'Gaming scores with advertisers', *Media Week,* 14 (26). (Cited in Calvert, S. L. (2008) 'Children as consumers: Advertising and Marketing', *Future of Children,* 18 (1): 205–234.

Moore, E. and Rideout, V.J. (2008) 'The online marketing of food to children: is it just fun and games?', *Journal of Public Policy & Marketing,* 26: 202–220.

Nielsen (2009) 'How teens use media: a Nielsen report on the myths and realities of teen media trends, June. Available at http://blog.nielsen.com/nielsenwire/reports/nielsen_howteensusemedia_june09.pdf

Nordicom (2009) 'Young people in the European Digital Media landscape: a statistical Overview with an introduction by Sonia Livingstone and Leslie Haddon', The International Clearinghouse on Children, Youth and Media, Nordicom, University of Goithenburg.

Ramaat, R., Keller, M., Martensen, A. and Tufte, B. (2008) 'Young Estonians and Danes as online shoppers: a comparative study', *Young – Nordic Journal of Youth Research,* 16, 3.

Sharples, M., Graber, R., Harrison, C. and Logan, K. (2009) 'E-Safety and Web2.0 for children aged 11–16', *Journal of Computer-Assisted Learning,* 25: 70–84 (see Becta at. http://partners.becta.org.uk/page_documents/research/web2_esafety.pdf).

Siegel, D.L., Coffrey, J. and Livingston, G. (2001) *The Great Tween Buying Machine – Marketing to Today's Tweens.* Ithaca, NY: Paramount Market Publishing, Inc.

Strasburger, V.C. and Wilson, B.J. (2002) *Children, Adolescents, & the Media.* Thousand Oaks, CA: Sage.

Tufte, B. (1995) *Medier og skole* [Media and the School]. København: Akademisk Forlag.

Tufte, B. (2007) *Børn, medier og marked* (Children, Media and Market). Copenhagen: Samfundslitteratur.

Tufte, B., Puggaard, B. and Gretlund, T. (eds) (2009) *Børns opvækst med medier og forbrug* [Children Growing Up with Media and Consumption]. Copenhagen: Samfundslittleratur.

Tufte, B. and Rasmussen, J. (2005) 'Children and adolescents use of the internet – with a focus on tweens', in B. Tufte, J. Rasmussen and A.B. Christensen (eds), *Frontrunners and Copycats*. Copenhagen: Copenhagen Business School Press. Copenhagen: Samfundslitteratur.

US Department of Education (2003) 'Computer and internet use by children and adolescents in 2001', National Center for Education Statistics Report No. 2004–014.

Vettenranta, S. (ed.) (2007) *Mediedanning og mediepædagogik* [Media Culture and Media Education]. Gyldendal Akademisk.

Websites

Mediappro Project website at www.mediappro.org
The Open Source Initiative website at www.opensource.org
Forbrug (Danish Consumer Agency) at www.forbrugerstyrelsen.dk
Child and Teen Consumption 2010 website at www.tema.liu.se/tema-b/ctc2010
The World Advertising Research Center at www.warc.com

Notes

1 According to Cook and Kaiser (2004) the term 'tween' appeared for the first time in the mid-eighties (Hall, 1987) where it was described as a market comprising children aged 9–15 with 'distinct characteristics and powers all its own'. Since then the concept of tweens has had an increasing importance in marketing literature. Lindstrøm (2003) considers 8–14 year olds as tweens, whereas Siegel et al. (2001) believe that it is relevant to operate with the age group 8–12 year olds, drawing a possible further distinction between 8–10 year olds, and 11–12 year olds.

2 The background for the study was, among other things, the fact that the effect of traditional advertising is decreasing, which is the reason why the companies want to target children and adolescents through the new digital platforms, where they can be found as rather competent consumers.

12 Children and Fashion

Maria Piacentini

Chapter aims

- To examine the current market for children's clothes and the key trends that have informed the development of this market.
- To explore the range of influences on children's clothing choices (including peers, parents, media and the wider social context).
- To examine the importance of symbolic consumption in clothing choices.
- To consider some of the key childhood contexts where clothes play an important role, focusing on the way that clothes are used by children to mark social distinctions.
- To identify emerging issues and future research directions in the area of children's clothing consumption.

Vignette 1: Teen brands

'The better brands you wear, the more popular you are', says Becky Gilker, a 13 year old eighth grader from Sherwood Park in the Canadian province of Alberta. 'If you don't wear those things you get criticized'.

In many US schools, the most expensive designer goods, such as those by Chanel or Louis Vuitton, have the highest social ranking among girls. But popular teen brands such as American Eagle, Abercrombie and Fitch, and Aeropostale are also important. But, even the wrong colour can bring put-downs. When Becky wears pinks, she says, 'I get the snarky "Nice clothes!" when people walk by in the halls'. Her mom, Karin Gilker, who is 44, says she has tried to explain to her daughter that she should ignore such comments and wear what she likes.

Source: Vanessa O'Connell, *Wall Street Journal*, 25 October 2007

Introduction

Clothing can be viewed as an essential social tool in the lives of children and teenagers, and branded clothes are often used as a way of surviving in their social worlds. For children, clothes play a key role in defining who they are and communicating this to others around them (see Vignette 1). The clothes worn by children and teenagers are closely bound to their self concept, and are used both as a means of self-expression and as a way of judging the people and situations they face (Jamison, 2006; Wooten, 2006). Clothes also help them to 'fit in' with their peers, and signify belonging and an affiliation with other children. The use of clothes as markers of identity is particularly important at times of uncertainty, such as the transition from childhood to adolescence. Clothes are important symbolic resources for children, marking out one's social position, not just in terms of economic capital, but also in terms of social and cultural capital (Piacentini and Mailer, 2004). All this suggests that clothing choice is a central part of how and why children consume. This is an area of behaviour that is not only interesting in its own right but one that can provide us with insights into children's consumption behaviour in general.

Context of the children's clothing market

The UK children's wear market was valued at £5.29bn in 2008.[1] Major players in this market are Mothercare, Marks and Spencer, Debenhams, ASDA, Tesco, and Primark. The economic downturn and recession that began in the UK in 2008 sharpened retailers' focus on price and recent estimates show that nearly 40 per cent of all children's wear sales are via the value sector.[2] This suggests that price rather than quality is a key driver of this market. Despite the difficult economic climate, retailers operating at the more upmarket end continue to invest in children's fashion brands. For example, GapKids/BabyGap are collaborating with celebrity designer, Stella McCartney, to develop a range of accessibly priced clothing.[3]

According to the market research company Keynote[4] (2009), older children can often be more discriminating about the source of their purchases, preferring to opt for fashion stores. This suggests that opportunities remain for those companies operating in the mid to higher end of the market. 'Tweenagers' is the term used to refer to children who are in the pre-teen age group of 8–12 years old (Clarke, 2003). A key characteristic of this group is that they are beginning to make some independent purchases as well as influencing and directing their parents' expenditure (Banister and Nejad, 2004). The consumption power of tweenagers has been recognized by marketers, and the clothing industry has evolved in recent years in response to changes in their consumption behaviour. Key to this group is the idea of 'being cool and fitting in' (Grant and Stephen, 2005: 451), and in many ways they are like mini-teenagers, starting to exhibit similar emotional and symbolic aspects of purchasing clothes. This is an increasingly important market and marketers recognize the value of these young consumers as future customers (see Introduction chapter).

Influences on children's clothing choices

Children's tastes, preferences and identities become embodied through fashion consumption – in part shaped by the media and popular culture, but also mediated through social networks, parental choices, controls and economic capital (Crewe and Collins, 2006). Key influences on children's clothing consumption include celebrities, peers and parents.

Popular music and sports *celebrities* tend to be key influences and reference points in children's lives (Pole et al., 2005). Banister and Nejad (2004) conducted a qualitative study of the role of celebrity endorsement and fashion clothing among young girls. They found that girls aged 8 and 9 years old were only vaguely aware of the celebrity endorsement aspect of clothes, but nonetheless were interested in having these clothes. Slightly older girls, aged 10 and 11 years old, were very conscious of celebrity endorsers, and were able to associate the various celebrities with television programmes and the images communicated through these programmes and other media. Girls aged 12 and 13 years old were also very aware of celebrity endorsement in fashion, but tended to have a more complex understanding of the images portrayed and how this impacted on their own self image and the need to be different. For older girls, approaching their teenage years, if a fashion brand or product was considered to be too popular it was rejected.

Other studies looking at clothing products and brands among children have pointed to the importance of sporting brands for boys (Swain, 2002), but for girls the trend is more towards the purchase and consumption of clothes that in some way reflect more adult and teenage trends. This 'adultification' of children's clothing (Pole et al., 2005) has been the subject of much debate in the media, especially in relation to girls' clothing and the overtly sexualized clothing found in many high street retailers. Recent examples of overtly sexualized clothing items sold to young children include: the British retailer Next selling T-shirts for girls under 6 with the slogan 'So many boys, so little time';[5] and the Asda supermarket chain being accused of selling pink and black lace lingerie aimed at girls as young as 9 years old.[6] The concern here is that children are less able than adults to comprehend the cultural messages conveyed in these kinds of clothes (Strasburger and Wilson, 2002), and that they are more susceptible to the messages expressed by them. These symbols and influences from marketing and retail environments as well as popular culture and the media inform the construction of children's gendered identities (Swain, 2002).

A second main influence on children's clothing is that of *peers and social networks*. Peers and social networks have a very important influence on children's clothing choices, most often in the form of peer pressure to fit in with the prevailing norms of the group. Approval-seeking is a central concern here, and there is considerable pressure on children (and their parents) to make the 'right' decisions. Bullying and the resulting emotional distress can be the outcome of a child failing to 'fit in' and be accepted by their peers and cultural knowledge is required in terms of what is 'in' and 'out' of fashion at the time (Elliott and Leonard, 2004). Beaudoin and Lachance (2006) conducted a quantitative survey of 1,012 high school students, looking at the determinants of brand sensitivity on adolescents' clothing choices. They found that peers played the greatest influence on children's brand choices, which is hardly surprising given the important role that clothes play in helping children to fit in. This is emphasized in the findings of a study of group identity and clothing among US teenagers by Jamison (2006), who reported that brand named clothes, especially sportswear brands such as Nike and Fila, were central to children's 'fitting in' strategies.

Parents are another important socializing influence on children's consumption behaviour, although their influence on clothing consumption changes dramatically as the child approaches adolescence. During consumer socialization children interact with their parents to learn instrumental aspects of being a consumer (e.g., comparing quality and price), but also the expressive or social motivations of consumption (e.g., forming views on the symbolic meanings of brands) (Beaudoin and Lachance, 2006). As children get older this dynamic shifts and they become less dependent on their parents in terms of learning which brands/products are acceptable. At the same time many children are still reliant on their parents to fund their clothing purchases. Recent social trends, such as the increase in the number of older parents, smaller family sizes, and more dual-income families have contributed to the increased per capita spending on children's clothing. There is a trend towards parents spending more on their children due to feelings of guilt, hence giving more power to this group of consumers. Children, and their roles as influencers on parent's clothing consumption, are starting to emerge as an area of interest. Banister and Nejad (2004) looked at the relative influence of the child in relation to the parent in the consumption situation. In the case of younger children, aged 8–9 years old, the parent was influenced by the child but retained control – and power – over the purchase. In contrast the older children, 10–13 years old, emphasized their greater involvement in and control over the purchasing process, although ultimately it was still the parent who was the buyer. Recent evidence suggests that 'children are assuming an authority to modernise parent's tastes and that the behaviour of parents is being compromised by a peer pressure on them to consume as urged by their children' (Boden, 2006: see also Ekström, Chapter 3 in this book).

Linked to this discussion of influences is the demographic context within which consumption takes place, and a number of studies have highlighted the role of materialism in relation to clothing purchases (often linked to parent's economic resources) and the consequences for social inclusion (Elliott and Leonard, 2004; Piacentini and Mailer, 2004; Pole et al., 2005). Children from all social groupings recognize the value of clothing brands and their importance for facilitating social acceptance and conformity. According to McCracken and Roth (1989), not only does a lack of economic resources limit access to the purchase of goods, but the experience of poverty and isolation can also pose limitations on understanding and accessing code information, essential for the shared understanding of cultural meanings attached to clothing consumption. Moreover, cultural meanings attached to clothing brands can vary greatly within social groups, an issue discussed later in this chapter.

What clothes say about us: self-concept, symbolic meaning and fashion consumption

Clothing is important as an aid for managing first impressions (Holman, 1980). The use of goods as symbols for communicating with other consumers is related to the idea of goods in the development of self-identity. A recent study by Jamison (2006: 20) comments that: 'clothes, and specifically brand named clothes, are among the most important symbolic representations of group identity and belongingness within the sub-cultures of late childhood-early adolescence in the US'. Clearly, clothes have a role to play in communicating something about children's identity. McCracken (1986) emphasizes the transfer of symbolic meanings from the cultural world to material goods and thus to the individual consumer. There is evidence that people use consumption as a means of encoding messages to others through their consumption, and also for decoding messages from others' consumption practices (Holman, 1980). According to McCracken and Roth (1989), females have more code knowledge than males, young people have greater code knowledge than older consumers, and generally inexpensive and unfashionable looks are more 'readable'. All of this suggests that there are unwritten rules about how people should dress and what items of clothing go well together which are recognized and acted upon. Among children and teenagers, clothes can act as powerful signals for communicating what's 'in' and what's 'not in' (Banister and Hogg, 2004). As Rose et al. note: 'Clothing is a particularly visible means of consumption and self-presentation is both a preoccupation of adolescents and a central motivation in clothing selection' (1998: 197).

Vignette 2: Looking cool

'The clothes I like are my kind of style. I like to wear jean shorts and a shirt. I like the clothes I wear because they are me. My mom does not mind what I wear. She doesn't get on my nerves because she knows it is me and she knows they are comfortable to wear ... I would like to wear Nike and Guess shorts and shirts that are Nike and Guess. I also like to wear Bongo and No Fear and the shirts and shorts they make ... I like Nike and Fila because they are cool. I like Nike because they are cool and because they make a lot of shoes in variable styles' (female, aged 12).

Source: Jamison (2006: 30)

Understanding how children interpret these rules and the codes around clothing, and the ways that 'different groups of young people make different judgements about the same brand of clothing is critical to clothing manufacturers and their advertising agencies' (Auty and Elliott, 1998) is necessary, and yet, not every child will decode the symbolic message in the same way. Whether or not children are consciously aware of what they are trying to 'say' through their clothes is problematic. As the Banister and Nejad (2004) study showed, even within the defined category of children, there is great variation in terms of how children understand the symbols and messages communicated via celebrity endorsers of clothes. In their study, 8 year old children interpreted and understood messages quite differently from 13 year olds. Clothing messages will be successfully communicated only if the symbolism is socially recognized (Grubb and Grathwohl, 1967). The cultural messages that are socially relevant for 8–9 year olds may not be relevant for 12–13 year olds. This represents a major challenge for those communicating with children and, as some studies have suggested, older children are more similar to teenagers (aspire to be like them) than they are to younger children (Banister and Nejad, 2004). The literature on symbolic consumption tells us that individuals will use the symbolic content of chosen consumption objects to reflect their affiliation or connection to a particular social group (Elliott and Wattanasuwan, 1998). This applies to children too, and as noted already, children use clothing symbolically in many different ways. The level of importance attached to the symbolic qualities of clothes is influenced by factors such as their level of self-monitoring (Auty and Elliott, 1998); their knowledge of clothing codes (McCracken and Roth, 1989); and their attitudes towards materialism (Browne and Kaldenberg, 1997).

Self-monitoring relates to the extent to which a person is sensitive to the social cues around them, and, in the consumption domain, high self-monitors are typically more sensitive to social cues when making their consumption decisions. In the context of fashion choices, Auty and Elliott (1998) found that high self-monitors will judge a product's functional features based on the product's symbolic brand image. If, for example, a particular brand of trainers, say Nike, are perceived to be 'trendy', they will also be perceived to be good quality and have a high performance rating. This contrasts with the way low self-monitors are inclined to base their judgements more on practical reasons. For high self-monitors there is greater emphasis on the social acceptability of the clothing brands consumed, and this outweighs the functional aspects of the clothes. Linked to this, high self-monitors' clothing choices are concerned with the 'elimination of the unacceptable' rather than with the positive selection of brands. This distancing from certain brands and items of clothes is comparable to Bourdieu's (1984) theory of 'refusal of other tastes' whereby the choice is concerned with rejecting that which is most distasteful rather than choosing the most pleasing option. In this way, symbolic purchasing behaviour also encompasses aspects of aversive consumer choice (Hogg, 1998).

This view was supported by more recent research into fashion consumption by Banister and Hogg (2004), where they concluded that understanding the negative drivers for consumption (that is, what we are trying to avoid through our consumption behaviour) is 'as important as understanding how consumers attempt to approach an "ideal self"' (2004: 862). Among children this can relate to not wanting to wear clothes that are seen as too 'babyish' or young, and the importance of being seen to be rejecting clothes that signify childhood. For example, O'Connell (2007) reports girls avoiding wearing the colour pink since this signifies younger childhood. Similarly, the popularity of toy-related logos on clothing diminishes as children get older – for young girls, Barbie and Bratz images are popular on clothes, but as they get older they actively reject these symbols and are attracted to teenage and adult brand names, often linked to specific retailers, such as New Look and Gap. This paradoxically results in children conforming to a set of norms that are relevant to their specific age group – the point being that the social norms around clothing change quite significantly as children grow older and there are major differences in the cultural meanings attached to clothes and fashion brands among the different age levels (Banister and Nejad, 2004).

Knowledge of clothing codes and understanding is linked to cultural and sub-cultural norms, and, as stated earlier, the transfer of cultural meaning through goods to the individual is the important mechanism of meaning transfer whereby cultural codes become enacted and brought to life by the group (McCracken, 1986). This is the case for young people and children and the key issue for children is how these codes are used as part of their approval seeking and identity formation projects. Understanding, and using, these codes as a form of symbolic capital can be an important part of group identity and any failure to do so can lead to exclusion or a rejection from the group. Wooten's recent (2006) work, exploring adolescents and the ways in which ridicule is used to encourage/discourage certain forms of clothing consumption behaviour, sheds more light on this issue. In an in-depth retrospective study Wooten found that ridicule was a powerful tool among groups of adolescents, serving the important social functions of: reflecting, and affecting adolescents' feelings of belongingness; communicating something about the norms and values of the peer group; and assisting young people in their acquisition of consumption information and thus ultimately affecting their consumption decisions. According to Wooten, ridicule helps young people refine their understanding of the social symbolism of objects, and ultimately helps them in their efforts to construct their own identities and label others.

Clothing symbols are a useful mechanism for conforming, especially important for teenagers, who are known to attach great importance to fashion and physical appearance (Beaudoin and Lachance, 2006). Many studies have shown that 'fitting in' with the peer group is of great importance to many young consumers and clothing is used to symbolize the link between the individual and the group they wish to be accepted by (Creekmore, 1980; Auty and Elliott, 1998). In some cases displaying the appropriate symbols shields the insecure teenager from teasing and name-calling (Wooten, 2006). In their study of teenagers, Auty and Elliott examined these issues further, and concluded that 'teenagers are not trying to be *like* other people as much as trying to be *liked* by them' (2001: 240). This need for social approval is key to understanding adolescents' brand behaviour in relation to clothes. Equally, by rejecting the symbols worn and recognized by the majority, clothing can be used to express someone's individuality.

A key dilemma for a child entering into early teenage years is weighing up the costs and benefits of either conforming to social norms or expressing individuality. Clothes help children to satisfy their need for conformity, which is a key value of childhood and adolescence (Danesi, 1994), and also helps them to deal with this period of increased social awareness. Balanced against this need for conformity and belonging is the need for some expression of rebellion, often to signify their difference from various social categories that they do not want to be associated with, including certain peer groups, younger children, and demonstrating their independence from parents. However, as Danesi (1994) notes, the 'rebel' or 'outsider' is a defined sub-culture, with its own cultural norms of behaviour and rules of conformity, and even among children and adolescents this is evident (as demonstrated in Vignette 2).

The role of clothes in the transition to adolescence

When consumers enter new phases of their lives, or take on new roles, they tend to be insecure and feel uncertain about how to behave. Understanding the important rites of passage in people's lives can lead to an improved understanding of consumer behaviour. Rites of passage are personal and social experiences that are partially constructed through the use of material objects (Fischer and Gainer, 1993), and are generally characterized by a separation, transition or reintegration with former roles (van Gennep, 1960). As consumers experience these rites of passage they enter a period of disequilibrium, and begin to assimilate a new status and make appropriate role adaptations (van Gennep, 1960). Studies of children and clothing consumption have identified that adolescence is a key transition point where clothes play an important role (Meyer and Anderson, 2000). As already mentioned, group identity and belonging are of great importance for adolescents and pre-adolescents. At this time, adolescents are trying to separate from their childhood self as they make the transition to early adolescence, and clothes are used to signify their success in this transition and to reject those groups they regard as different from themselves. Adolescence is a time of heightened social awareness, which can be stressful, and at this time adolescents are trying to avoid identity confusion and derive a sense of identity (Erikson, 1950), and often this is done through clothing.

The transition from childhood to adulthood is a major rite of passage in all societies, and involves a significant change in status and behaviour (Hill, 1992). In the absence of initiation rites, consumption habits take on a greater role in distinguishing the pre-adult from the adult (Ozanne, 1992). Young people, particularly in the West, tend to have a strong desire to communicate their maturity and 'adultness' to their peers through their consumption, and often this is done through clothes and fashion. Gathering material possessions is a way of establishing their identity and gaining much-needed prestige (Belk, 1988), especially at this time of 'identity crisis' for many adolescents. Often clothes are used to make the wearer feel more confident and better equipped to fulfil certain roles. Wearing certain clothes can have the psychological effect of reducing insecurities among adolescents (O'Connell, 2007). Clothes are used not only as a symbol for communicating with others but also for the purposes of conversing with oneself, to reinforce self-identity or the 'symbolic self-completion', which tends to occur after a role transition has taken place.

Clothing as a marker of social distinction

Clothes and fashion can play an important role in marking distinction and reflecting social position. According to Bourdieu (1984), people draw on three different types of resource (economic, social and cultural capital) to compete for status in the form of symbolic capital (Holt, 1998). Economic capital relates to the financial resources available to the individual, while social capital covers the relationships and social networks that influence individual behaviour. Bourdieu (1984) wrote about 'cultural capital' as knowledge that is accumulated through upbringing and education, which confers social status. Cultural capital consists of a set of 'socially rare and distinctive tastes, skills, knowledge and practices' (Holt, 1998). According to Bourdieu, cultural capital is the lynchpin of a system of distinction in which cultural and social hierarchies correspond and people's tastes are predominantly a marker of class. Although an individual may have economic capital that can be used to consume certain brands and products that may confer social standing, without the necessary skills associated with high cultural capital they will not occupy a higher social position. Cultural capital is critical to the communication of social position through symbolic consumption. The interaction of the different forms of capital on children's clothing consumption is not straightforward, and is complicated by the fact that often children do not have the economic capital to make purchases independently, with their consumption often sanctioned by parents. However, children do influence their parents' decisions around clothes and often parents and children will negotiate and arrive at a shared consumption decision. Further, parents play a role in transmitting an understanding about social and cultural forms of capital in particular, and this is likely to influence the ways that children consume clothes.

Piacentini and Mailer (2004) found that British school children in two socially contrasting schools had quite different understandings of the role of clothing in signifying their social position. For those attending the comprehensive school there was evidence that clothing choices were made to demonstrate economic competence. Buying branded clothes was important to demonstrate that they were not poor, and brands were a useful way of 'keeping up' with others in the school.

Interviewer: Is it important for you to have branded clothes?

Participant: Not really but I'd prefer to have it because it makes you mix in. You don't want to be any worse than what your friends have got and you don't want to be any better so you just get the same logos as your friends just to keep up with them ... I wouldn't want to stand out of the crowd; I just want to be part of it. I wouldn't want to be the big man. (Male, 15 years old, comprehensive school)

In contrast, those participants attending the private school expressed their distaste for heavily branded clothes, and generally distanced themselves from such clothes.

Interviewer: Why do you think some people want to show off how expensive their clothes are?

Participant: Some people think that it shows they have money and that that makes them a better person.

Interviewer: Would it impress you if someone came into school with a brand new pair of expensive trainers or a top of the range jacket?

Participant: In my opinion, I think it makes them look quite sad that they've went to all that trouble just to come to school. (Female, 12 years old, private school)

and

Participant: ... I think there's an alternative fashion going on with all these skate-punks being anti-fashion and it's become a fashion itself. I think that's very funny. I do try and shy away from brands and whatnot, it's just advertising how much money you've got, which I don't think is necessary. (Male, 17 years old, private school)

These perspectives are the product of social conditioning, and will be determined by family, school and neighbourhood, reflecting the material conditions that are experienced as a result of one's position in society (Allen and Anderson, 1994). Taste in clothing and ways of dressing are based on distinctions, and enable people to judge and classify one another (Holt, 1998). This echoes Bourdieu's (1984) ideas about the cultural elite, where 'aesthetic distancing' occurs as a way of marking an elite group. The high aesthetic ideal is defined as 'against the popular' and informs the tastes and preferences of those in this group. In the context of young people and fashion, adopting an alternative fashion position in their clothing choices (and therefore not making 'popular' clothing choices) demonstrated the private school pupils' different level of cultural, rather than economic, capital. These examples illustrate the ideas of cultural capital among the two social class groups, where knowing what to wear serves as a marker of belonging and understanding the norms and values for both groups (see Nairn, Chapter 6 in this book).

There was evidence of a confidence underpinning these participants' tastes and preferences, learned effortlessly and unconsciously through their social world. For the participants in the comprehensive school (where clothing as a display of 'economic capital' was an important theme) the emphasis was on acceptance by peers, and social learning occurred via friends, through the media and popular culture. These are interesting findings, as they indicate the complex interplay of social, economic and cultural forms of capital. These data were collected at a time of relative economic boom; in the current recessionary climate it would be interesting to examine these themes in more depth to observe any shifts in the relative importance of the different forms of capital among different social groupings.

Conclusion

The issues affecting children as clothes consumers have been explored within this chapter. A key issue to emerge is that clothes serve a valuable social function for children, and therefore the social context of consumption is especially important for this age group. Belonging and affiliation are expressed through clothing, but clothes are also used by children and adolescents to signify what groups they are rejecting. This leads to the paradoxical nature of clothing consumption for children. Clothes help children to satisfy their need for conformity, which is a key value of childhood and adolescence (Danesi, 1994), which helps them to deal with this period of increased social awareness. Set against this need for conformity and belonging is the need for some sense of self-expression and rebellion. The challenge is to strike a suitable balance between the two competing needs. Some of the mechanisms by which these social groupings emerge were discussed, including the role of ridicule for reinforcing social groupings and also the way that the different forms of capital impact on children's clothing consumption.

Sociological and cultural studies offer a perspective on children's fashion consumption that address issues about the wider social and cultural context within which consumption takes place (e.g., Swain, 2002; Pole et al., 2005). This is relevant for marketing, particularly if we start to look at children's clothing from an interpretivist standpoint, where the emphasis is on understanding the wider socio-cultural and historical context within which children's consumption takes place. Linked to this wider social and cultural context is the debate around the construction of gendered identities through clothes, and this is a particular concern in relation to the sexualization of young girl's clothing. This last section will identify some future research directions in the area of children's clothing consumption.

Future research directions

A key theme in all the studies looking at children's clothing consumption is the importance of the social context and peer pressure. However, more recent research suggests that children are placing pressure on their parents in ways that influence the parents' clothing consumption, and that this is not wholly unwelcome by the parents (Boden, 2006). Aligned to this is the importance of understanding the cultural codes that are being used by children to denote what's 'in' and what's 'not in' fashion. The pursuit of understanding 'cool' is important here, and in the USA and the UK there are agencies dedicated to understanding cool (e.g., Coolhunters; Cool Hunting). From a commercial perspective, there is an advantage to understanding the current trends among young people and children, and ensuring that products/brands speak to children in a culturally meaningful way, but critical to success in this area is an ability to research and communicate with children in age and culturally appropriate ways, i.e., entering their worlds. Despite the interpretivist turn in much consumer behaviour research, research in this area is still dominated by experimental and survey methodologies (often testing brand acceptance) and qualitative studies are often descriptive rather than embracing interpretivist approaches. Such a shift towards interpretivism would ensure the fuller representation of children's voices in the research into fashion consumption, which is currently lacking (see Davis, Chapter 4 in this book).

The impact of recessionary pressures on the market may have interesting effects on the way that clothes are consumed by children – as parents face greater economic constraints then this may impact on the way that they purchase clothes. Although industry analysts predict that longer term the mid-market brands will continue to do well, it will be interesting to see what impact the recession has on children in their endeavours to balance the need for individuality against conformity in their clothing choices.

Discussion questions

1 There are clear differences in the clothing consumption of younger children (8–10 years old) in comparison to older children (say, 12–14 years). What are the implications for conducting research into children's clothing consumption?
2 Discuss the paradoxical issues around individualism vs group identifications.
3 Given the importance of group pressure on children's clothing purchases, what suggestions would you have for a government agency tasked with developing a social marketing campaign to stop bullying based around clothing?

Further reading

Cardoso, A., de Araujo, M. and Coquet, E. (2008) 'Modelling children's choice decisions of clothing', Journal of Fashion Marketing and Management, 12 (3): 415–428.

Hogg, M.K., Bruce, M. and Hill, A.J. (1998) 'Fashion brand preferences among young consumers', International Journal of Retail and Distribution Management, 26 (8): 293–300.

Meyer, D.J.C. and Anderson, H. (2000) 'Preadolescents and apparel purchasing: conformity to parents and peers in the consumer socialization process', Journal of Social Behavior and Personality, 15 (2): 243–257.

Poole, C. (2007) 'Researching children and fashion: an embodied ethnography', Childhood. 14 (1): 67–84.

Russell, R. and Tyler, M. (2002) 'Thank heaven for little girls: "Girl Heaven", and the commercial context of feminine childhood', Sociology, 36 (3): 619–637.

References

Allen, D.E. and Anderson, P.F. (1994) 'Consumption and social stratification: Bourdieu's distinction', *Advances in Consumer Research*, 21: 70–74.

Auty, S. and Elliot, R. (1998) 'Fashion involvement, self-monitoring and the meaning of brands', *Journal of Product and Brand Management*, 7 (2): 109–123.

Auty, S. and Elliot, R. (2001) 'Being like or being liked: identity vs. approval in a social context', *Advances in Consumer Research*, 28 (1): 235–241.

Banister, E.N and Nejad, H. (2004) 'Young consumers: the influence of celebrity on clothing choices', in Margaret Bruce, Christopher Moore and Grete Birtwistle (eds), *International Retail Marketing*. London: Butterworth-Heinemann.

Banister, E.N. and Hogg. M.K. (2004) 'Negative symbolic consumption and consumers' drive for self-esteem: the case of the fashion industry', *European Journal of Marketing*, 38 (7): 850–868.

Beaudoin, P. and Lachance, M.J. (2006) 'Determinants of adolescents' brand sensitivity to clothing', *Family and Consumer Sciences Research Journal*, 34: 312–331.

Belk, R.W. (1988) 'Possessions and the extended self', *Journal of Consumer Research*, 15 (2): 139–168.

Boden, S. (2006) '"Another day, another demand": how parents and children negotiate consumption matters', *Sociological Research Online*, 11 (2): Available at http://www.socresonline.org.uk/11/2/boden.html

Bourdieu, P. (1984) *Distinction: A Social Critique of the Judgement of Taste* (translated by Richard Nice). London: Routledge.

Browne, B.A. and Kaldenberg, D.O. (1997) 'Conceptualizing self-monitoring: links to materialism and product involvement', *Journal of Consumer Marketing*, 14 (1): 31–44.

Clarke, B. (2003) 'The angst, anguish and ambitions of the teenage years', *Young Consumers: Insights and Ideas for Responsible Marketers*, 4 (3): 27–33.

Creekmore, A.M. (1980) 'Clothing and personal attractiveness of adolescents related to conformity, to clothing mode, peer acceptance and leadership potential', *Home Economic Research Journal* 8 (3): 213–215.

Crewe, L. and Collins, P. (2006) 'Commodifying children: fashion, space, and the production of the profitable child', *Environment and Planning A*, 38: 7–24.

Danesi, M. (1994) *Cool: The Signs and Meanings of Adolescence*. Toronto: University of Toronto Press.

Elliott, R. and Leonard, C. (2004) 'Peer pressure and poverty: exploring fashion brands and consumption symbolism among children of the 'British Poor'', *Journal of Consumer Behaviour*, 3 (4): 347–359.

Erikson, E.H. (1950) *Childhood and Society*. New York: Norton.

Fischer, E. and Gainer, B. (1993) 'Baby showers: a rite of passage in transition', *Advances in Consumer Research*, 20: 320–324.

Grant, I.J. and Stephen, G.R. (2005) 'Buying behaviour of "tweenage" girls and key societal communicating factors influencing their purchasing of fashion clothing', *Journal of Fashion Marketing and Management*, 9 (4): 450–467.

Grubb, E.L. and Grathwohl, H.L. (1967) 'Consumer self-concept, symbolism and market behaviour: a theoretical approach', *Journal of Marketing*, 31 (4): 22–27.

Hill, R. (1992) 'Transition in turmoil: when becoming an adult involves criminal behaviour', *Advances in Consumer Research*, 19: 399–401.

Hogg, M.K. (1998) 'Anti-constellations: conceptualization and content', *European Advances in Consumer Research*, 3: 44–449.

Holman, R.H. (1980) 'Clothing as communication: an empirical investigation', *Advances in Consumer Research*, 7: 372–377.

Holt, D.B. (1998) 'Does cultural capital structure american consumption?', *Journal of Consumer Research*, 25: 1–25.

Jamison, D.J. (2006) 'Idols of the tribe: brand veneration, group identity and the impact of school uniform policies', *Academy of Marketing Studies Journal*, 10 (1): 19–37.

McCracken, G. (1986) 'Culture and consumption: a theoretical account of the structure and movement of the cultural meaning of consumer goods', *Journal of Consumer Research*, 13, June, 71–84.

McCracken, G. and Roth, V.J. (1989) 'Does clothing have a code? Empirical findings and theoretical implications in the study of clothing as a means of communication', *International Journal of Research in Marketing*, 6: 13–33.

Meyer, D.J.C and Anderson, H. (2000) 'Pre-adolescents and apparel purchasing: conformity to parents and peers in the consumer socialisation process', *Journal of Social Behaviour and Personality*, 15 (2): 243–257.

O'Connell, V. (2007) 'Fashion Bullies Attack-In Middle School', *Wall St Journal*, 25 October. Available at http://online.wsj.com/public/article/SB119326834963770540.html (accessed 10 August 2009).

Ozanne, J.L. (1992) 'The role of consumption and disposition during classic rites of passage: the journey of birth, initiation and death', *Advances in Consumer Research*, 19: 396–397.

Piacentini, M.G. and Mailer, G. (2004) 'Symbolic consumption in teenagers' clothing choices', *Journal of Consumer Behaviour*, 3 (3): 251–262.

Pole, C., Pilcher, J., Edwards, T. and Boden, S. (2005) '*New Consumers? Children, fashion and consumption*'. Summary paper from Cultures of Consumption ESRC programme of research. Available at www.consume.bbk.ac.uk/publications.htm

Rose, M.R., Bush, D.M. and Friestad, M. (1998) 'Self-esteem, susceptibility to interpersonal influence, and fashion attribute preference in early adolescents', *European Advances in Consumer Research*, 3: 197–203.

Strasburger, V.C. and Wilson, B.J. (2002) *Children, Adolescents, and the Media*. Thousand Oaks, CA: Sage.

Swain, J. (2002) 'The "Right Stuff": fashioning identity through clothing in a junior school', *Gender and Education*, 14 (1): 53–69.

van Gennep, A. (1960) *The Rites of Passage* (trans. M.B. Vizedom and G.L. Caffee). Chicago, IL: University of Chicago Press.

Wooten, D.B. (2006) 'From labelling possessions to possessing labels: ridicule and socialization among adolescents', *Journal of Consumer Research*, 33 (2): 188–198.

Notes

1 *Just Style* (2009) 'UK: Children's wear challenges offset birth rate', June 2009 http://www.just-style.com/article.aspx?id=104425 (accessed 10 August 2009).

2 Verdict (2009) 'UK Childrenswear Retailers 2009: Dominance of grocers and value retailers suppressing growth in resilient sector', http://www.verdict.co.uk/dmvt0456-UK_Childrenswear_Retailers_2009.htm (accessed 10 August 2009).

3 *Retail Week* (2009) 'Stella McCartney to design childrenswear range for Gap', June 2009 http://www.retail-week.com/retail-sectors/fashion/stella-mccartney-to-design-childrenswear-range-for-gap/5003398.article (accessed 10 August 2009).

4 Keynote (2009) 'Childrenswear Market Report 2009', http://www. researchand markets.com/reports/1054419/childrenswear_market_report_2009 (accessed 7 August 2009).

5 *Independent*, 'Shocking truth about tweens', 2/9/06, http://www.independent. ie/opinion/analysis/shocking-truth-about-tweens-76287.html (accessed 10 August 2009).

6 *Daily Mail*, 'Tesco and Asda attacked for lingerie and pole dancing kits for kids', 6/5/07, http://www.dailymail.co.uk/news/article-447057/Tesco-Asda-attacked-lingerie-pole-dancing-kits-kids.html (accessed 10 August 2009).

Part IV
Looking Forward

13 The Ethics of Marketing to Children

Sarah Todd

Chapter aims

- To understand the ethical implications of marketing to children.
- To gain an understanding of the different perspectives regarding the ethics of marketing to children.
- To look at how different theories and concepts have been used to inform this debate.
- To bring together the different areas of marketing to children within which ethical issues have been raised, and emerging issues.

Vignette 1: The ongoing consequences of marketing to children

'Although children have long participated in the consumer marketplace, until recently they were bit players, purchasers of cheap goods. They attracted little of the industry's talent and resources and were approached primarily through their mothers. That has changed. Kids and teens are now the epicentre of American consumer culture. They command the attention, creativity and dollars of advertisers. Their tastes drive market trends. Their opinion shapes brand strategies. Yet few adults recognise the magnitude of this shift and its consequences for the futures of our children and cultures'.

Source: Schor (2004: 9)

Introduction

The debate surrounding the ethics of marketing to children, and particularly advertising to children, is not new. However, it has gained more attention in the last few years than it has done in the previous couple of decades. While much of the focus of earlier research in this area has been around the role of advertising, as will be discussed in this chapter, there is now growing concern about a range of marketing practices, as well as the ethical implications associated with researching children. Over the past three decades, in particular, some fundamental questions have been raised about the fairness of marketing to children (Moore, 2004), but many remain unresolved. Such questions include the ethics of targeting children with messages about products and brands designed for an older market. For example, while the value of the children's market has been well-documented over the past decade or so, it is also important to note that they are frequently viewed as a future market, and thus many campaigns aimed at children are designed not to generate immediate sales but, rather, to forge brand loyalty from an early age (McNeal, 1998; Moore et al., 2002). This chapter will examine such concerns, and the heightened interest that has resulted from emerging technology and the adoption of increasingly sophisticated marketing techniques, while also acknowledging the perspective of those who argue that children have a right to be heard and informed, and that they need to 'learn to consume'.

The age debate

Much of the discussion regarding the rights and wrongs of marketing to children has centred on the issue of age. That is, at what age do children understand the persuasive intent of marketing? The rationale has been that, once the 'true nature' of advertising or other forms of marketing is understood, children are no longer 'vulnerable', and targeting them as a consumer market is therefore 'fair'. The focus in this area has predominantly been around concerns about children's ability to comprehend and evaluate selling or promotional messages: 'Embedded within this debate is the contention that advertising to children is inherently "unfair"' (Moore, 2004: 161).

Based on the stages people are said to progress through in terms of their cognitive skill development, it has long been argued that, minors, unlike adults, don't have the cognitive skills required to differentiate among marketing messages (see Chapters 9 and 7 respectively by Roland-Lévy, and Young, in this book). As well as the necessary skills, it has also been argued that children don't have the 'life experience' to resist persuasive claims.

Before looking at the broader ethical question about the fairness or unfairness of marketers' actions, we need to understand the developmental capacities of children. Information processing theories and developmental stage theories have been used to study what children understand from commercial messages, how their responses change as they mature or get older, and under what conditions they are more likely to be persuaded (see Roedder-John, 1999; also see de la Ville and Tartas, Chapter 2 in this book).

Basically, it is suggested that younger and older children differ in their ability both to understand advertising's general purpose and, importantly, in how they deploy that understanding when responding to specific advertisements. The two key skills that are required, then, are to distinguish commercial versus non-commercial content, and to recognize persuasive intent and be able to use that knowledge when interpreting messages. Most researchers are in agreement that, by about age 5, most children can distinguish between commercials and television programmes (the context within which most of this research has been conducted) (e.g., Blatt et al., 1972). However, being able to articulate that advertisements are 'shorter' or 'funnier' than programmes is not the same as having a conceptual understanding of the content of advertisements. Rather, it is the capacity to recognize the persuasive intent that has been seen as a key developmental milestone by policy makers and researchers. Again, there is relative consensus that most children have at least an initial understanding of the aim of advertising by 8 years of age (e.g., Roberts, 1982; Macklin, 1987). Once they understand the intent, it has been considered that they become more sceptical, and therefore less susceptible, to commercial messages. Arguably though, scepticism in itself may not be enough, with research revealing that, unless prompted explicitly to do so, even children from 8 to 12 years of age do not invoke that knowledge of the persuasive intent when viewing television commercials (Brucks et al., 1988).

More recent research has reinforced the important role that consumption experience (rather than age per se) plays, with the suggestion being made that older children are actually more attentive to the entertainment dimension of advertising, and therefore it is more likely that this will shape their interpretation of product usage. Thus, because of (rather than in spite of) their increased understanding of the multiple levels of meaning in advertisements and their ability to appreciate both the literal and figurative elements, their relative inexperience in the marketplace means that they are actually more permissive of advertisers having 'creative licence' in what is said about various brands. While the popular press frequently makes claims that children are more sophisticated consumers than previously, there is, as yet, little evidence to suggest how their understanding of advertising can be accelerated beyond their cognitive capacities at key points (Moore, 2004). Even less evidence exists to indicate children's understanding of the plethora of other types of marketing messages and techniques to which they are exposed, many of which are arguably more subtle in their targeting of children than is mass advertising.

The American Children's Advertising Review Unit (CARU), like many similar self-regulatory bodies around the world, has developed guidelines for advertising to children and, in addition to the words commonly found in such codes or guidelines, specifically states that certain 'techniques which may be appropriate for adult directed advertising may mislead children if used in child-directed advertising'. CARU notes that their guidelines are deliberately subjective, and go beyond the conventional issues of the truthfulness and accuracy of advertising, 'to take into account the uniquely impressionable and vulnerable child audience' (http://www.bbb.org/us/caru). Others have also used the term 'vulnerable' when describing children as a market, with the reasons for this including not only their limited cognitive development, but also their lesser experience and general maturity (e.g., Bergadaa, 2002).

While such self-regulatory mechanisms and an understanding of the different cognitive abilities of children go a long way to providing a reference point against which to review individual cases, what they do not do is answer the fundamental question of whether or not it is fair to advertise to children at all (Kunkel, 2001). Nairn and Fine (2008) progressed that debate with their thesis that 'discussion of the effects and ethics of marketing to children will continue to be incomplete as long as discussants fail to acknowledge, and address in the form of a mature debate, the role of implicit cognition in consumer psychology' (2008: 896). They argue that what they term as the 'persuasion knowledge framework' (i.e., the contention that evidence of scepticism about marketing is a basis for children being a fair target for marketing) is not as important as was previously thought in understanding the effect of advertising on children. Rather, they use the dual process model of attitudes (see Gawronski and Bodenhausen, 2006) to contend that there are both implicit and explicit attitudes, with the former being an 'automatically evoked evaluation of a stimulus' and the latter requiring more 'cognitive control' or self-regulatory checks which are dependent on both the individual's motivational state, and his/her cognitive control resources (Nairn and Fine, 2008). In support of Moore (2004)'s findings, although using a different theoretical basis, Nairn and Fine (2008) note that older, supposedly more 'marketing-savvy', children are no less susceptible to marketing than younger children, and therefore understanding the persuasive intent of advertising is not, in itself, sufficient. Rather, evaluative conditioning (through advertising and other marketing techniques) will lead to an implicit attitude change in children and drive their consumer behaviour as they lack the required 'control' resources to form an explicit attitude.

With much of the current marketing aimed at children arguably taking the form of evaluative conditioning (e.g., product placement in movies, use of celebrities and advergames) rather than propositional product information, there is an increased likelihood that age alone will not be enough to 'protect' children from marketing initiatives. The ethical implications of such a thesis are profound, as it suggests that advertising does not necessarily affect children through a process of conscious, rational evaluation, even among those older 'marketing-savvy' children previously seen to be 'fair game' as targets for marketing initiatives. While Ambler (2008) considers it contentious to suggest that there is something unfair about advertising to consumers who are unable to resist implicit persuasion, the hypothesis that the lesser self-regulatory capacity of both children and adolescents compared to that of adults affects their ability to resist marketing techniques has significant implications when considering the ethics of marketing to children. Rather than just considering the age at which children have 'persuasion knowledge', or can identify the selling intent of marketing, Nairn and Fine's (2008) hypothesis suggests the need to investigate the ways in which contemporary marketing practices are able to bring about an attitude change without the consumer's 'explicit' permission or awareness.

The rights of children

As well as opponents of marketing activities targeted at children, there are also proponents, who argue that children's vulnerabilities have been over-stated and that children have the right to product information to make better informed choices. To be able to make choices, it is argued, children need to be aware, and awareness comes from being exposed to marketing messages: 'Of course, we want and need to tell children about new products, where they can get them, how much they cost, how they work and the other usual essentials of marketing' (Davidson, 1998: 10). However, Davidson also notes that marketers who push this line too far will face a social backlash, ranging from letters from upset parents through to restrictive legislation and regulations. Similarly, Paine et al. (2002: 71) note the need for marketers to monitor trends carefully, as the 'targets of media attention vary and the sources of public indignation among adults can lead to great umbrage when children are involved'.

A study of adults' views on marketing to children (Roper Starch Worldwide, 1994, cited in Heubusch, 1997) found that while a general scepticism about advertising aimed at children was observed there was not necessarily an objection to the practice. Eight out of ten adults said it was 'all right' to advertise toys, cereal and clothing during children's television programmes, but they were more likely to object to commercials selling 'sex' and poor nutrition (Heubusch, 1997: 55). While summarizing that 'Americans do not overwhelmingly object to the way TV sells to kids', Heubusch also poses the notion that 'maybe they figure it's good training for them'.

The UN Convention on the Rights of Children was first adopted in 1980 and has been the basis for many subsequent codes and charters regarding children's rights. Two quite different views of children's rights are promulgated by the Convention, with both the child's right to protection and their right to participation being advocated. The former conceptualizes children as helpless and defenceless, while the latter suggests children are active, autonomous agents (Nairn and Monkgol 2007). In other words, children are portrayed as both active and passive. This same tension is evident in much of the debate around the ethics of marketing to children, with their right to be socialized in a way that allows them to grow up as responsible and knowledgeable consumers put up against their lesser capacity to cope in the marketplace.

The consumer rights advocated by J.F. Kennedy in the 1960s are often referred to when discussing this issue. For example, children, as with all consumers, are said to have the right to choose, to be informed and to be heard. Obviously, these rights have significant implications for a range of areas covered by 'marketing' and have been used at various times to justify advertising to children, as well as the development of products and brands targeted at young consumers. They have also been used in the debate held at different times and in different places around the world regarding calls to ban advertising to children. Arguably, with the consumption of products and brands now a fundamental part of social life, children have the right to be educated, but it is the form that such an education should take that is up for debate.

Similarly, in the field of marketing research, there are increasing calls for the right of children to 'have a voice'. Alongside such calls has been the developing sophistication in research methodologies used to collect information about children as consumers (see Davis, Chapter 4 in this book). Such developments have lead to psychologists, among others, joining in the debate about the ethics of researching children, especially when they may not be consciously aware that they are the subjects of research: 'Deploring what they see as an unfair and conflict-ridden manipulation of the young, a group of psychologists and other professionals has called on the American Psychological Association to restrict the use of psychological research by advertisers pitching toys, video games, snack foods, and other products to children' (Hays, 1999). Not all would agree however, with others saying that, if you're going to market to children, it should be done in the most responsible way possible, which includes using all the insights available to make a successful children's product. The American Psychological Association responded to the concern by stating that it was important to note that psychological techniques were also being used by marketers for 'socially redeeming issues' (Hays, 1999).

Many market research associations' codes of ethics now include a specific reference to the special implications of researching children (e.g., the Market Research Association), but these tend to focus on issues such as parental consent and the 'mechanics' of the research, such as disclosing the length of time that is required and any special tasks, rather than dealing with the fairness, or otherwise, of using children as respondents in research they may not readily understand or recognize as being research. (Interestingly, the age of the child at which parental consent is no longer required varies considerably across the different codes, reflecting another issue that dominates this area, namely, defining a 'child' consumer.)[1] Children participating in studies using particular techniques, such as focus groups and projective techniques, may well believe they are simply 'having a chat', without realizing they are providing 'data' (Todd, 2000). In other cases, such as observation studies, children may have no idea that they are being watched. Almqvist's (1997) study that involved content analysing children's letters to Santa Claus, while undoubtedly an innovative method by which to measure the effect of pre-Christmas advertising campaigns on children's wish-lists, raises other ethical queries about taking personal letters, written for a specific purpose, as research data. As Almqvist (1997) notes, analysing children's letters to Santa Claus 'opens the door to quite a number of otherwise hidden domains of children's play, thinking and learning'. Such insights are undoubtedly valuable, but it is the purpose to which those insights are put that determines the ethics or otherwise of acquiring data in such a way. While many research associations' codes of ethics talk about research contributing to the subjects' welfare, there has been little specific discussion as to whether the researching of children, for marketing purposes, can truly be said to contribute to those children's welfare (see Davis, Chapter 4 in this book).

The ill-effects of marketing to children

Various authors have argued that exposing children to consumer culture increases the likelihood they will suffer from a raft of different ills, in addition to potentially making bad purchases, and that list includes depression, anxiety and poor self-esteem (Schor, 2004). Schor goes on to argue that, furthermore, the urgings of marketers to minors to use their 'discretion' and decide carefully what they reveal to parents and friends about what they are doing inherently teaches them to deceive and act dishonestly. Ward (cited in Rigby 2005: 22) describes the reason he founded www.iknow.it as being his concern about the 'negative effect of marketing on children'. He includes parental debt (as a result of children asking for brands they can ill afford) and 'social exclusion in the playground, bullying and theft' among those effects.

As well as concerns about children's vulnerability due to their limited cognitive skills and understanding of commercial intent, there is also concern that, without the necessary critical thinking skills, they are more likely to develop values such as materialism (Macklin, 2003). An American psychologist, Dr Kanner, was one of those who wrote the previously referred to letter concerning psychologists' involvement in the development of marketing strategies targeting children, and claimed that his concerns were based on conversations with children that were, as a group, 'blatantly materialistic': 'I'll ask kids what they want to do when they grow up, and lots of times they'll tell me "Make money"' (Kanner, quoted in Hays, 1999). The argument is based on the tenet that, rather than just selling a product, marketers are promoting a larger value system which reinforces the idea that making money, and spending money on material things, will make you happy.

Thus, marketers are criticized for encouraging children to 'consume in an increasingly trivial manner' (Bergadaa, 2002: 55), with many products seen to ascribe social status, or give the buyer the feeling of being one of the 'tribe'. Related to concerns about the encouragement of materialistic values is the observation that consumers are increasingly 'selfish and playful' (Bergadaa, 2002: 56), far more influenced by their emotions than by reason.

Similarly, the encouragement (or, some would argue, manipulation) of children into consuming certain products or brands to appear 'cool' is a criticism often levelled at marketers. The importance of a product's symbolic value is generally agreed upon (e.g., Belk, 1988; Holt, 1998; Holbrook, 1999) and children, for whom peer approval is of significant importance, are understandably attracted to marketing appeals suggesting their consumption of a certain product or brand will enhance their 'coolness' (see Nairn, Chapter 6 in this book). While the New Zealand Advertising Standards Authority is not alone among self-regulatory bodies for making reference to this issue, it is interesting to note that its relevant statement approaches this issue from the opposite of coolness. Namely, it is stated that 'Advertisements should not suggest to children any feeling of inferiority or lack of social acceptance for not having the advertised product' (www.asa.co.nz/code_children.php, 2(e)). Thus, while it is considered 'wrong' to show a child suffering social exclusion for lack of a particular product or brand, it is not explicitly stated that it is 'wrong' to show a child being ascribed social status, or 'coolness', as a result of their consumption. From a different but related perspective, McNeal (1992) argues that the increasing practice of encouraging children's attachment to a brand, rather than a tangible product, through imagery and positive reinforcement, also means that young consumers will have problems learning to compare products and choose the one with the best quality-price ratio.

One of the problems with attempts to either control or monitor marketing to children is that practices are no longer limited to commercials on mass media such as television but rather 'ads have proliferated far beyond the television screen to virtually every social institution and type of public space, from museums and zoos, to college campuses and elementary school classrooms, restaurant bathrooms and menus, at the airport, even in the sky' (Schor, 2004: 9). Marketing practices commonly used to target children include not only television and print advertising but also product placements, sales promotions, packaging design, public relations and, in some countries, in-school marketing (both directly and indirectly via sponsorship arrangements). While various countries have moved to ban advertising to children due to concerns about children's ability to cope with it, there is a problem in determining exactly which kinds of advertising children are exposed to. For example, Lindstrøm and Seybold's (2003) study of 'tweens' (9–14 year olds) showed the participants could readily supply opinions about brands of cars, fashion and cell phones. In addition, there is the argument that, as representatives of the future, children cannot be isolated by simply banning advertising but rather we need to remember it is 'the practice of consumerism that exposes children to the necessary socialisation process for them to develop into aware adults' (Bergadaa, 2002: 53).

Some of the most well-known cases in the debate about marketing to children involve products for which children, arguably, are not the direct target market. For example, Budweiser's frogs and lizards, Bud Light's cuddly 'Spuds McKenzie' and, of course, Reynolds' Joe Camel (Broder, 1997) have long been contentious icons associated with adult brands and products, but undoubtedly appealing to children. In the case against Joe Camel, studies reportedly found that he was one of the most recognized corporate advertising symbols in the United States, and recognized by 86 per cent of children aged 10 to 17. As part of the Congress petition to the FTC to reopen its earlier investigation, it was claimed that 'Joe Camel is directly designed to appeal to 12-year-olds to hook them on smoking' (Broder, 1997). The sale of hazardous products is thus seen as another example of unethical marketing to children, with young consumers considered a 'development market' by alcohol and cigarette producers. Arguably, knowing that the consumption of such products is a health hazard makes the marketing of these to children a moral issue. Nader (1999) went further, describing marketers to children in general as 'electronic child molesters', whose actions in promoting alcohol, tobacco, violent entertainment and junk or fast food were particularly repugnant.

The role of parents

Traditionally, many marketing messages for children's products were aimed at their parents who made the buying decisions and the actual purchase. For many product categories now though, in terms of products both directly and indirectly consumed by children, the message is more likely to be targeted directly at children. Davidson (1998) quotes one advertising executive who candidly stated 'We're relying on the kid to pester the mom to buy the product'. Parents, interestingly, have been found to be no more likely than the average to object to advertising directed at children (Heubusch, 1997), with some apparently more lenient than those without children. For example, those over 60 years of age (and therefore unlikely to have young children) are most likely to object to advertising during children's programmes.

Increasingly, as discussed above, concerns are being expressed around the practice of developing brand loyalty from a very early age for products not designed for children, and thus parents may not be as aware that their children are being targeted. Reflecting this contemporary practice, the senior VP (Marketing) at Nickelodeon is quoted as saying (in Dobrow, 2002), 'nobody says we're going to go after newborns ... but if you don't get this audience now, you're going to lose them in 10 years'. Parents might view such a statement as shameless and unethical, but the reality is that such targeting commonly occurs – both in recognition of the future value but also in recognition of the 'pester power' children can exert on adults' purchase decisions. For example, the Ford Motor Co linked up with Nickelodeon's *Blues Clues* and named the animated dog character (Blue) official 'spokes-puppy' for their minivan safety campaign.

From a utilitarian and pragmatic perspective, the marketer's role is to put goods and services on the market. As the children's market increases in value, it is not surprising that more and more products are targeted at them. From an ethical standpoint though, the encouragement of children to 'pester' or exert influence on parental purchase decisions is worthy of debate. While it may be one way for them to develop the necessary skills for their own future consumption, it is also a way for children to test the leverage they have over their parents by deploying manipulative strategies (McNeal, 1998). Under such circumstances, it is difficult to decide whether or not it is 'fair' or 'right' to let children acquire this special behaviour (Bergadaa, 2002: 58). The significance of this concern is reflected in the codes of various self-regulatory bodies that include statements such as 'Children should not be urged in advertisements to ask their parents, guardians or caregivers to buy particular products for them' (www.asa.co.nz/code_children.php, 2(d)). What such regulatory statements do not cover, however, is the indirect or more subtle targeting of children that encourages them to attempt to influence their parents' purchasing behaviour.

It has been argued (e.g., Bergadaa, 2002: 65) that the 'decision-making responsibility of parents ... is to assist their children in developing a sceptical attitude to the information in advertising'. With the results regarding the effect of such scepticism on children's actual consumption behaviour now considered somewhat inconclusive, a better suggestion may be that parents have a responsibility to actively participate in the socialization of their children as consumers, particularly in terms of letting them develop experience in the marketplace and allowing them to learn from their mistakes. For example, giving children pocket money and control over how that money is saved and/or spent gives them firsthand experience of how product claims translate into product performance.

Census data from many parts of the world indicate that children are increasingly living in households where there is a gap in the time that children are at school and parents return from work. This means that a large proportion of children have unsupervized access to a wide range of media and are potentially subject to increased peer influence, with parents simply not available or able to protect them in the current marketplace (Paine et al., 2002). Thus, there is also an increasing need for marketers and organizations to take on more of an *in loco parentis* role, working with parents in a similar way as schools have done on ethical and other issues.

It should also be remembered that through what Rummel et al. (2000) describe as a 'reactance' process, there is often a tendency among children to reject parental attempts to influence their purchase and consumption behaviour. Marketing practices which target the 'dark side' (i.e., that side in younger children that responds to slapstick, toilet humour, etc.) are therefore likely to appeal to children and make it more difficult for parents to intervene and influence their consumption choices.

Vignette 2: Are marketers or parents to blame?

It's Thanksgiving Day and 8 year old Jason Jones has just finished stuffing himself with turkey, cranberry sauce, and pumpkin pie *à la mode*. He sits at his PC, frantically typing a list of presents he hopes to receive from Santa Claus for Christmas. He plans to deliver the list to Santa the next day, opening day of the Christmas shopping season and, incidentally, of affluenza season. Jason's list contains ten items, including a trip to Disney World, a mountain bike, a cell phone, a DVD player, and several compact disks.

Jason is no dummy; he doesn't really believe in Santa Claus, but he knows his parents give him what he asks Santa for, so he gets up bright and early on Friday to play the game.

Source: De Graaf et al. (2001: 11)

The merging of media

The widespread adoption of the internet, and the various opportunities it opens up for new marketing initiatives, has led to renewed interest in the 'fairness' or otherwise of marketing to children: 'Emerging media such as the internet have further expanded advertising's reach and offer novel opportunities to target this young audience … as a result they face new challenges in terms of their capacity to interpret and assess commercial messages' (Moore, 2004: 161). While researchers in the past have focused on children's ability to distinguish between advertisements and programmes (primarily within the context of television), the web and its chat rooms, animated game sites, virtual communities and the potential for viral marketing techniques has meant that the question of what children understand and are aware of is once again up for debate (see Chapters 11 and 6 respectively, by Tufte and Rasmussen, and Nairn in this book). The time that children spend online, with less room for a parental discussion about what they're seeing and doing than that which may naturally occur when watching television, has led to renewed concerns about the impact of marketing techniques.

For example, in 2004 the (US) National Institute on Media and the Family initiated an investigation into marketers' use of websites to attract 'secret agents' who were then sent free products to promote among their peers. Various companies that have adopted what Walsh (2004) describes as 'contrived "cool" names', such as Proctor & Gamble's 'Tremor', or SoulKool and BzzAgent, have been accused of exposing children to adult-oriented concepts, using them as an inexpensive and unsuspecting distribution force, as well as the (unintended, non-marketing) consequence of creating forums that are easy targets for child predators. Such serious allegations have been countered with claims that sites require young children to get parental consent and that this is merely an online form of 'word-of-mouth advocacy'. However, on many sites the proof of age is easily changed and, apart from the ongoing argument regarding children's cognitive ability to differentiate marketing messages, the issue of whether or not children have the necessary self-esteem to resist the lure of free products and the opportunity to be 'cool' is heightened in the online world (Mayo and Nairn, 2009).

As early as 1996, CARU had added a special section to their guidelines to highlight such issues that are unique to the internet, and particularly for sites that are aimed at children less than 12 years old. Despite such protections, children are still frequently required to fill out a questionnaire about themselves, their families and their friends before being able to access the entertainment offered online, providing marketers with a vast array of information to store in databases and use for future marketing initiatives. Nairn and Monkgol (2007) note that two central concepts when examining online privacy are those of 'control' and 'knowledge'. That is, online consumers should have control over unwanted intrusions, but, equally, it should be recognized that, without knowledge, they are unable to exercise control. What is of particular concern to those interested in the ethical issues surrounding the increasing use of online media to communicate with children is the capacity of young consumers to both understand and, therefore, control the process of information collection.

The changing media landscape now means that children are exposed to complementary and reinforcing messages on multiple media. For example, commercials shown on television often link in with website games and activities featuring the same brand characters, while the use of product placement in children's movies further blurs the distinction between advertising and entertainment, with the ability to make such a distinction traditionally used as an indicator of the age to which it is 'fair' to target children. As noted by Moore (2004), older children's ability to integrate both the fantasy elements of an advertisement with the brand reality, but their relative inability to enlist the necessary defences to resist such messages, may actually make them more susceptible than their younger counterparts to the blurring of advertising messages and activities apparently designed to entertain.

While the growth and pervasiveness of the internet have lead to renewed public debate about the way in which children are targeted by marketers, other offline techniques have raised concerns about the ethics or otherwise as well. The late 1980s/early 1990s saw significant growth in the use of 'clubs' (predecessors to the online virtual communities) to promote products and brands to children. Typically, these clubs involved membership cards, newsletters and 'initiation prizes' (e.g., stickers or badges) and many included the chance to enter competitions or win prizes. With an increasing number of children living in families where the sole or both parents were working when the child arrived home after school, these clubs were seen to 'hold great psychological allure' (Bruzzese, 1991: 45), appealing to children who wanted to belong and be part of something. Such clubs also coincided with the increased affordability of databases, allowing marketers to track children's buying habits and develop long-term relationships. For example, Burger King's explicit goal was to 'increase loyalty to its chains among both parents and children' (Bruzzese, 1991: 46), and its regular club newsletters featured animated characters that were promoted on television and through franchises. Others, such as Fox Television's *Kids' Club*, focused solely on children, recognizing their academic attainment with discount coupons or similar as rewards, as well as sending out a magazine. In addition to developing loyal viewers among the children's market, Fox could also use the Club to convince advertisers of a steady child audience. While advocacy groups saw such marketing programmes as unethical and manipulative, others claimed that, as long as the children received something of value from their membership, there was no need for concern.

With many schools and other educational institutions increasingly required to look at non-traditional funding sources, new opportunities have been opened up for marketers looking to access a very defined and specific target market. With schools offering an undoubtedly cost-effective and appealing alternative promotional channel for businesses to use, there are just as obviously a number of ethical issues that need to be considered. Often, the potential negative impact of advertisements in schools has been dismissed by the 'circular argument that since advertising itself is pervasive in our society, there is nothing wrong with placing advertising in the schools' (Curran, 1999: 534).

Vignette 3: Viral marketing – clever promotion or a 'disease'?

'Got girls?' That was the subject of an email last month from a professional marketing firm to a 13-year-old boy. If he read past the subject line, he was promised access to 'loads of gorgeous girls for you to check out and vote on'. An isolated example? Unfortunately not. Consider this email sent to another 13-year-old, a girl who was invited to a second company's chat room, where she can 'flirt with visitors'. Both emails are part of an increasingly common strategy among a new breed of youth marketers: they use sexual titillation and age-inappropriate language and images to entice kids into helping sell products and services.

Source: Walsh (2004: 16)

The practitioner's perspective

While children, their parents and policy makers have tended to be the participants in research examining the fairness or otherwise of marketing to children, a recent survey conducted by Harris Interactive gathered the views of 878 people in the industry and compared them with those of their target market, or young consumers' own perceptions. As Grimm (2004: 44) notes, the impression gained is that there is a level of 'conflicted ambivalence' among marketing professionals charged with targeting the younger market. Interestingly, there was overwhelming agreement with the suggestion that marketers today are 'going overboard in pursuit of kids' dollars and minds', although far fewer indicate that their own employer 'crosses any ethical lines' (Grimm, 2004: 44). Such a mentality is worrying as it suggests a reluctance to recognize their own part, or to take ownership of any of the negative consequences associated with marketing to children. One of the key findings was that the marketers tended to define children in terms of their characteristics as consumers, whereas children defined themselves first and foremost as children. That difference in perception casts some doubt on the idea that today's children are mature and savvy consumers, and the age at which, in all good conscience, they can be appropriately considered as 'consumers'. Marketers, as the people who both create and implement the marketing tools and concepts, cannot afford to ignore the ethical implications of what they are doing, even if they do believe that 'ethics is the domain of the CEO' (Bergadaa, 2002).

There are, of course, various codes of ethics that govern marketing practices, some of which are at the level of the individual organization while others are promulgated by professional associations, nationally or internationally (e.g., the American Marketing Association, the Business Marketing Association). Additionally, there are those that have been developed to cover specific marketing practices (e.g., the Word of Mouth Marketing Association, Online Marketing Association). Unlike those that have been created to govern advertising though, many others do not specifically discuss the ethical implications involved when dealing with child consumers.

Conclusion

Advertainment has proved to be one of the most effective tools in marketing to tweens, and 'disguising promotions as games and comics makes it harder for tweens to be sceptical of advertising messages' (Lindstrøm and Seybold, 2003: 225). The advent of digital television means that we are going to see increasingly the seamless integration of television and commercial websites, and the time is ripe for the debate regarding marketers' use of increasingly sophisticated techniques to target children to be resurrected (Moore, 2004).

Marketers have tended to prefer self-regulation over laws and regulations when it comes to monitoring marketing to children, in part because of the ability to respond in a more timely fashion to situations that emerge from the development of new products and media. For such self-regulation to survive though, in an area around which there is much emotion, it needs to prove itself to be reliable and trustworthy. As soon as commercial instincts start to override a sense of responsibility, marketers run the risk of genuinely manipulating children and generating an emotional backlash where legislation will be imposed in place of a reliance on marketers' ethics (Davis, 1997).

One of the ongoing and unresolved issues when examining marketing to children has been defining exactly what is acceptable, and what isn't. 'Ethics' comes from the Greek *ethos*, meaning 'values' and ways of taking action. The etymology of the word 'morality' comes from the Latin *mores*, meaning 'character'. In other words, much of the determination of what is moral and/or ethical is not the subject of some universal law, but rather is up to an individual's interpretation. Marketing, as a business function, requires a pragmatic approach in the majority of cases, but this needs to be balanced with an ethical perspective. That is, to be able to confront and counter the criticism of various marketing practices, marketers need to take a stance as individuals and see children as children and not just as consumers, subjects for research or potential customers.

Future research directions

Recent and future practices need to be reviewed in light of new research, as well as being cognizant of society's tolerance for children to be treated as consumers. While several countries have gone down the path of banning advertising to children, the reality is that the plethora of different marketing techniques and media now available with which to access children make a ban increasingly impractical. Additionally, there is also the socialization and consumer rights perspectives, which argue that children need to learn to consume, and, indeed, have the right to information and choices as consumers. Undoubtedly, the area of ethics in relation to marketing to children is in its infancy, with much of the work focusing primarily on advertising and undertaken some considerable time ago. There is a definite need for both practitioners and academics alike to re-look at what is happening, in the context of the environment in which today's children are growing up.

Discussion questions

1 Describe some of the tensions that might occur because of a conflict between an individual marketer's own ethics and the objectives of the organization when targeting an online promotion at children less than 12 years old.
2 Given the various rights that children are entitled to, examine the arguments in favour of a total ban on advertising to children.
3 Marketers, organizations, society, parents, or children themselves – who is responsible for keeping children safe in the marketplace?
4 Choose a particular aspect of marketing (e.g., advertising, research, sales promotions) and analyse the ethical implications of using that technique when dealing with young consumers.
5 Given recent research findings which indicate that it is the consumption experience rather than a sceptical attitude to advertising alone which best indicates children's capacity to make good consumer decisions, how should we ensure that children acquire that experience without being put at risk in the marketplace?

Further reading

Archard, D. (2004) *Children: Rights and Childhood*. London: Routledge.
Grimm, M. (2004) 'Is marketing to kids ethical?', *Brandweek* 5 (April): 44–48.
Kouzelas, K. (2005) 'Direct marketing and children – how far can you go?', *Database, Marketing and Customer Strategy Management* 12(3): 257–265.
Whiton, S., Stewart, K. and Kruger, E. (2002) 'Preventing ethical problems when marketing to minors', *Advertising & Marketing to Children*, Jan–Mar: 69–80.

References

Almqvist, B. (1997) 'Letters to Santa Claus: An indication of the impact of toy marketing on children's toy preferences', *Fordrag Presenterat vid NFPFs Jubilenmskangress Goteborg*. Available at http://www.hh.se/dep/ncflweb/the impact.html
Ambler, T. (2008) 'Whose minds are messed up? A response to Nairn and Fine', *International Journal of Advertising*, 26 (2): 283–286.
Belk, R. (1988) 'Possessions and the extended self', *Journal of Consumer Research*, 15 (2): 139–168.
Bergadaa, M. (2002) 'Children and business: pluralistic ethics of marketers', *Society and Business Review*, 2 (1): 53–73.
Blatt, J., Spencer, L. and Ward, S. (1972) 'A cognitive developmental study of children's reactions to television advertising', in G. Comstock and E. Rubenstein (eds), *Television and Social Behaviour* (vol. 4). Washington, DC: US Government Printing Office.

Broder, J. (1997) F.T.C. 'Staff Seeks Action Against Joe Camel', *The New York Times.* 27 (March): B14.

Bruzzese, A. (1991) 'Little people, big market', *Incentive*, 165 (5): S1: 45–47.

Brucks, M., Armstrong, G. and Goldberg, M. (1988) 'Children's use of cognitive defenses against television advertising: a cognitive response approach', *Journal of Consumer Research*, 14 (March): 471–482.

Curran, C. (1999) 'Misplaced marketing – a best buy in advertising: schools selling students as media audiences', *Journal of Consumer Marketing*, 16 (6): 534–535.

Davidson, K. (1998) 'Opportunities, threats when marketing to kids', *Marketing News Chicago*, 32 (17): 10.

Davis (1997) 'Time to Write New Rules for Ads that are Out of Bounds' *Campaign*, 25 September.

De Graaf, J., Wann, D. and Naylor, T. (2001) *Affluenza: The All-Consuming Epidemic.* London: Berrett-Koehler.

Dobrow, L. (2002) 'How old is old enough', *Advertising Age Chicago*, 73 (5): S4.

Gawronski, B. and Bohdenhausen, G. (2006) 'Associative and propositional processes in evaluation: an integrative review of implicit and explicit attitude change', *Psychological Bulleting*, 132 (5): 692–731.

Grimm, M. (2004) 'Is Marketing to Kids Ethical?', *Brandweek*, 5 (April): 44–48.

Hays, C. (1999) 'A Call for Restrictions on Psychological Research by Advertisers into Products for Children', *New York Times*, 22 (October): C6.

Heubusch, K. (1997) 'Is it OK to sell to kids?', *American Demographics*, 19 (1): 55.

Holbrook, M. (1999) *Consumer Value: A Framework for Analysis and Research.* London: Routledge.

Holt, D. (1998) 'Does cultural capital structure American consumption?', *Journal of Consumer Research*, 25 (1): 1–25.

Kunkel, D. (2001) 'Children and television advertising', in D. Singer and J. Singer (eds), *Handbook of Children and the Media.* Thousand Oaks, CA: Sage. pp. 375–393.

Lindstrøm, M. and Seybold, P. (2003) *Brand Child.* London: Kogan Page.

Macklin, M. (1987) 'Preschoolers' understanding of the informational function of television advertising', *Journal of Consumer Research*, 14 (Sept): 229–239.

Macklin, M. (2003) 'Children: targets of advertising', in J. McDonough and K. Egolf (eds), *Encyclopaedia of Advertising.* New York: Fitzroy Dearborn. pp. 294–298.

Mago, E. and Nairn, A. (2009) *Consumer Kids: How Big Business is Grooming our Children for Profit.* London: Constable.

McNeal, J. (1992) *Kids as Customers: A Handbook of Marketing to Children.* New York: Lexington.

McNeal, J. (1998) 'Tapping the three kids' markets', *American Demographics*, 20 (April): 37–41.

Moore, E. (2004) 'Children and the changing world of advertising', *Journal of Business Ethics*, 52 (2): 161–167

Moore, E., Wilkie, W. and Lutz, R. (2002) 'Passing the torch: intergenerational influences as a source of brand equity', *Journal of Marketing*, 66 (April): 17–37.

Nader, R. (1999) 'Why is the government protecting corporations that prey on kids', *The Public Interest*, 22 September.

Nairn, A. and Fine, C. (2008) 'Not seeing the wood for the imaginary trees: or, who's messing with our article?', *International Journal of Advertising*, 27 (5): 896–908.

Nairn, A. and Monkgol, D. (2007) 'Children and privacy online', *Journal of Direct, Data and Digital Marketing Practice*, 8 (4): 294–308.

Paine, W., Stewart, K. and Kruger, E. (2002) 'Preventing ethical problems when marketing to minors', *Advertising & Marketing to Children*, Jan–March: 69–80.

Rigby, E. (2005) 'Can Brands Promote Goods Ethically to Kids Online', *Revolution*, February: 22.

Roberts, D. (1982) 'Children and commercials: issues, evidence and interventions', *Prevention in Human Services*, 2: 19–35.

Roedder-John, D. (1999) 'Consumer socialization of children: a retrospective look at twenty-five years of research', *Journal of Consumer Research*, 26 (Dec): 183–213.

Rummel, A., Howard, J., Swinton, J. and Seymour, D. (2000) 'You can't have that! A study of reactance effects & children's consumer behavior', *Journal of Marketing Theory and Practice*, 8 (1): 38–45.

Schor, J. (2004) *Born to Buy: The Commercialised Child and the New Consumer Culture*. New York: Scribner.

Todd, S. (2000) 'Researching children: ethical issues'. *Proceedings of the 4th Academy of Marketing Conference*, University of Derby, UK (CD-ROM).

Walsh, D. (2004) 'Children for Sale', *Adweek*, 6 December, 4 (46): 16.

Websites

American Marketing Association Code of Ethics www.helleniccomserve.com/marketingcodeofethics.html

Business Marketing Association Code of Ethics http://www.marketing.org/i4a/pages/index.cfm?pageID=3286

Children's Advertising Review Unit http://www.bbb.org/us/caru

Online Marketing Code of Ethics http://www.interactivereturn.com/ethics-code.htm

Making Kids Brand Aware www.iknow.it

Market Research Association Code of Ethics http://www.mra-net.org/pdf/expanded_code.pdf

New Zealand Advertising Standards Authority http://www.asa.co.nz/code_children.php

National Institute on Media and the Family http://www.mediafamily.org/

Note

1 Examples include 'Children means all persons below the age of 14' http://www.asa.co.nz/code_children.php; 'in 1996 CARU added a section to its *Guidelines* that highlight issues, including children's privacy, that are unique to the Internet and online sites directed at children age 12 and under' http://www.caru.org/about/index.aspx; 'For purposes of this Code, the term child refers to someone who has not reached his or her 13th birthday' http://www.the-cma.org/?WCE=C=47|K=225849#11; 'not target children under the age of six ... take account of the relative sophistication of audiences, especially between the ages of six and eleven' http://www.afgc.org.au/cmsDocuments/GWF%20CAP.pdf

<table>
<tr><td>**14**</td><td></td></tr>
</table>

14 Children as 'Competent' Consumers

Stephen Kline

Chapter aims

- To consider children's consumer competencies in an increasingly risk averse society.
- To revisit the media panic surrounding the marketing and advertising of food to children.
- To examine the research into consumer socialization and children's marketplace literacies.

Introduction

In 2000, the WHO (World Health Organization) launched a health promotion initiative rather out of keeping with its usual reports on global malnutrition, refugees, and viral epidemics. Their report, entitled *Obesity: Preventing and Managing the Global Epidemic*, claimed that the risks associated with the rising incidence of obesity in both the developed and developing world was a greater global health issue than malnutrition. The WHO (2000) noted that the over-consumption of energy dense foods coupled with 'sedentary lifestyles' was becoming shockingly visible – especially in the USA and Britain where nearly 65 per cent of the adult population was considered either overweight or obese: 'If immediate action is not taken, millions will suffer from an array of serious health disorders' they concluded. The link between childhood obesity and adult obesity is illustrated in the following Vignette 1.

> **Vignette 1: 'Children don't lose puppy fat'**
>
> This was the headline on a 2006 piece on *CBBC*, the British Broadcasting Company's children's channel. It reported on a study of more than 5000 children conducted for Cancer Research which found that children who were obese or overweight at 11 years old were still carrying too much weight at 16 years old. The site claims that while many parents tell their children that the 'puppy fat' melts away as they get older the scientists did not find this.
>
> Another UK study from the University of Newcastle upon Tyne, which began in 1947, looked at the heights and weights of over 400 participants at age 9, age 12 and age 50. Researchers found that although overweight teenagers were more likely to carry this into adulthood a number of overweight adults were not overweight as children.
>
> *Source*: http://news.bbc.co.uk/cbbcnews/hi/newsid_4970000/newsid_4975800/4975830.stm http://news.bbc.co.uk/1/hi/health/1680995.stm

Putting the panic in the obesity pandemic

The increasing coverage of the obesity 'pandemic' focused public debate on the availability and promotion of a wide variety of good tasting, inexpensive, but excessively energy dense food and drink products. The report was quickly hailed by the critics of commercialism in the USA protesting the Golden Arches Awards for advertising to children: 'Intensive marketing harms children. It harms their health and sense of wellbeing. It compromises their safety and undermines their family life. In this era of unprecedented and rampant exploitation of children as a consumer group, it's time for people who care about kids to take a stand against an industry that seeks to manipulate for profit our most vulnerable citizens' (CCFC, 2000).[1]

Schlosser's best selling *Fast Food Nation* escalated the controversy by pointing a finger at the food industry. American lawyer Samuel Hirsh launched a multi-million dollar class action law suit against the fast food Goliaths, accusing them of deceptive marketing, and young film-maker Morgan Spurlock made a 'biting' documentary about his declining health on an unremitting diet of McDonald's meals. Journalists increasingly turned their spotlights on children as the key 'at risk population'. In 2002, the WHO released another report claiming that children's habitual consumption of soft drinks constituted a world-wide health risk. Globesity became 'the leading science story of 2002' (AAAS, 2002). By 2004 fast food had become 'the new tobacco' at the heart of a media panic galvanized by the public battle over food marketing to kids (Kline, 2004). Around the world, the fast food and constant snacking diets of American children were brandished in a moralizing tale about deregulated markets and irresponsible corporations. Augmented by projections of soaring health care costs, 'fat kids' became symptomatic of

Epidemic

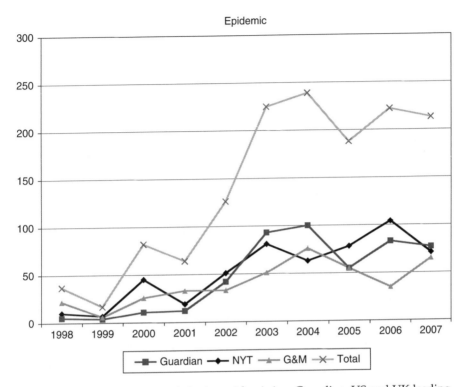

Figure 14.1   News coverage of obesity epidemic in a Canadian, US and UK leading broadsheet

the looming lifestyle risks associated with a food chain driven by irresponsible marketers (Lang and Heasman, 2004).

As illustrated in Figure 14.1, media coverage of the child globesity epidemic peaked in 2004 with 40 per cent of all stories about children's health mentioning the weight gain associated with fast food and sedentary lifestyles.[2] Overweight children became the fulcrum of a broadening debate about banning marketing to children. The American Psychological Association's (APA) Task Force on Advertising to Children reviewed the impact of advertising on children under age 8, concluding in 2003 'that all advertising to children is, by its very nature, exploitive. Long-standing public policy holds that all commercial content must be clearly identifiable as such to its intended audience, in order to allow the consumer to consider the source of the message in evaluating its claims. Advertising that violates this standard is deemed deceptive, and a violation of federal law' (APA, 2004). In Britain also the media coverage of obesity precipitated a similar debate, as a coalition of health, parenting and children's advocacy groups escalated their lobbying effort to stop 'big food' industries from exploiting children by lobbying for a 'ban' on food advertising to children. Reports on the effects of food marketing to children were commissioned (Hastings et al., 2003;

Livingstone and Helsper, 2004) which were immediately heralded by anti-commercialization advocacy groups calling for the regulation of food advertising aimed at children under 8 years old. The globesity pandemic reignited a long standing ideological struggle over children's ambiguous standing as consumers in the media saturated marketplace.

Déjà vu all over again

If this politicization of children's marketing seems familiar that is because it is. As Americans watched the Baby Boomers grow into maturity in front of their TVs during the 1970s, escalating concerns about food and toy advertising precipitated very similar arguments thirty years ago. As Jeffery et al. noted in 1982:

> In the past decade increased attention has been paid to the potential mediating role of television food advertising in the development and maintenance of food preferences. The Federal Trade Commission (FTC) has conducted hearings about whether or not to regulate television advertising directed mainly at children. Critics claim that television food commercials are adversely affecting our children's health by influencing them to develop enduring preferences for foods which are high in calories and sugar, but possess little else of nutritional value. Advertisers assert that they are helping to teach children appropriate consumer behavior, that children's food preferences are shaped most strongly by parents not advertisers, and that deciding what a child watches on TV is a parental function in which there is no need for federal regulation. (Jeffery et al., 1982: 98)

I cite this comment here to remind readers that the media panic galvanized by child globesity simply re-ignited both the moral uncertainties surrounding children's commercial television and the unresolved, but crucial, policy issues underscoring children's ambiguous status as consumers in the mediated marketplace. The central assumptions of fair market competition are crucial in commercial law: markets are efficient as long as consumers have a choice between alternative products; when they are fully informed about the qualities of products available to them; and when they are capable of making rational decisions based on the costs, benefits and risks associated with their use. Commercial free speech is warranted as long as the information that sellers provide is truthful, not misleading, and meets community standards. Which is why FTC commissioner Azcuenaga (1997) concluded that it was important for US governments to regulate advertising in the interests of ensuring informed choice as the *sine qua non* of fair markets. But at what age can children be considered rational economic subjects capable of making informed choices?

This question was first put to the test by the Kroger Food Foundation in an experiment in the early 1950s which followed a group of pre-teen boys and girls who were taken to a supermarket to choose 20 free items. The observers were surprised to note that these child consumers had considerable knowledge not only of various food and beverages, but also of clothes, toys and games, appliances, tools and cars. The researchers moreover were shocked to discover that the children acted more like price conscious adults than a horde of out of control brats: they didn't pig out on candy, toys, chocolate, and ice cream, but instead chose large bags of flour and other consumer durables that their parents might value. Commenting on this study, Riesman and Roseborough (1955) concluded that children born just after the Second World War had acquired many of the skills, knowledge and attitudes required in the mass marketplace – the ability to shop for a good buy in a supermarket. Moreover these children seemed to understand the roles, norms, and restraints of adults. But were those traditional values of thrifty consumption being eroded by the emerging normative order of mass materialism?

Consumer socialization in the mediated marketplace

During the 1950s, the perfect storm of laissez faire parenting, mass media and direct-to-child marketing began to agitate anxiety about children's vulnerability in mass markets (Kline, 1993). The issue of children's consumerism was presaged eloquently in Eric Fromm's (1947) attempt to apply Freudian psychoanalysis to the problems associated with the emerging 'market orientation' of post-war America. Fromm concerned himself with the changing dynamics of post-war childrearing: 'In order that any society may function well, its members must acquire the kind of character which makes them want to act in the way they have to act as members of the society or of a special class within it' (1947: 66). Fromm took pains to differentiate his own view of consumption from that of Freud by asserting that 'the fundamental basis of character is not about the organization of the libido', but instead about how, in the process of living, a person relates himself to the world in two ways: 'by acquiring and assimilating things' and 'by relating to people (and himself) in a process of socialisation' (1947: 66). Early economic socialization, he noted, took place within the family as bodily drives were channelled, tastes and preferences were formed, money was introduced and shopping was first experienced.

Fromm was careful not to blame children for these new priorities of market socialization, arguing 'The character of the child develops in response to the character of the parents' whose 'methods of child training are in turn determined by the social structure of their culture'. Fromm's student, David Riesman (Riesman et al., 1950), extended this reflection on the broader consequences of these changing agencies of socialization in post-war America where parents were becoming more concerned about providing the skills and knowledge required in the mass mediated marketplace – the ability to save, shop for, and find a good buy among the vast array of goods. He argued that changes in childrearing and popular culture were transforming the inner-directed moralities formed by the Protestant ethos into an outer directed character of mass consumerism.

Lloyd DeMause (1974) noted that after the Second World War new ideas about childrearing were circulated, widely emphasizing the child's need for autonomy, self-expression and control over their body. Benjamin Spock's bestselling book *Baby and Child Care* (1964), for example, advocated a less repressive approach to childrearing which abandoned punishment in favour of rewards which supported the child's development as an autonomous, self-regulating 'individual' capable of enjoying life. As the war economy gave way to a rapidly expanding commercial culture, the Spock psychology of supportive parenting was woven into public discourses about leisure and consumption for the Baby Boom generation. Unrestricted leisure and free play were no longer perceived as 'devil's work', but were now seen as necessary conditions for promoting rational, autonomous and self-expressive individuals. Berger et al. suggested the 'gentle revolution' brought about by new childrearing methods sought to cultivate individuals 'generally unaccustomed to harshness, suffering or for that matter, any kind of intense frustration' (1974: 173).

Children had been targeted in selling strategies since the 1920s, but it was in the 1950s that commercial television propelled advertising to the fore-front of the critiques of mass society. Advertisers raised alarm bells, for as J.K. Galbraith (1958) warned 'the power of these corporations extends into commercial culture and politics, allowing them to exercise considerable influence upon popular social attitudes and value judgments', and as McNeal (1964) pointed out, there were three reasons why children were increasingly being integrated into the marketing plans of those corporations: in so far as they purchased goods, because they could influence their parents' purchasing behaviour, and because they were future consumers-in-the-making. Children's induction into the marketplace therefore came to symbolize the crisis of consumerism as the 'new forms of electronic media together with the flow and forces of capital converged in the last quarter century fomenting a post-modern childhood inseparable from media use and media surveillance' (Cook, 2001: 82). Would the future generation of TV kids continue to choose wisely when left to choose for themselves?

Television brought a daily supply of direct-to-child ads into the American household (Kline, 1993). Watching TV for three hours a day not only rivaled the influence of schools but also exposed children to 20,000 messages per year from corporations. Early research was providing some indication that children could be influenced in their toy and food preferences by ads on TV (Robertson and Rossiter, 1974) and that children were playing a more active role in parental shopping decisions (Atkins, 1978). In short, like it or not, children's consumer socialization had become intricately bound up with children's time spent in front of the screen. Parents began to see that the invisible hand of marketing was also leaving smudgy fingerprints on that same screen: the cereals it promoted were too sweet and the toys were too war-like for many parents. Pestered to buy Coon Skin Hats, Frosted Flakes and Barbies as advertised on TV, parents became alarmed by the marketers' growing influence on their children's consumer preferences which made conflicts over goods a part of familial dynamics. But without the guiding hand of parents and teachers would the immature child have the knowledge and perspective necessary to discriminate between the healthy and safe in a commercialized popular culture promoted by the mediated marketplace? Acknowledging children's developmental vulnerability as consumers, in 1974 the FCC limited the amount of advertising to 9.5 minutes and called for the separation of programming and advertising content. But these regulations proved insufficient to meet the growing public panic about the impact of commercial TV.

One systemic effect of commercialized TV was the forging of a dialogue between merchants and children about toys and food which vied with parental influence. What many believed was that numerous young children had trouble distinguishing advertising from programming. The question of direct-to-child marketing became the flashpoint of a contentious public debate about the knowledge, understanding and skills which enabled young people to perform as audiences for commercial TV. Although younger children demonstrated little understanding of advertising it was also clear that many older ones understood advertising's intent to persuade and were somewhat sceptical of advertising claims (Robertson and Rossiter, 1974). It was in this context of uncertainty that children's consumer competence erupted as the last battleground for the preservation of childhood innocence in the mediated marketplace.

According to Ward (1974: 2), 'consumer socialisation is the process by which young people acquire skills, knowledge, and attitudes relevant to their functioning as customers in the marketplace'. The importance of this definition was that it focused on competencies rather than processes. Yet one of the most comprehensive early studies found that neither developmental capacity (measured by age/grade), nor the external influence of parents, schools and marketers (such as heavy media use, SES, parenting styles, materialist attitudes and lifestyles) were *sufficient in themselves* to explain the acquisition of a child's consumer competences (Ward et al., 1977). Cognitive factors like reasoning, numeracy and information processing were clearly crucial for children to know about and judge goods and shop, whereas familial norms, training and the modelling of parents were related to the way children learned about money, brand orientation, scepticism and lifestyle preferences. Recognizing the multiple factors involved in consumer socialization, these researchers suggested that the regulation of advertising to children might be helpful not only in protecting very young children but also in reducing family conflicts over lifestyle choices. Other researchers confirmed that many young children nagged their parents for products that interested them (like food and toys) which they saw on television. Moreover, as children got older (8 years and up), these requests were largely for advertised brands (Moschis and Churchill, 1978; Moschis and Moore, 1979).

In 1978, ACT (Action for Children's Television) called on the FCC for a ban on advertising to kids based on this research. The advocates claimed that young children were developmentally incapable of understanding advertising as persuasive communication. This was a useful political strategy as Martin notes, for 'if children are unaware of the persuasive intent of advertising, all advertisements aimed at them are, by definition, unfair and/or misleading' (1997: 205). Here the policy and psychology parted company for at what age do legislators draw a line in an ongoing consumer socialization process based on the criterion of informed choice in the marketplace? Yet the evidence-based policy question proved of little consequence when Ronald Reagan appointed a neo-Conservative to the FTC in 1981 who de-regulated children's TV in the interests of commercial free speech. As Grossbart and Crossby (1984: 79) warned this ideological decision would not mark the end of the matter: 'Children's advertising is not a dead issue ... The FTC's defeat will do little to alleviate their concern or eliminate the possibility of direct action by concerned parents to mitigate advertising's effects'. They were right. When the obesity pandemic hit, the influence of advertising on children's diets moved right back into the public spotlight.

Rethinking consumer competencies in the mediated marketplace

Following those pioneering studies, research into children's capacity to understand products, money and market persuasion has developed into a field focusing on three marketplace competencies. First is the issue of *advertising and media literacy*, which asks at what point children come to understand that the claims made in advertising are intended to persuade them. The second concerns the question of *consumer literacy*, namely the point at which children acquire the ability to compare rationally the relative benefits and risks associated with the different goods necessary for comparative shopping. Third is the issue of children's *economic literacy*, that is their financial skills and the cognitive capacity to evaluate competing goods along a standard yardstick of monetary value and more generally their understanding of prices in a competitive market.

Advertising literacy and product knowledge

As I have already mentioned, the policy issues surrounding child consumers highlighted the development of children's understanding of persuasive communication. As Roedder-John (1999) states, regulation depended on five issues – namely children's ability to distinguish commercials from television programmes; children's understanding of advertising's persuasive intent: children's ability to recognize bias and deceptions in advertising: children's beliefs about the truthfulness of advertising; children's knowledge of advertising tactics and appeals; and children's use of a cognitive defence against advertising.

The most controversial competence concerns children's advertising processing abilities, particularly their capacity to make decisions for themselves or critically evaluate advertising campaigns. Researchers generally find that child consumers are interested in advertising. They actively chose to watch commercials, not only because they are fun, but also because ads provide them with one of the few sources of information about the products they want to consume (snacks, treats, cereals, movies, toys and games). Because they watch a lot of TV even the 8 year olds can identify an advertisement as a distinct genre, are more or less aware of its selling intent, and are competently deciphering the selling points and persuasion techniques. These research literatures have been reviewed with a broad agreement on the developmental limitations of the majority of children under the age of 8 (Roedder-John, 1999; Young, 2003). At this age, many are only able to describe ads as short and funny programmes, but rarely as 'trying to get people to buy something'. But as Roedder-John (1999) concludes: 'there is little reason to believe that the vast majority of children younger than seven or eight years of age have a command of advertising's persuasive intent'.

There are, however, a number conceptual issues troubling the study of advertising literacy. Blosser and Roberts' (1985) view of advertising was as a multi-dimensional form of communication which simultaneously informs, educates, persuades, entertains, and sells, to the viewer. Rossiter and Robertson (1974), for example, distinguished between children's capacity to read ads as information about products as opposed to reading ads as a persuasive social influence. Methodological problems have also confounded attempts to provide a clear developmental breaking point for children's understanding of intent to influence. Some argue that young children understand advertising but simply cannot articulate that understanding (Donohue et al., 1980). But using visual measures Macklin (1987) counters that it is not a lack of verbal capacity but children's lack of understanding of how advertising persuades that matters.

Research has also shown that by the time children reach their eighth birthday 'negative or mistrustful predispositions toward advertising are well established' (Boush et al., 1994). Yet as Rossiter and Robertson (1974: 19) noted long ago: 'Children's ability to recognize persuasive intent in commercials should not be taken as implying immunity to all commercials'. As Brucks et al. (1988: 480–481) point out, to be informed consumers, children 'need more than just a skeptical or critical attitude toward advertising. They also need a more detailed knowledge about the nature of advertising and how it works'. Marshall et al. (2007) report that, although 8 year old children in Canada and New Zealand could distinguish ads from programming, recognize the intent of advertisers, and have a general scepticism to all messages, their understanding of the economic arrangements of commercial media systems was marginal. Children understand advertising as a genre but not as a commercial media institution. In a meta-analysis of 23 studies with a cumulative N of 2934, Martin (1997) finds an r of .34–40 between age and children's understanding of advertising's intent to persuade. When all the studies are combined, research confirms that the younger children (<8) have difficulties in understanding persuasive communication generally: they do not understand that the advertising source has different perspectives and interests from that of the receiver; that the ad is attempting to persuade them to do something; and that the messages are potentially biased by the seller's interest. But Martin also points out that there is still considerable variation in the studies which 'reveals several issues that largely have been ignored in the literature, which has limited our understanding of children's development of understanding of ad intent'. Noting that an understanding of advertising is a function of changing social context (decade) as well as cognitive development (age), Martin suggests that the remaining variance in the study can best be explained by the fact that advertising practices changed between the 1960s and 1980s, and by other socio-demographic factors which also influence consumer socialization.

Vignette 2: Blurring the lines between promotion and product

While children's cereals have often featured free gifts and on pack promotions, some of the latest cross-marketing and product offerings in the snack sector are raising concerns about the ability of children to distinguish between products and promotion. Renée Carver, of Chicago Children's Toys Examiner, discusses Kellogg's new Operation fruit flavoured snacks styled on the Hasbro operation game and Lego snack bars based on the classic building blocks. Aside from the concerns over young children not being able to distinguish between the snacks and the actual toys potentially encouraging children to put game pieces in their mouths and to associate the games with 'tasty fun', the author notes that this amounts to advertising for these toys. While not new this raises the question of what constitutes advertising and promotion and highlights the issue of young consumers' competencies, in this case to distinguish between the two.

(See the article at http://www.examiner.com/x-6192-Chicago-Childrens-Toys-Examiner~y2009m6d11-Kelloggs-Operation-FruitFlavored-snacks—free-advertising-and-teaching-kids-to-eat-toys)

Given recent changes in branded marketing strategies (i.e., cross-marketing, guerrilla marketing, product placements, web advertising, and synergistic strategies) (McChesney, 2003), it is hardly surprising that even 12 year olds have trouble distinguishing programming and advertising content (see Vignette 2). Besides which, these tactics are less directed to informing product choice than bolstering brand attitudes and affect. Advertising works by establishing brand awareness through affective rather than cognitive channels by establishing a liking for the brand (Hitchings and Moynihan, 1998; Borzekowski and Robinson, 2001), so scepticism and a knowledge of intent to persuade are irrelevant to preference formation. When it comes to the internet, it is far from clear that children can avoid the pop-ups and pornography, distinguish the commercial intent of sites such as Neopets, avoid cyber-lurkers, or understand how the information they input is being used by marketers (see Tufte and Rasmussen, Chapter 11 in this book). The escalating importance of online food advertising to children has provoked concerns about the extent of children's new media literacies (*Which?*, 2006; Holt et al., 2007).

In this respect, we must note that research into children's comprehension of the tactics and appeals used by advertisers, and their understanding of the role that advertising plays in the broader media system, are not consolidated until early adolescence (Moschis and Moore, 1979; Boush et al., 1994; Obermiller and Spangenberg, 2000). Moreover, as Hobbs (2004) points out, even teenagers who go through a media literacy course do not necessarily become more careful consumers. Chernin's (2008) study of this issue confirms what has long been evident: that the youngest children are simply unable to conceptualize the persuasive communication contexts of mediated communication and that critical skills and scepticism are of little use in 'resisting' the persuasive influence of marketing. Given the changes taking place in marketing and the evidence provided by thirty five years of research, children's advocates seem justified in wondering whether children are fully competent consumers.

Customers, products and economic literacy

Paine (1983) suggests that comprehending the persuasive intent of ads and forming the ability to communicate to parents about brand preferences are perhaps the least complex aspects of consumer socialization. She goes on to argue that children cannot be regarded as competent consumers if they lack the 'understanding of time, self, and money' implied by consumer sovereignty. This includes the ability to search for reliable information, understand the risks of long-term consumption, and to compare brands for price and quality on multiple attributes before making a choice. Most commentators agree that by age 8 most children are interested in, and knowledgeable about, a wide variety of consumer goods. Parents are obviously keen to help their children become consumers, taking them along when shopping and coaching them in the routines of selection and purchase from a young age (Carruth et al., 2000).

Clearly young children can recognize brand logos and recite advertising slogans for heavily advertised food products. By age 8, children's marketers believe they possess knowledge about a vast array of toy and food brands, and also media, cars and clothes (Sutherland and Thompson, 2002). Yet studies of their favourite ads and reported product requests rarely include a mention of healthier foods (Taras et al., 1989; Valkenburg and Buijzen, 2005). From a very young age children are also communicating their preferences to their parents at home and in the supermarkets (O'Dougherty et al., 2006). Carruth et al. (2000) found that 60 per cent of the 5 year olds in their study had formed preferences for snacks, displaying consistent product choices in a point of sale simulation game. They recognized and discriminated between brands they liked but they could also communicate those preferences to their parents. Yet children in the preoperational stage of development mostly based their food preferences on the advertised dimension – usually a sweet taste, brand elements or the colour – rather than the product category ('I like oatmeal'; 'Because it's yogurt') or nutrition.

Moreover, as McNeal notes, children also begin to make purchases for themselves by age 6. By age 7, most have become 'active shoppers' in their own right, searching through toy catalogues, using pocket money for discretionary purchases, window shopping, chatting with sales personnel, carefully investigating their favourite products, and learning to influence their parents on what to buy them (McNeal, 2000). Many 8 year olds also receive allowances that they are allowed to spend freely on discretionary consumption: when they do make discretionary purchases, children will commonly spend money on playthings, snacks, clothing and entertainments, although this depends on their SES (Dotson and Hyatt, 2000). They know where to look for price information and understand that there are price variations among products and stores. And by age 12 most young people have learned how to save for a major purchase, enter a shop, chose their favourite products (or influence their parents to buy these) and check their change (McNeal, 2000).

It is generally expected that in order to be considered competent consumers children must also possess cognitive defences which allow them to 'resist' the brand message by being able to rationally compare the products for price and benefits. In the mid 1970s Turner and Brandt (1978) argued that knowledge was the lowest level of cognitive functioning required of consumers and that the application of knowledge was a much better measure of competence. They used a simulated market test to evaluate children's ability to perform three basic consumer skills: to decide which of three options was a 'best buy'; to compare the quantity of product in different packages; and to compute a unit price for comparing similar products. The test score was based on a child's ability to complete these three tasks. They found that 70 per cent of the 4 year old children were incapable of even the first task and only 16 per cent of the 10 year olds completed all three of the product choice assignments correctly. Money experience and home responsibilities assigned by the parents were related to the acquisition of consumer competencies however. The authors of this unusual study concluded by noting that the parents were interested in the simulated market test because it provided them with a way of teaching their children about mindful shopping.

Nutritional knowledge is also essential in evaluating children's purchase decisions about snacks, yet surveys show that most teens lack a sufficient understanding of body metabolism and diet to make healthy choices (Pirouznia, 2001). Marketers' own studies of what kids buy with their own money have indicated that 75 per cent of a British sample chose fizzy soft drinks as their most frequent discretionary purchase, compared with fruit juice at 11 per cent. Although by age 10 these children were aware of the health issues associated with snacking, chocolate topped their snacking list and fruit was rarely mentioned. When pressed marketing researchers found there was a lot of confusion in all age groups as to what constituted 'junk food'. In this respect children's relative lack of nutritional knowledge may lead them to make unhealthy requests of their parents (Roberts et al., 2003). However, given that parents chose most of their daily foods, it is not surprising that in the UK children buy a very limited range of foods with their pocket money – mostly snacks or sweets. Until they have an adequate nutritional education, it seems unlikely that even 10 year olds would be able to evaluate advertised snacks and drinks based on nutritional criteria (see Marshall and O'Donohoe, Chapter 10 in this book).

Economic psychologists argue that market rationality also implies more than a practical shopping script. Today's customers need a pro-active shopping strategy that evaluates the price–benefits–risk of a product in a highly fluid pricing environment (Lunt and Furnham, 1996). Surveys indicated that when assessed for pricing accuracy, consumer affairs knowledge, and socially desirable consumer behaviours, children's consumer competencies depended on developmental factors but also differed by gender and social class. Youth from wealthy backgrounds had more opportunities to learn and practise consumerism (Moschis and Moore, 1979). There was also evidence that parents were playing a declining role in the adolescent acquisition of shopping skills when measured by consumer affairs knowledge, money management skills, and brand preferences (Moschis and Moore, 1982). Surprisingly, parents and schools accounted for very little variance in the acquisition of basic economic knowledge whereas the amount of television viewing did predict both consumer satisfaction and attitudes to the marketplace, although it was negatively related to 'puffery filtering' and advertising scepticism. Nor did consumer-related courses at school have much of a positive impact on young people's knowledge and attitudes (Moschis and Churchill, 1978). Money skills, attitudes and saving strategies have been shown to be a matter of social and economic circumstances (Lunt and Furnham, 1996). But studies of children's economic knowledge and attitudes reveal that like adults, adolescents are limited in their understanding of basic economic concepts (Doss et al., 1995; see also Roland-Lévy, Chapter 9 in this book).

The various reviews of the literature suggest that children's marketplace literacy is partial at best for children under the age of 12, and shaped as much by social circumstance, education, peers and parental coaching as by advertising. Moreover, their information searches for competitive products and prices may be limited by their lack of economic knowledge about the marketplace more generally and also a lack of price information in the advertising available to them. There is limited evidence that even teens possess the ability to perform the complex price–benefits–risk calculation involved in exercising rational choice, especially in relationship to goods that have long-term risks associated with them such as cigarettes or violent video games. Children's decision strategies tend to use fewer attributes in forming preferences and comparing products and rarely acknowledge the long-term health risks associated with some products. Yet as Ward et al. (1977) noted long ago, parents continue to wield power over children's consumer behaviour well into their teens. In a series of recent studies, it has been demonstrated that parenting style, familial negotiations, and restrictions on children's discretionary consumption are crucial aspects of consumer socialization (Dotson and Hyatt, 2005). I must conclude with others therefore that children must be regarded as neither victims nor possessing savvy – but rather as consumers-in-training, *learning to behave* in accordance with the variable standards established in the media-saturated family.

Conclusion

Galvanized by media panic, the public debate about food advertising on children's TV became politically charged: on one side stood the health advocates with their rhetoric of 'vulnerable' children, and on the other stood the food industry quick to dismiss the accusations that they were the ones making children fat. But the underlying question was really moral: were corporations, schools or parents responsible for children's diet? For legal reasons the debate highlighted children's questionable ability to perform as rational consumers in a mediated marketplace. To be competent shouldn't children be able to (a) access and evaluate the information about goods in various media in order to assess rationally the quality, usefulness and price (product attributes, utility and brands); (b) weigh up both the short- and long-term risks associated with regular use of specific products; (c) understand competitive pricing in markets, choices and the protocols of social transactions in shops (shopping scripts); and (d) able to acquire, save and exchange money for products (financial management skills)? In short the ideology of market rationality implies that consumers must be able to search out and evaluate information in order to compare the various goods available to them; they must be able to critically evaluate persuasive communications about product utility, cognitively weighing up the various benefits offered by competing sellers across the whole range of products; and they must also be able to assess product utility and multiple performance characteristics. To do so with food they must have a basic understanding of both nutrition and body metabolism and the risks associated with imbalanced diets. So to say that children under the age of 8 have been empowered by their parents to express themselves through consumer choices does not imply that they are fully rational economic subjects or should be regarded as such by marketers. Few adults, let alone children, meet these stringent criteria proposed by the theory of rational and informed market choice.

Still both sides looked to the established research literatures on children's consumer competencies to make their case – and both found it of limited relevance in solving the problem of globesity. What fifty years of research into children's consumer behaviour have taught us is that in many ways modern children have been historically empowered as customers in the consumer society (compared with previous generations), yet their interest in and practical knowledge about branding, shopping scripts and store pricing are no guarantee that they are competent consumer decision makers. Clearly today's children have and spend more money than previous generations; they have more say in what their families consume; and they are more knowledgeable about a wider range of brands and marketing techniques. Yet in the media-saturated markets of today, it remains highly unlikely that a ban on TV advertising to children alone would significantly reduce the prevalence of overweight children. The reasons are clear: firstly because there are many other factors shaping diet and exercise besides food advertising, secondly, because children would still be exposed to food ads on prime time TV and the internet, and thirdly, because parents continue to influence most of their dietary choices.

Future research directions

All this does not mean that revisiting the issue of children's marketing was a waste of time. The revival of the debate from the 1970s has forced researchers to acknowledge that marketing practices targeting children are indeed changing (Calvert, 2008). Firstly, because new speciality networks and digital media have changed children's media use patterns, because new techniques of advertising such as synergistic promotion and product placement in movies and online are common, and because children's discretionary leisure, consumption and influence on the family may have significantly changed. Secondly, because this controversy has forced a rethinking of the unintended effects of the promotional system not of individual consumer behaviour, but of family lifestyle dynamics and children's attitudes (Buijzen and Valkenburg, 2003; Schor, 2004). And thirdly, because we have become more aware of the risky lifestyle choices that might seem tolerable for adults as matters of free choice in the market – like smoking, drinking, not wearing seatbelts – but remain problematic because of children's limited knowledge of what is required for the price–benefits–risk analysis. The consequenice of media panic therefore is that we have been forced to rethink both the competencies that child consumers require in a risk society and also reminded that children must be educated in lifestyle and environmental risks as part of their growing marketplace literacy. Perhaps it is time to make marketplace literacy a mandatory aspect of public education.

Discussion questions

1 Outline the main concerns around marketing to children.
2 What are the main differences between the politicization of children's marketing today compared to the Baby Boom generation?
3 Is childhood protection a matter for the state or should this be left to parents?
4 Consider the role of parents, schools and the state in developing children's consumer competencies. Do marketers have a role to play in this?
5 Discuss the three children's marketplace competencies in relation to new forms of media such as the internet and specific applications such as social networking sites.

Further reading

Buckingham, D. (2009) 'Beyond the competent consumer: the role of media literacy in the making of regulatory policy on children and food advertising in the UK', *International Journal of Cultural Policy*, 15 (2) (May): 217–230.

Keller, M. and Kalmus, V. (2009) 'Between consumerism and protectionism: Attitudes towards children, consumption and the media in Estonia', *Childhood*, 16 (3): 355–375.

McNeal, J. (2007) *On becoming a consumer: the development of Consumer Behavior Patterns in Childhood*. London: Elsevier Science & Technology.

References

AAAS (2002) Available at http://www.aaas.org/news/releases/2002/topten.shtml

American Psychological Association (2004) '*APA task force report on advertising and children: psychological issues in the increasing commercialization of childhood*', edited by D. Kunkel, B.L. Wilcox, J. Cantor, E. Palmer, S. Linn and P. Dowrick, APA, Washington, DC, February.

Atkins, C. (1978) 'Observation of parent–child interaction in supermarket decision-making', *Journal of Marketing*, October: 41–45.

Azcuenaga, M. (1997) 'The Role of Advertising and Advertising Regulation in the Free Market'. Federal Trade Commission website.

Berger, P., Berger, B. and Kellner, H. (1974) *The Homeless Mind*. London: Penguin.

Blosser, B. and Roberts, D. (1985) 'Age differences in children's perceptions of message intent: responses to TV news, commercials, educational spots, and public service announcements', *Communication Research*, 12: 455–484.

Borzekowski, D. and Robinson, T. (2001) 'The 30-second effect: an experiment revealing the impact of television commercials on food preferences of preschoolers', *Journal of the American Dietetic Association*, (Jan) 101 (1): 42–46.

Boush, D., Friestad, M. and Rose, G. (1994) 'Adolescent skepticism toward TV advertising and knowledge of advertiser tactics', *Journal of Consumer Research*, June: 165–175.

Brucks, M., Armstrong, G.M. and Goldberg, M. (1988) 'Children's use of cognitive defenses against television advertising: a cognitive response approach', *Journal of Consumer Research*, 14: 471–482.

Buijzen, M. and Valkenburg, P.M. (2003) 'The unintended effects of advertising: a parent child survey', *Communication Research* (Oct) 30 (5): 483–503.

Calvert, S. (2008) 'Children as consumers: advertising and marketing', *Journal of Communication: The Future of Children?* (Spring) 18 (1): 205–34.

Carruth, B.R., Skinner, J.D., Morran, J.D. and Coletta, F. (2000) 'Preschoolers' food product choices at a simulated point of purchase and mothers' consumer practices', *Journal of Nutrition Education* (May/Jun) 32 (3): 146.

CCFC (2000) 'Intensive marketing harms children'. Available at http://www.commercialexploitation.org/pressreleases/goldenmarbles2000.htm

Chernin, A. (2008) 'The effects of food marketing on children's preferences: testing the moderating roles of age and gender', *The ANNALS of the American Academy of Political and Social Science*, January, 615: 101.

Cook, D. (2001) 'Exchange value as pedagogy in children's leisure: moral panics in children's culture at century's end', *Leisure Sciences*, 23 (2): 81–98.

DeMause, L. (1974) *The History of Childhood*. New York: Psychohistory Press.

Donohue, T.R., Henke, L.L. and Donohue, W.A. (1980) 'Do kids know what TV commercials intend?', *Journal of Advertising Research*, 20 (October) (5): 1–57.

Doss, V., Manawe, J. and Godwin, D. (1995) 'Middle school children's sources and view of money', *Journal of Consumer Affairs*, 29(1): 219–241.

Dotson, M.J. and Hyatt, E.M. (2000) 'A comparison of parents' and children's knowledge of brands and advertising slogans in the United States: implications for consumer socialization', *Journal of Marketing Communications*, 6 (4): 219–230.

Dotson, M.J. and Hyatt, E.M. (2005) 'Major influence factors in children's consumer socialization', *Journal of Consumer Marketing*, 22: 35–42.

Fromm, E. (1947) *Man For Himself: An Inquiry into the Psychology of Ethics*. New York: Holt, Rinehart and Winston.

Galbraith, J.K. (1958) *The Affluent Society*. New York: Pelican.

Grossbart, S.L. and Crosby, L.A. (1984) 'Understanding the bases of parental concern and reactions to children's food advertising,' *Journal of Marketing*, 48 (Summer): 79–92.

Hastings, G., Stead, M., McDermott, L., Forsyth A., MacKintosh, A., Rayner, M., Godfrey, C., Caraher, M. and Angus, K. (2003) 'Review of research on the effects of food promotion to children'. Report commissioned by the Food Standards Agency, September. Available at http://www.foodstandards.gov.uk/multimedia/pdfs/promofoodchildrenexec.pdf

Hitchings, E. and Moynihan, P.J. (1998) 'The relationship between television food advertisements recalled and actual foods consumed by children', *Journal of Human Nutrition and Dietetics*, 11: 511–517.

Hobbs, R. (2004) 'Does media literacy work? An empirical study of learning how to analyze advertisements', *Advertising & Society Review*, 5 (4).

Holt, D.J., Ippolito, P.M., Desrochers, D.M. and Kelley, C.R. (2007) *Children's Exposure to TV Advertising in 1977 and 2004: Information for the Obesity Debate*. Federal Trade Commission. Bureau of Economics Staff Report.

Jeffery, D.B., McLelland, R.W. and Fox, R.T. (1982) 'The development of children's eating habits: the role of television commercials', *Health Education Quarterly*, 9 (23): 78–93.

Kline, S. (1993) *Out of the Garden: Toys, TV and Children's Culture in the Age of Marketing*. London: Verso.

Kline, S. (2004) *Sedentary Lifestyle or Fast Food Culture? Lessons from the Battle of the Bulge*, in Umashankar Shastri (ed.) *Fast Food Industry – Issues and Implications Executive*. Reference Books Institute of Chartered Financial Analysts of India (ICFAI University).

Lang, T. and Heasman, M. (2004) *Food Wars: The Global Battle for Mouths, Minds, and Markets*. London: Earthscan.

Livingstone, S. and Helsper, E. (2004) 'Advertising foods to children: understanding promotion in the context of children's daily lives'. Review of the literature prepared for the Research Department of OFCOM, available at http://www.ofcom.org.uk

Lunt, P. and Furnham, A. (1996) *Economic Socialization*. Cheltenham: Edward Elgar.

Macklin, M.C. (1987) 'Preschoolers' understanding of the informational function of television advertising', *Journal of Consumer Research*, 14 (September): 229–239.

Marshall, D., O'Donohoe, S. and Kline, S. (2007) 'Families, food, and pester power: beyond the blame game?', *Journal of Consumer Behaviour*, 6 (4): 164–181.

Martin, M. (1997) 'Children's understanding of the intent of advertising: a meta analysis', *Journal of Public Policy and Marketing*, 16 (2): 205–216.

McChesney, R.W. (2003) 'Theses on media regulation', *Media, Culture & Society*, 25 (1): 125–133.

McNeal, J. (1964) *Children as Consumers*. Austin, TX: Bureau of Business Research, University of Texas.

McNeal, J. (2000) *The Kids' Market: Myths and Realities*. Ithaca, NY: Paramount Market.

Moschis, G.P. and Churchill, G.A. Jr (1978) 'Consumer socialization: a theoretical and empirical analysis', *Journal of Marketing Research*, 15 (November): 599–609.

Moschis, G.P. and Moore, R.L. (1979) 'Decision making among the young: a socialization perspective', *Journal of Consumer Research*, 6 (September): 101–112.

Moschis, G.P. and Moore, R.L. (1982) 'A longitudinal study of television advertising effects', *Journal of Consumer Research*, 9 (3): 279–286.

Obermiller, C. and Spangenberg, E.R. (2000) 'On the origin and distinctness of skepticism toward advertising', *Marketing Letters*, 11 (4): 311–322.

O'Dougherty, M., Story, M. and Stang, J. (2006) 'Observations of parent child co-shoppers in supermarkets: children's involvment in food selections, parental yielding and refusal strategies', *Journal of Nutrition, Education and Behavior*, 38 (3): 183–188.

Paine, L.S. (1983) 'Children as consumers: an ethical evaluation of children's advertising', *Business and Professional Ethics Journal*, 3 (3–4): 119–146.

Pirouznia, M. (2001) 'The influence of nutrition knowledge on eating behavior – the role of grade level', *Nutrition & Food Science*, 31 (2): 62–67.

Riesman, D., Denney, R. and Glazer, N. (1950) *The Lonely Crowd: A Study of the Changing American Character*. New Haven, CT: Yale University Press.

Riesman, D. and Roseborough, H. (1955) 'Careers in consumer behavior', in L. Clark (ed.), *Consumer Behaviour II: The Life Cycle and Consumer Behavior*. New York: University Press.

Roberts, B., Blinkhorn, A. and Duxbury (2003) 'The power of children over adults when obtaining sweet snacks', *International Journal of Paediatric Dentistry*, 13: 76–84.

Robertson, T.S. and Rossiter, J.R. (1974) 'Children and commercial persuasion: an attribution theory analysis', *Journal of Consumer Research*, 1: 508–512.

Roedder-John, D. (1999) 'Consumer socialization of children: a retrospective look at twenty-five years of research', *Journal of Consumer Research*, 26 (December): 183–213.

Rossiter, J.R. and Robertson, T.S. (1974) 'Children's television commercials: testing the defenses', *Journal of Broadcasting*, 23: 33–40.

Schor, J.B. (2004) *Born to Buy*. New York: Scribner.

Spock, B. (1964) *Baby and Child Care*. New York: Pocket Books.

Sutherland, A. and Thompson, A.T. (2002) *Kidfluence: Why Kids Today Mean Business*. Toronto: McGraw-Hill.

Taras, H., Sallis, J.F., Patterson, T.L., Nader, P.R. and Nelson, J.A. (1989) 'Television's influence on children's diet and physical activity', *Journal of Developmental and Behavioral Pediatrics*, 10: 176–180.

Turner, J. and Brandt, J. (1978) 'Development and validation of a simulated market to test children for selected consumer skills', *Journal of Consumer Affairs*, 12 (2): 266–276.

Valkenburg, P. and Buijzen, M. (2005); 'Identifying determinants of young children's brand awareness: television, parents and peers', *Applied Developmental Psychology*, 26: 456–468.

Ward, S. (1974) 'Consumer socialization', *Journal of Consumer Research*, 1 (September): 1–16.

Ward, S., Wackman, D.B. and Wartella, E. (1977) *How Children Learn to Buy: The Development of Information Processing Skills*. Beverly Hills, CA: Sage.

Which? (2006) 'Childcatchers: the tricks used to push unhealthy food to your children'. Available at http://www.which.co.uk

World Health Organization (2000) *Obesity: Preventing and Managing the Global Epidemic (no. 894)*. Geneva: WHO.

Young, B. (2003) 'Does food Advertising make children obese?', *International Journal of Marketing and Advertising to Children*, 4 (3): 21–26.

Notes

1   Stop Commercial Exploitation of Children (SCEC) changed its name to Campaign for a Commercial Free Childhood in November 2004. I have referenced this organization according to its current name.

2   The charts are based on Lexis/Nexis searches plotted by year, revealing the number of stories that featured various key words that help us trace the underlying themes that were woven into the coverage of the globesity pandemic.

Index